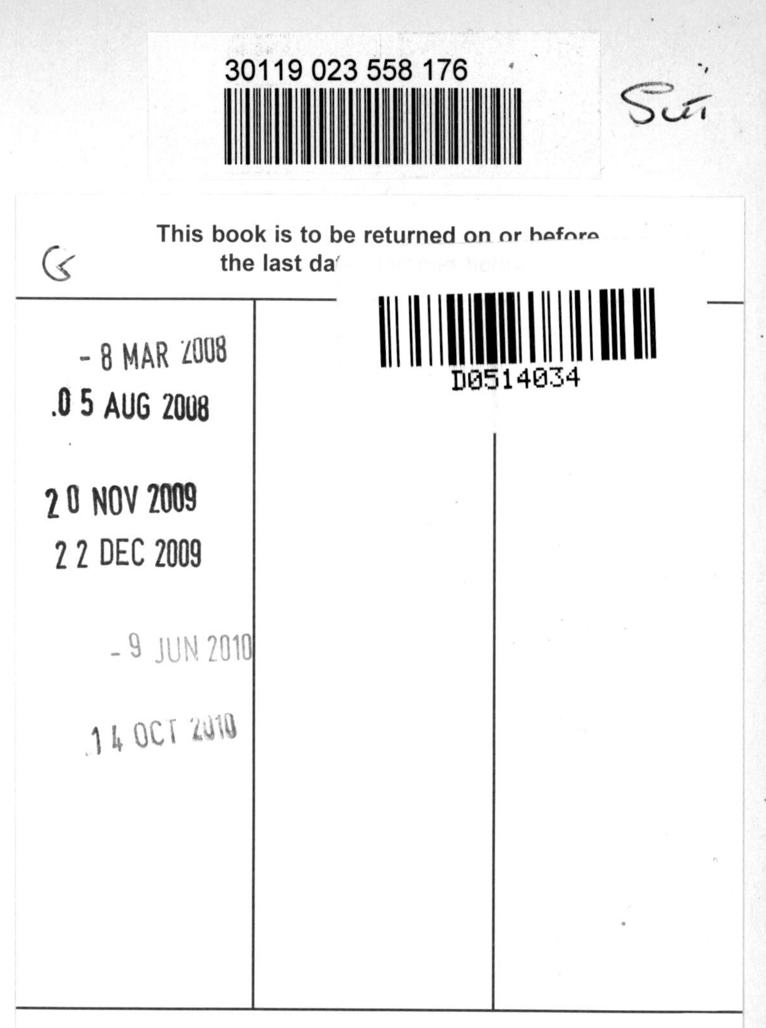

Other B&W titles by John Buchan

JOHN BURNET OF BARNS
THE COURTS OF THE MORNING
A LOST LADY OF OLD YEARS
THE BLANKET OF THE DARK
SICK HEART RIVER
MIDWINTER
THE POWER-HOUSE & THE THIRTY-NINE STEPS
THE GAP IN THE CURTAIN
SUPERNATURAL TALES
A PRINCE OF THE CAPTIVITY

THE FREE FISHERS

JOHN BUCHAN

Introduced by David Daniell

B&W PUBLISHING

First published 1934
This edition published 1994
by B&W Publishing Ltd
Edinburgh
Reprinted 2000

ISBN 1 873631 32 4

British Library Cataloguing in Publication Data:
A catalogue record for this book is available
from the British Library.

Cover illustration: Detail from
Spencer, 2nd Marquess of Northampton (1821),
by Sir Henry Raeburn.
Photograph by kind permission of
The Marquess of Northampton.

Cover Design by *Winfortune & Associates*

Printed by WS Bookwell, Finland 2000

CONTENTS

INTRODUCTION

David Daniell

John Buchan began *The Free Fishers* early in the summer of 1933 at his house at Elsfield, just outside Oxford, where he had lived in great contentment with his growing family for fourteen years. By then, though continuing his work as Deputy Chairman of Reuter's, and keeping an interest in Nelson's the publishers, he had been for six years Member of Parliament for the Scottish Universities. In May 1933 he was the King's representative as Lord High Commissioner to the General Assembly of the Church of Scotland. In October eighteen months later he was to leave Britain to become, as Lord Tweedsmuir of Elsfield, the King's representative in an altogether grander way as Governor-General of Canada. When *The Free Fishers* was published, in June 1934, he was approaching his sixtieth birthday. It was his eighty-fourth book, and twenty-fourth novel.

That June it appeared as a book from Hodder and Stoughton. It had been serialised in seven monthly parts in *Chambers's Journal* since January 1934, where it had pride of place in a number which ended with notes on 'A useful ladder gadget' and a new high tension re-chargeable accumulator (rather than wasteful dry batteries) for household wireless sets: the gadget and the accumulator did not last. John Buchan's historical adventure did.

A writer already most famous for the Richard Hannay thrillers, Buchan had a strong following as a journalist, biographer, historian, and especially, historical novelist. His first fiction, written forty years before, when he was an undergraduate at Brasenose College Oxford, was historical romance in Scottish settings, and in a way he never stopped. Written ten years before *The Free Fishers*, his *Midwinter* had been set in eighteenth-century Oxfordshire: *The Blanket of the Dark* eight years later was set in the sixteenth-century Cotswolds, close to his home. Both were important for Buchan when writing *The Free Fishers*, set at the time of the Napoleonic threat to England. The first half of *The Free Fishers*, however, and more, is set in Scotland—and a Scotland exceptionally important to Buchan.

He had been born, and spent his first years, on the Fife coast between Edinburgh and St Andrews, where the book opens. His school and university holidays had been spent exploring the dales of the Borders, to which the book moves. The later journey deep into England allows strange adventures among the highest in the land: the young John Buchan's first experience of English life was at the age of nineteen with the Gilbert Murrays in their Norfolk house, and there are qualities of Lady Mary Murray in many of his historical heroines. There is a significant sense in which *The Free Fishers* is more personal to Buchan than even his other historical novels; Anthony Lammas, the scholar-cum-dashing-adventurer who is his hero, represents two sides of his maker's mind—more deeply touched in *Witch Wood* of 1927, perhaps, but not so lightly taken. Many years before, in 1910, Buchan had set the opening of an adventure on the Fife coast of his childhood; the young hero of that story went on to do amazing deeds in Africa, personally subverting a great Zulu uprising under the eponymous leadership of Prester John. Buchan's rather solitary experiences in South Africa at the end of the Boer War gave that book a strong immediacy. Here in *The Free Fishers*, the threat of an invasion of England by Napoleon is kept far in the background, allowing full prominence to a set of characters who work the whole time in small groups, reacting among themselves—a particularly happy device. The immediacy is in the variations of shared mood and activity.

The Free Fishers is a holiday book, with neither the international threat nor the villainy being enough to disturb a sense of young adventure. It shares that off-duty quality with, in particular, his 1925 novel, *John Macnab*, a modern romance where high professional people find new truths about themselves in the rains and mists of Highland deer-stalks and salmon-fishing, against curious odds. As the plot of *The Free Fishers* unravels, the threat to the sanity, and life, of a remarkable young woman gradually appears at its centre. She, Gabriel Cranmer, is approached slowly: she is at first seen at a great distance, and quite wrongly, as a most unseemly problem in the life of a young Scottish lord. Step by step the various groups get closer to her, until she dominates the plot. Yet even she, and even the emerging qualities of the main heroes, are secondary to the wonderful sense of terrain, from the first pages to the last. Moods and weathers change quickly throughout the book: the landscapes change even more, 'from the echoing chambers and orderly terraces of Snowdoun or the deep heather of Catlaw to the windy beaches of Fife,' as an early sentence has it, and far beyond: but constant is a sense of that landscape, its shape, its trees and flowers and birds, and the sky above it—as, to take an example at random, in the opening pages of Chapter XV. The book is set in spring, and much of the happiness it brings comes from that steady sense of new life (a hasty journey is across 'rushy meadows full of nesting snipe').

By contrast, the villainy is deep inside various decaying houses which are neglected, inhospitable, imprisoning and unknowable. However apparently dangerous it might be, it is always good in this book to get out into the open air again: there everything can be understood. In the Borders house of Hungrygrain, or the old Norfolk inn the Merry Mouth, or even the Yonderdale inn, doors and windows are likely to show worse threats, and more secret dangers.

Though Buchan's influences are to a little extent Sir Walter Scott, and Byron (both mentioned), and slightly more Stanley Weyman or Georgette Heyer, his true avatar is Stevenson.

Buchan's book is his own, and he is not writing pastiche 'R.L.S.': but scene after scene is properly Stevensonian, like Professor Lammas's interview in Edinburgh with Lord Mannour; and the vital individual life of the characters, as well as the range of them (both novelistic qualities able to surprise the reader) belong to Stevenson's achievements.

Yet Buchan is his own man. An example might be the way the change in Sir Turnour Wyse's understanding of Mrs Cranmer is managed. In Chapter XVI, Sir Turnour becomes convinced of the lady's husband's devilry, but still finds her innocence and vulnerability impossible to believe, being more stirred by a fine horse for the *manège* than by any woman. He and others are in the now-deserted Overy House in Norfolk, a home of the Cranmers until a few hours before. In an upstairs room secret documents have been found which were forged with the intent of being fatal to the lady. Even they did not convince the baronet. Then:

> He strode from the room, but at the top of the staircase came to a sudden halt. There was an alcove there which may once have held a statue. In that alcove there was a wicker basket, and in that basket there was a dog.

Those forty-five words make a surprise: in the rush of high events in the plot the dog—a wounded spaniel—is the last thing a reader expects. It is swiftly characterised, and casts light on Sir Turnour. 'He [Benjamin, the dog] knew with the certainty of all wise dogs that here was a friend.' Sir Turnour suffers a violent change of heart. One could argue that Stevenson's *Kidnapped* and *Catriona* together are never far from *The Free Fishers*: but the little spaniel is Buchan's own (very different, but equally catalytic, small dogs appeared in his *John Macnab* and *Castle Gay*).

Also his own is the secret society, the freemasonry known as the Free Fishers, which is a brotherhood of worthy North Sea fishermen on the Fife coast and far afield—and far inland. The true Buchan touch is their astonishing power of secret communication over great distances. Individual Fishers are given portraits rather than characters; developed natures would have not let them melt back into the landscape, as they need to do. Indeed, one of them, a land-based Fisher, the pack-shepherd Tam Nickson, comes less to life than his dogs in his one significant scene in Chapter X.

In a sense, this device is simply the landscape come to life. For those who have eyes to see, the ground is 'all of blue and gold, the blue of the tiny bugle and the gold of ranunculus and primrose' (Chapter XV). Those who really understand the terrain, however, know that the woods or the hedges or the sea-shores have hidden eyes, and remain alert for sudden secret messages. Buchan had been here before in *Midwinter*, for example, where he made a Cotswold landscape in which those who know can tap into an ancient secret network: it is an idea never far from his historical fiction. But he had also been here before in *Prester John*, where the African *veld* hides the same abilities: and, in a different form, in the first of his 'shockers' written as the First World War started, *The Power-House* and *The Thirty-Nine Steps*. In those two novels it is the enemy who has the power of fitting the setting so perfectly that he can learn or communicate what he wants.

As usual with Buchan, the villain, Cranmer, is a deceiver, an apparently unthreatening man who is secretly a master of evil, like, supremely, Moxon Ivery in *Mr Standfast* or Dominick Medina in *The Three Hostages*. (It is tiresome that it has still to be pointed out that none of these is a Jew. Buchan's villains are not Jews, though some of his heroes are. The notion that there are anywhere in his books characters that can be called 'Buchan's Jewish villains' is an invention, produced in New York in 1960, and still, sadly, influential.) It is given out that Cranmer is a boorish, even booby, squire, henpecked by his politically-subversive wife: we are slowly shown that this is a picture of his own creation for his own sinister purpose, which is nothing less than the betrayal of his country to the French, by way of an assassination. It has to be said that Cranmer is more plot-device than character. Though called in Chapter XI 'the most dangerous man now alive on earth', he is really of little interest to his creator except in passing as 'an immense perverted genius', the negative to the Free Fishers' positive. To have a nearly-invisible spider at the centre of the decaying web, a trick probably learned from Scott, is effective, however, and not a blemish. Like his wife, Cranmer is only fully present in the last pages.

Ever since the appearance of a famous, and wrong-headed, essay by Graham Greene, 'The Last Buchan', it has been fashionable to accuse Buchan in his fiction of worshipping worldly success. Almost impossible to substantiate anywhere, in all the historical fiction it is plainly and simply untrue. The hero of the book is young, 'a licensed minister of the Kirk and a professor of the University of St Andrews', who sets out to do one thing and is diverted to a far greater, and secret, task; who falls in love, travels the land in quest of the threatened lady, and has high, astounding adventures. Yet at the very end he is content to feel 'the gentle hand of old homely things', to return to his 'little study and the drawer with the manuscript of his great treatise on the relation of art and morals'; 'dear and familiar things' which include his landlady's burnt porridge. The key to the way the book works is that device of diversion. A hero set on worldly success would press steadily on from St Andrews to the great man in Edinburgh and then on to London to impress the very great on behalf of the university, winning high rewards. From the beginning 'Nanty' Lammas is set apart from colleagues ambitious in university or national politics by being made chaplain to the secret, and particularly unelevated, Free Fishers. His double commission, from the university and from Lord Mannour, is set aside with the spontaneity found in true romance, and his successive larger quests, growing out of each other, are similarly desperate rather than realistic. The Regency baronet Sir Turnour Wyse changes tack several times, across great distances of feeling and of mileage, his lightly sketched energy making a symbol of possible achievement: success for this man is simply arrival somewhere in time. This trait Buchan brings alive through the splendid details not just of horsemanship, but of superb skill in high-speed posting along impossible roads: the reader longs for a light carriage and a pair of fine horses, confident of expert hands—it feels fabulous, and easy. Buchan as always treats his reader as skilful and knowledgeable: familiarity with Bunyan, Shakespeare, classical poetry and the Bible, as well as different Scottish dialects, is expected, even to seeing when a characteristic is shaded in through misquotation: Bob Muschat says in Chapter XIV 'We maun put our trust in horses, as the Bible says', when the Bible says the opposite. Buchan, a son of a Scottish Manse, enjoyed such popular mis-sayings.

Spring landscapes and April weather, a little dog, a Corinthian baronet; a young woman in great danger from an evil traitor; a secret organisation; a young Scottish professor of logic diverted into romance; several passionate young men and a pretty young woman or two—these are the ingredients of an unpretentious and highly enjoyable fiction. The great and successful, like the Prime Minister himself, are thin compared to crowded scenes of strange comings-together in humble places. One of these is in the tiny spare bedroom of the Yonderdale Manse, where in candlelight an old minister, his formidable housekeeper, the unstoppable little town-clerk of Waucht, and Sir Turnour Wyse crowd round the big four-poster containing the young Lord Belses, still romantically wounded from a murderous attack, as he tells his extraordinary story—a tale prefaced by mutton ham, new scones and ale for all: 'four pairs of jaws were busy in the little room'. It is in Chapter VIII: but there are many such excellent moments of humble romance in *The Free Fishers*.

TO

JOHN KEY HUTCHISON

IN MEMORY OF OUR BOYHOOD
ON THE COAST OF FIFE

CHAPTER I

IN WHICH A YOUNG MAN IS AFRAID OF HIS YOUTH

MR. ANTHONY LAMMAS, whose long legs had been covering ground at the rate of five miles an hour, slackened his pace, for he felt the need of ordering a mind which for some hours had been dancing widdershins. For one thing the night had darkened, since the moon had set, and the coast track which he followed craved wary walking. But it was the clear dark of a northern April, when, though the details are blurred, the large masses of the landscape are apprehended. He was still aware of little headlands descending to a shadowy gulf which was the Firth. Far out the brazier on the May was burning with a steady glow, like some low-swung planet shaming with its ardour the cold stars. He sniffed the sharp clean scent of the whins above the salt; he could almost detect the brightness of their flowering. They should have been thyme, he thought, thyme and arbutus and tamarisk clothing the capes of the Sicilian sea, for this was a night of Theocritus. . . .

Theocritus! What had he to do with Theocritus? It was highly necessary to come to terms with this mood into which he had fallen.

For Mr. Lammas, a licensed minister of the Kirk and a professor in the University of St. Andrews, had just come from keeping strange company. Three years ago, through the good offices of his patron and friend, Lord Snowdoun, he had been appointed to the Chair of Logic and Rhetoric, with emoluments which, with diet money and kain-hens, reached the sum of £309 a year, a fortune for a provident bachelor. His father, merchant and boat-builder in the town of Dysart, had left him also a small patrimony, so that he was in no way cumbered with material cares. His boyhood had been crowded with vagrant ambitions. At the burgh school he had hankered after the sea; later, the guns in France had drawn him to a soldier's life, and he had got as far as Burntisland before a scandalized parent reclaimed him. Then scholarship had laid its spell on him. He had stridden to the top of his Arts classes in St. Andrews, and at Edinburgh had been well thought of as a theologian. His purpose then was the lettered life, and he had hopes of the college living of Tweedsmuir, far off in the southern moorlands, where he might cultivate the Muses and win some such repute as that of Mr. Beattie at Aberdeen.

But Lord Snowdoun had shown him the way to better things, for to be a professor at twenty-five was to have a vantage-ground for loftier ascents. In the Logic part of his duties he had little interest, contenting himself with an exposition of Mr. Reid's *Inquiry* and some perfunctory lectures on Descartes, but in the Rhetoric classes, which began after Candlemas, his soul expanded, and he had made himself a name for eloquence. Also he had discovered an aptitude for affairs, and was already entrusted with the heavy end of college business. A year ago he had been appointed Questor, a post which carried the management of the small academic revenues. He stood well with his colleagues, well with the students, and behind him was Lord Snowdoun, that potent manager of Scotland. Some day he would be Principal, when he would rival the fame of old Tullidelph, and meantime as a writer he would win repute far beyond the narrow shores of Fife. Had he not in his bureau a manuscript treatise on the relations of art and morals which, when he reread it, astounded him by its acumen and wit, and a manuscript poem on the doings of Cardinal Beatoun which he could not honestly deem inferior to the belauded verse of Mr. Walter Scott!

So far the path of ambition, in which for a man of twenty-eight he had made notable progress. Neat in person, a little precise in manner, his mouth primmed to a becoming gravity, his hair brushed back from his forehead to reveal a lofty brow, Mr. Lammas was the very pattern of a dignitary in the making. . . . And yet an hour ago he had been drinking toddy with shaggy seafarers, and joining lustily in the chorus of "Cocky Bendy", and the tune to which his long legs had been marching was "Dunbarton's Drums". He was still whistling it:

> "Dunbarton's drums are bonnie O—
> I'll leave a' my friends and my daddie O—
> I'll bide nae mair at hame, but I'll follow wi' the drum,
> And whenever it beats I'll be ready O."

This was a pretty business for a minister of the Kirk, the Questor of St. Andrews, and a professor of divine philosophy.

There was a long story behind it. As a boy his playground had been the little rock-girt port of Dysart, and as the son of honest David Lammas, who could build a smack with any man between Berwick and Aberdeen, he had been made free of the harbour life. His intimates had been men who took their herring busses far north into the cold Shetland seas, whalers who sailed yearly for the Färoes and Iceland and still stranger waters, skippers of Dutch luggers and Norway brigs who leavened their lawful merchantry with commodities not approved by law. He learned their speech and the tricks of their calling, and listened greedily to their tales through many a summer twilight. Sometimes he went to the fishing himself in the shore-cobles, but his dream was to sail beyond the May to the isles of the basking sharks and the pilot-whales and the cliffs snowy with sea-fowl. Only the awe of his father kept him from embarking one fine morning in a Middelburg lugger with tulips in its cabin, and a caged singing-bird whose pipe to his ear was the trumpet of all romance.

There was a brotherhood among the sea-folk as close and secret as a masonic order. Its name was the Free Fishers of Forth, but its name was not often spoken. To be a member was to have behind one, so long as one obeyed its rules, a posse of stalwart allies. It had been founded long ago—no man knew when, though there were many legends. Often it had fallen foul of the law, as in the Jacobite troubles, when it had ferried more than one much-sought gentleman between France and Scotland. Its ostensible purpose was the protection of fisher rights, and a kind of co-operative insurance against the perils of the sea, but these rights were generously interpreted, and there had been times when free-trade was its main concern, and the east-coast gaugers led a weary life. But the war with France had drawn it to greater things. Now and then the ship of a Free Fisher may have conveyed an escaping French prisoner to his own country, but it is certain that they brought home many a British refugee who had struggled down to the Breton shore. Also the fraternity did famous secret services. They had their own private ways of gleaning news, and were often high in repute with an anxious Government. Letters would arrive by devious ways for this or that member, and a meeting would follow in some nook of the coast with cloaked men who did not easily grasp the Fife speech. More than once the Chief Fisher, old Sandy Kyles, had consulted in Edinburgh behind guarded doors with the Lord Advocate himself.

To the boy the Free Fishers had been the supreme authority of his world, far more potent than the King in London. He cherished every hint of their doings that came to him, but he fell in docilely with the ritual and asked no questions. As he grew older he learned more, and his notion of the brotherhood was clarified: some day he would be a member of it like his father before him. But when he chose the path of scholarship he had to revise his ambitions, since the society was confined strictly to those whose business lay with the sea. Yet the harbour-side was still his favourite haunt, and he went on adding to his seafaring friendships.

"I'll tell you what," he told his chief ally, Tam Dorrit. "If I cannot be a member, I'll be your chaplain. When I'm a minister you'll appoint me. King George has his chaplain, and Lord Snowdoun, and all the great folk, and what for no the Free Fishers?"

The notion, offered half in jest, simmered in the heads of the brotherhood, for they liked the lad and did not want to lose him, if fate should send him to some landward parish. So it came about that when Mr. Lammas had passed his trials and won his licence to preach, a special sederunt of the Free Fishers took place, and he was duly appointed their chaplain, with whatever rights, perquisites and privileges might inhere in that dignity. In due course he was installed at a supper, where the guests, a little awed by the shadow of the Kirk, comported themselves with a novel sobriety. Then for a year or two he saw nothing of them. He was engaged by Lord Snowdoun as the governor of his heir, the young Lord Belses, and passed his time between the great house of Snowdoun under the Ochils, the lesser seat of Catlaw in Tweeddale, and his lordship's town lodgings in Edinburgh. Ambition had laid its spell on him, high-jinks were a thing of the past, and he was traversing that stage of ruthless worldly wisdom which follows on the passing of a man's first youth. It was a far cry from the echoing chambers and orderly terraces of Snowdoun or the deep heather of Catlaw to the windy beaches of Fife.

But with his return to St. Andrews he found himself compelled to pick up the threads of his youth. The stage of premature middle-age had passed, and left him with a solid ambition, indeed, but with a more catholic outlook on the world. He had to deal with young men, and his youth was his chief asset; he had strong aspirations after literary success—in youthful spheres, too, like poetry and fantastic essays. He dared not bolt the door against a past which he saw daily in happier colours. The Free Fishers had not forgotten him. They had solemnly congratulated their chaplain on his new dignity, and they invited him to their quarterly gatherings at this or that port of the Firth. The message was never by letter; it would come by devious means, a whispered word in the street or at the harbour-side or on the links from some shaggy emissary who did not want to be questioned.

At first Mr. Lammas had been shy of the business. Could a preceptor of youth indulge in what was painfully akin to those extravagances of youth against which the Senatus warred? He had obeyed the first summons with a nervous heart, and afterwards the enterprise was always undertaken in the deepest secrecy. No chaise or saddle-horse for him; his legs carried him in the evening to the rendezvous, however distant, and brought him back in the same fashion. From the side of the Free Fishers, however, he knew that he need fear nothing, for they were silent as the tomb. So into the routine of his life came these hiatuses of romance with a twofold consequence. They kept his hand in for his dealings with his pupils. He became "Nanty" to the whole undergraduate world, from the bejant to the magistrand. His classes were popular and orderly, and many consulted him on private concerns which they would not have broached to any other professor. Also, as if to salve his conscience, he began to cultivate a special gravity in his deportment. Among his colleagues he spoke little, but what he said was cogent; he acquired a name for whinstone common sense; he was a little feared and widely trusted. Soon his gravity became a second nature, and his long upper lip was a danger-signal to folly. Yet all the while he was nursing his private fire of romance in the manuscripts accumulating in his study drawers, and once in a while those fires were permitted to flicker in public. After a dull day of Senatus meetings, when he would reprehend the plunderings by his colleagues of the College library, or frame new rules for the compulsory Sunday service in St. Leonard's Kirk and the daily Prayer-hall at St. Mary's, or bicker with Dr. Wotherspoon, the Professor of Moral Philosophy, over the delimitations of his subject, he would find himself among his boyhood's friends, bandying queer by-names and joining in most unacademic choruses.

This night the supper had been at Pittenweem. All day Mr. Lammas had been engaged on high affairs. There was trouble over the University revenue from the Priory lands, which was a discretionary grant from the Exchequer; Government had shown itself unwilling to renew it on the old terms, and it had been decided that Mr. Lammas should proceed forthwith to London, lay the matter before Lord Snowdoun, and bespeak his lordship's interest. It was a notable compliment to the young man, and a heavy responsibility. Also he had received a letter from Lord Mannour, who as Mr. Peter Kinloch had been the University's standing counsel, begging him to wait upon him without delay in Edinburgh. Mr. Lammas, cumbered with such cares and about to set out on a difficult journey, had been in no mood for the Free Fishers, and had almost let the occasion slip. But some perverse loyalty had set his feet on the shore-road, and for some hours he had been absorbed, not unhappily, into a fantastic world.

The sederunt had been the queerest in his recollection. The great boat-shed on the edge of the tide had been bright at first with a red sunset, but presently the April dusk had gathered, and ships lanterns, swung from the rafters, had made patches of light among its shadows. Beneath, round the rude table, had sat fifty and more shaggy seafarers, each one entering the guarded door with the password for the night. Old Sandy Kyles was dead, and in the chair of the Chief Fisher sat Eben Garnock, a mountainous man with a beard like Moses and far-sighted blue eyes beneath penthouse brows. There were gaps in the familiar company, and Mr. Lammas heard how one had lost his boat and his life off the Bass in the great January storm, and another had shipwrecked at Ushant and was now in a French gaol. But there was a goodly number of old friends—Tam Dorrit, who had once taken him on a memorable run to the Eastern Banks; Andrew Cairns, who had sailed his smack far into the unpermitted Baltic; the old man Stark who, said rumour, had been a pirate in western waters; and young Bob Muschat, a new member, who had bird-nested with him many a Saturday in the Dunnikier woods. There were faces that were new to him, and he noted that they were of a wilder cast than those he first remembered. The war was drawing the Free Fishers into odd paths. There were men there who had been pressed for the Navy and had seen Trafalgar, men who had manned privateers and fought obscure fights in forgotten seas, men who on Government business had talked in secret chambers with great folk and risked their lives in the dark of the moon. It was not his recovered boyhood that Mr. Lammas saw, but a segment of a grimmer world whose echoes came faintly at intervals to St. Andrews halls.

The company had been piped to meat by a bosun's whistle, and they had said the Fisher's Grace, which begins:

> "For flukes and partans, cakes and ale,
> Salty beef and seein' kale—"

and concludes with a petition for the same mercies at the next meeting. There was no formality round their table, but there was decorum, the decorum of men for whom the world was both merry and melancholy. They faced death daily, so even in their cups they could not be children. Mighty eaters and drinkers, good fare only loosed their tongues. Mr. Lammas heard tales which he knew would haunt his dreams. When they forsook ale for whisky-toddy, brewed in great blue bowls of Dutch earthenware, the first songs began. He drank liquors new to him, in particular a brew of rum, burned and spiced, which put a pleasant fire in his veins. His precision was blown aside like summer mist; he joined lustily in the choruses; himself he sang "Dunbarton's Drums" in his full tenor; his soul melted and expanded till he felt a kindness towards all humanity and a poet's glory in the richness of the world.

This high mood had accompanied his striding under the spring moon for three-quarters of his homeward journey. His fancy had been kindled by glimpses into marvels—marvels casually mentioned as common incidents of life. One man had sailed round the butt of Norway to Archangel, and on returning had been blocked for five days among icebergs. "Like heidstanes in a kirkyaird," he had said—"I hae still the grue of them in my banes." Another had gone into the Arctic among the great whales, and stammered a tale—he had some defect in his speech—of waters red like a battlefield, of creatures large as a hill rolling and sighing in their death-throes, and of blood rising in forty-foot spouts and drenching the decks like rain. Still another, a little man with a mild face and a mouth full of texts, had been cast away on the Portugal coast, and had shipped in a Spanish boat and spent two years in the rotting creeks of the Main. "God's wonders in the deep!" he had cried. "Maybe, but it's the Deil's wonders in yon unco land," and, being a little drunk, he had babbled of blood-sucking plants and evil beasts and men more evil. Poetry churned in Mr. Lammas's head, and he strung phrases which ravished him. . . .

But the excitement was ebbing, and "Dunbarton's Drums" was dying in his ears. He was almost across the King's Muir, and could see the first lights of St. Andrews twinkling in the hollow. With an effort he pulled himself together. He was returning to duty, and must put away childish things.

Suddenly he was aware of a figure on his left. He saw it only as a deeper shadow in the darkness, but he heard its feet on the gravel of the track. A voice caused him to relax the grip which had tightened on his staff, for it was a voice he knew.

"You have the pace of me, sir." The owner of the voice dropped into step.

Had there been light to see, the face of Mr. Lammas would have been observed to fall into lines of professorial dignity.

"You walk late, Mr. Kinloch," he said.

"Like yourself, sir, and for the same cause. I too, have been *in loco. . . . Dulce est desipere*, you know. Old Braxfield used to translate the line, 'How blessed it is now and then to talk noansense'!"

"I do not follow."

"I mean that I had the honour of supping in your company, sir. Of supping under your benediction. I am the latest recruit to the honourable company of the Free Fishers."

Mr. Lammas was startled. Here was his secret disclosed with a vengeance, for one of his own pupils shared it. His safety lay in the Fishers' Oath and also in the character of the participant. By the mercy of Providence this lad, Jock Kinloch, and he had always been on friendly terms. The only son of Lord Mannour, the judge whom he was trysted to meet on the morrow, he was unlike the ordinary boys from the country manse, the burgh shop or the plough-tail. Among the two hundred there was at the moment no "primar", that is, a nobleman's son, and Jock ranked as one of the few "secondars" or scions of the gentry. He was a stirring youth, often at odds with authority, and he had more than once been before the Rector and his assessors at the suit of an outraged St. Andrews townsman. He was popular among his fellows, for he had money to spend and spent it jovially, his laugh was the loudest at the dismal students' table in St. Leonard's, on the links he smote a mighty ball, he was esteemed a bold rider with the Fife Hunt, and he donned the uniform of the Fencibles. No scholar and a sparing attendant at lectures, he had nevertheless revealed a certain predilection for the subjects which Mr. Lammas professed, had won a prize for debate in the Logic class, and in Rhetoric had shown a gift for declamation and a high-coloured taste in English style. He had written poetry, too, galloping iambics in the fashionable mode, and excursions in the vernacular after the manner of Burns. Sometimes of an evening in the Professor's lodgings there would be a session of flamboyant literary talk, and once or twice Mr. Lammas had been on the brink of unlocking his study drawer and disclosing his own pursuit of the Muses. For most of his pupils he had a kindliness, but for Jock Kinloch he felt something like affection.

"It is an old story with me," he said primly. "It goes back to my Dysart boyhood, when I was never away from the harbour-side. I have kept up the link out of sentiment, Mr. Kinloch. As one grows older one is the more tenderly affectioned to the past."

The young man laughed.

"You needn't apologize to me, sir. I honour you for this night's cantrip—maybe I had always a notion of something of the sort, for there must be that in you that keeps the blood young compared to the sapless kail-runts of the Senatus. I had thought it might be a woman."

"You thought wrong," was the icy answer. Mr. Lammas was a little offended.

"Apparently I did, and I make you my apologies for a clumsy guess." The boy's tone was respectful, but Mr. Lammas knew that, could he see it, there was a twinkle in the black eyes. Jock Kinloch's eyes were dark as a gipsy's and full of audacious merriment.

"Maybe yon queer folk at Pittenweem," he went on, "brew a better elixir of youth than any woman. They were doubtless more circumspect at your end of the table, but at my end the tongues were slack and I got some wild tales. It would have done the douce St. Andrews folk a world of good to sit down at yon board and hear the great Professor ask the blessing. . . . But no, no," he added, as if conscious of some mute protest from his companion, "they'll never hear a word of it from me. There's the Fishers' Oath between us. You'll be Professor Anthony Lammas as before, the man that keeps the Senatus in order and guides my erring steps in the paths of logic and good taste, and Nanty Lammas will be left among the partans and haddies and tar-pots of Pittenweem."

"I am obliged to you, Mr. Kinloch. As you say, the oath is between us, and the Free Fishers sup always under the rose."

The boy edged closer to his companion. The lights of the town were growing near—few in number, for the hour was late. He laid a hand upon Mr. Lammas's arm.

"There's more in the oath than secrecy, sir," he said; "there's a promise of mutual aid. I took pains to make up on you, for I wanted to ask a favour from you as from a brother in the mystery. I want information, and maybe I want advice. Will you give it me?"

"Speak on." Mr. Lammas, his mind at ease, was well disposed to this garrulous youth.

"It's just this. When you finished college you were tutor in my Lord Snowdoun's family? You were the governor of his eldest son and prepared him for Oxford? Am I right, sir?"

"I was governor to the young Lord Belses, and for two years lived in his lordship's company."

"Well, I'd like to know what kind of a fellow he is. I don't want to hear about a brilliant and promising young nobleman—born to a great estate—a worthy successor of his father—bilge-pipe stuff like that. I want a judgment of him from an honest man, whose hand must have often itched for his ears."

"I assure you it never did. There was much in Harry I did not understand, but there was little to offend me. He was a most hopeful scholar, with taste and knowledge beyond his years. He was an adept at sports in which I could not share. His manners were remarkable for their urbanity, and in person he was altogether pleasing."

"In short, a damned pompous popinjay!"

"I said nothing of the kind, and let me tell you that it ill-becomes you, Mr. Kinloch, to speak thus of one of whom you can know nothing. Have you become a Jacobin to rave against rank? Have you ever seen the young lord?"

"Ay, I have seen him twice." The boy spoke moodily. "Once he came out with the Hunt. He was the best mounted of the lot of us, and I won't deny he can ride. At first I took the fences side by side with him, but my old Wattie Wudspurs was no match for his blood beast, and I was thrown out before the kill. He spoke to me, and he was so cursed patronizing I could have throttled him. Minced his words like an affected school-miss."

"I see in that no cause for offence."

"No, but the second time he gave me cause—weighty cause, by God. It was at Mount Moredun, at the Hogmanay ball, and he came with Kirsty Evandale's party. Kirsty was to be my partner in the first eightsome, and she jilted me, by gad—looked through me when I went to claim her—and danced all night with that rotten lordling."

"Your grievance seems to lie rather against Miss Christian Evandale."

"No—she was beguiled—women are weak things. There were the rest of us—country bumpkins compared to this spruce dandy, with the waist of a girl and the steps of a dancing-master. There was me—not a word to say for myself—boiling with passion and blushing and fuming—and all the time as gawky as a gander. . . . You say there has never been a woman in your life. Well, there's one in mine—Kirsty. I'm so crazily in love with her that she obscures daylight for me. They tell me that the Snowdouns want to make a match of it with Belses, for they are none too well off for grandees, and Kirsty will own half the land between Ore and Eden. . . . Now here is what I want to know. What about the popinjay? Is he scent and cambric and gold chains and silk waistcoats and nothing more, or is there a man behind the millinery? For if there's a man, I'm determined to come to grips with him."

The two were now under the shadow of the ruined tower of St. Regulus, and their feet were on the southward cobbles of the little city.

"Dear me, you are very peremptory," said Mr. Lammas. "You summon me like an advocate with an unfriendly witness."

"I summon you by the Fishers' Oath," said the boy. "I know that what you say will be honest and true."

"I am obliged, and I will answer you, but my knowledge stops short five years back. When I knew Harry he was immature—there was no question of a man—he was only boy and dreamer. But I can bear witness to a warm heart, a just mind and a high spirit. He may end as a fantastic, but not as a fop or a fool. He made something of a name at Christ Church, I understand, has travelled much in Europe, and has now entered Parliament. I have heard rumour of some extravagance in his political views, but I have heard no charge against his character. Your picture does not fit in with my recollection, Mr. Kinloch, and you will do well to revise it. A dainty dress and deportment do not necessarily imply effeminacy, just as rudeness is no proof of courage."

"You think he will fight, then?"

"Fight? What is this talk of fighting?"

"Simply that if he is going to cast his glamour over Kirsty, I'll have him out by hook or by crook. I'm so damnably in love with her that I'll stick at nothing."

"You are a foolish child. If I did my duty I would report you to—"

"The Fishers' Oath! Remember the Fishers' Oath—Nanty Lammas!" He darted down a side-street without further word, as the clock on the town-kirk steeple struck the hour of twelve.

CHAPTER II

IN WHICH LORD MANNOUR DISCOURSES

MR. LAMMAS tumbled into bed in the closet behind his living-room, and fell instantly asleep, for he was drowsy with salt air and many long Scots miles. There seemed but an instant between his head touching the pillow and the knuckles of his landlady, Mrs. Babbie McKelvie, sounding on his door. "It's chappit five, Professor," her voice followed. "Ye'll mind ye maun be on the road by seven."

He rose in a very different mood from that of the night before. Now he was the learned professor, the trusted emissary of his university, setting out on a fateful journey. Gravity fell upon him like a frost. He shaved himself carefully, noting with approval the firm set of his chin and the growing height of his forehead as the hair retreated. A face, he flattered himself, to command respect. His locks had been newly cut by Jimmy Jardine, the college barber, and he subdued their vagaries with a little pomatum. His dress was sober black, his linen was fresh, and he had his father's seals at his fob; but, since he was to travel the roads, he wore his second-best pantaloons and he strapped strong frieze leggings round the lower part of them. Then he examined the rest of his travelling wardrobe, the breeches and buckled shoes to be worn on an occasion of ceremony, the six fine cravats Mrs. McKelvie had hemmed for him, the six cambric shirts which were the work of the same needle-woman, the double-breasted waistcoat of wool and buckram to be worn if the weather grew chilly. He was content with his preparations, and packed his valise with a finicking neatness. He was going south of the Border into unknown country, going to the metropolis itself to uphold his university's cause among strangers. St. Andrews should not be shamed by her ambassador. He looked at his face again in his little mirror. Young, but not too young—the mouth responsible—a few fine lines of thought on the brow and around the eyes—he might pass for a well-preserved forty, if he kept his expression at a point of decent gravity.

As his habit was, he took a short turn in the street before breakfast. It was a wonderful morning, the wind set in the north-west, the sky clear but for a few streamers, and the bay delicately crisped like a frozen pool. The good-wives in the west end of the Mid Street were washing their doorsteps or fetching water from the well, and as they wrought they shouted to each other the morning's news. There were no red gowns about, for it was vacation time, but far down the street he saw a figure which he knew for the Professor of Humanity, returning from his pre-breakfast walk on the links. His colleague was a sick man who lived by a strict regime, and Mr. Lammas thanked Heaven that he had a sound body. Never had he felt more vigorous, more master of himself, he thought, as he drew the sweet air into his lungs. He was exhilarated, and would have liked to sing, but he repressed the feeling and looked at the sky with the brooding brow of one interrupted in weighty thoughts. "Dunbarton's Drums" was a hundred years away. The housewives gave him good-morning, and he ceremonially returned their salutes. He knew that they knew that he was bound for London—not in the ramshackle diligence that lumbered its way daily westward, but riding post, as became a man on an urgent errand. In half an hour the horses from Morrison's stables would be at the door, for at Kirkcaldy he must catch the tide and the Leith packet.

As he re-entered his house his mouth had shaped itself for whistling, which he only just checked in time. "The Auld Man's Mare's Deid" was the inappropriate tune which had almost escaped his lips. He bent his brows, and straightened his face, and became the dignitary. A faint smell of burning came to his nostrils.

"Babbie," he thundered, "you are letting the porridge burn again. Have I not told you a hundred times that I cannot abide burnt porridge?"

The scarlet face of Mrs. McKelvie appeared from the little kitchen. " 'Deed sir, I'm sore flustered this morning. The lassie was late wi' the baps, and the fire wadna kindle, and I dauredna dish the parritch wi' you stravaigin' outbye. We maun haste, or Cupar Tam will be round wi' the horses afore ye have drucken your tea. . . . Eh, sirs, but ye're a sight for sair een, Mr. Lammas. I've never seen ye sae trig and weel set up. Tak my advice and keep out o' the lassies' gait, for they tell me there's daft queans about England."

An hour later Mr. Lammas had left the coast behind him and was in a landward country of plough and pasture. Cupar Tam on the horse which carried his mails rode discreetly some yards behind, and he was left free to think his own thoughts. He might even have whistled without scandal, but at first his mind was far from whistling.

Now that he was on the road, with every minute taking him farther from home, he was a little weighted by the importance of his mission. He, the youngest in the Senatus, had been chosen to fight this battle far away among subtle lawyers and cold men of affairs. London, which at other times he had dreamed of as an Hesperides of art and pleasure, now seemed like Bunyan's Vanity Fair, a hard place for a simple pilgrim. Also there was the meeting that very night in Edinburgh with Lord Mannour, a formidable figure as he remembered him, bushy-browed, gimlet-eyed, with none of the joviality of his son. He shook himself with difficulty out of a mood of diffidence. The harder the task, he reminded himself, the greater the credit. He forced himself to be worldly-wise. He was a man of affairs, and must view the world with a dignified condescension. "An old head upon young shoulders" had been the Principal's words. So he fell to repeating the arguments he meant to adduce about the Priory lands—"We are a little home of the humanities, my lords—Rome in her great days was always kindly considerate of Athens.". . .

But the motion of his horse sent the blood running briskly in his veins, the sun flushed his cheeks, and Mr. Lammas became conscious again of the spring. The rooks were wheeling over the ploughlands, and the peesweeps and snipe were calling in every meadow. The hawthorn bushes were a young green, every hedge-root had its celandines and primroses, and there were thickets of sloe, white as if with linen laid out to bleach. The twin Lomonds poked their blue fingers into the western sky, and over them drifted little clouds like ships in sail. A great wall of stone bounded the road for a mile or two, and he knew the place for the park of Mount Moredun, of which Jock Kinloch had babbled the night before. Far up on the slopes that rose north from the Eden valley he saw too the dapper new woodlands which surrounded Balbarnit, the house of Miss Christian Evandale, that much-sought lady.

The sight switched his thoughts to a new channel—the difficulties of youth, the eternal and lovable foppery of the world. He thought of the slim boy who had once been his pupil and the callow yearnings of which he had once been the confidant; now the boy was a grown man in a glittering world, of which a Scots professor knew nothing. He thought of Jock Kinloch eating out his heart for a girl who was destined for his betters. And at the recollection he was filled with a humorous tenderness, for was he not himself a preceptor of youth, with a duty to trim its vagaries and therefore to understand them?

The world around him was young—young lambs in the fields, young leaves on the trees, mating birds everywhere, whispering grasses and frolic winds. When he ate bread and cheese at midday in a village alehouse his head was brimming with fancies. The vale through which he was riding seemed to him to have a classic grace, with the austere little hills rimming the horizon and a sky as blue as ever overhung a

Sabine farm. He wished that he was Professor of Humanity, which had been his old ambition. He could have discoursed more happily on Horace and Virgil than on Barbara Celarent and the barren logomachies of Mr. Reid. . . . He took to repeating to himself what he held to be the best of his own verses, and when the ground began to fall away towards the west and he came in sight again of the sea, he was back in the mood of the night before, and impenitently youthful.

It was the sea that did it, and the sudden waft of salt from the gleaming Firth. Below him, tucked into a nook of the coast, lay Dysart, his childhood's home—he could see the steeple of its kirk pricking above a jumble of russet tiles, and the tall trees that surrounded the policies of its great new house, where once he had bird-nested. A schooner was tacking out with every sail set to catch the breeze—in the Norway trade, he judged from its lines. The air was diamond-clear, and on the Lothian shore he could make out the little towns, the thorn-bush which was the cluster of masts in Leith harbour, the Edinburgh spires on which the sun was shining, the lift of the Castle rock, and behind all the blue backbone of the Pentlands. He had a sudden vision of the world as an immense place full of blowing winds and a most joyous bustle. Classrooms and council chambers were well enough in their way, but here around him was the raw matter, the essential stuff of life, without which schools and statesmen would be idle.

The looms were clacking in every cot-house as he rode through the weaving village of Gallatown; hammers were busy among the nailmakers of Pathhead; the smell of a tan-pit came to his nostrils with a pleasing pungency; when he descended the long slope of the Path the sight of scaly fisherfolk and tarry sailormen gave him an inconsequent delight. As he saw the horses baited, and paid off Cupar Tam, and trod the cobbles of the harbour-walk he felt inexplicably happy. He stepped aboard the grimy Leith packet with the gusto of an adventurer.

The little ship had to tack far down the Firth to get the

right slant of wind, and Mr. Lammas stood in its bows, amid piles of fresh-caught haddocks and much tarry lumber, in a happy dream. "Nanty," Jock Kinloch had called him the night before, from which it appeared that the St. Andrews students knew him familiarly among themselves by his boy's name. Well, "Nanty" let it be. In a sense it was a compliment, for he could not imagine any of his starched colleagues being thus made free of the sodality of youth. He felt more like Nanty than Anthony, and the title of Professor seemed absurd. A recollection of his errand clouded him for an instant, but it was summarily dismissed. Time enough for those grave things later; let him indulge the flying minute. "It's not often I get such a lift of the heart," he told himself. This was the mood in which poetry was written; the thought of his literary ambitions gave a comforting air of prudence to his abandonment; there was an air jigging in his head to which fine verses might be set. Everything was making music—the light wind in the rigging, the rhythmical surge and heave of the vessel through the shining waters; and presently the blind fiddler squatted under the mast struck up, and the tune he played was "Dunbarton's Drums."

A figure, looking like a fisherman in his Sabbath best, sidled up to him. He did not know the face, but the man made a familiar sign—two plucks at an unshaven chin followed by a left forefinger drawn thrice along the brows. Mr. Lammas responded with the password, and a huge hand was extended, in the hollow of which lay a strip of dirty paper. "I've gotten this for your honour from ye ken who," said the man, and took himself off. "*Mum's the word to my father, J.K.*" were the words that Mr. Lammas read, before he crumpled the scrap and dropped it overboard.

Silly fellow to be at such pains, as if he were likely to confess a son's infatuation to a father with whom he had weighty business! But the message seemed to sharpen his exhilaration. It had come twenty miles that day up the coast with miraculous expedition, and a certainty beyond His Majesty's mails. The Free Fishers were a potent folk, and he was one of them. . . . A queer sensation stole into Mr. Lammas's mind, expectancy, wonder, a little fear. He was bound on a prosaic mission of which the bounds were strictly defined, but might not Providence, once he was on the road, take a hand in ravelling his purpose? He remembered something of a poem of Burns, which he had once turned into Latin longs and shorts:

> "The best-laid schemes of mice and men
> Gang aft agley."

He had had this sense of adventure upon him ever since he smelt the salt from the Pathhead braes. He had cherished it a little guiltily, as a lawful holiday mood, but might it not be a preparation for something momentous? Mr. Lammas stepped ashore on the pier of Leith with a not unpleasant solemnity upon his spirit.

A hackney carriage took him to his inn behind the Register House, for he had no time to lose if he would keep his appointment with Lord Mannour. There he spruced himself up, and set out briskly on foot for his lordship's residence in Queen Street. The butler who admitted him announced that his master was for the moment engaged with his confidential clerk, but that the Professor was expected. Mr. Lammas was ushered into the withdrawing-room on the first floor, which, owing to the lack of females in the family—for her ladyship was dead these many years—was cheerless as a tomb. But the windows were bright with late sunshine, and from them he had a wonderful prospect. He looked down over Lord Moray's meadows to the wooded glen of the Water of Leith, and beyond, across fields of ancient pasture, to a gleaming strip of firth. He saw the Fife shore smoking with its evening hearth-fires, the soft twin breasts of the Lomonds, and, to the left, at an infinite distance, the blue confusion of the Highland hills dappled with late snow. Ye gods, what a world of marvels! It was with an effort that he composed his countenance to gravity when he heard the street-door shut on the confidential clerk and his lordship's step on the stair.

Lord Mannour was but two years on the Bench. As Peter Kinloch he had been a noted verdict-getter, the terror of judges, whom he treated with small respect, and the joy of anxious clients. Mr. Lammas had first met him when he was counsel for the University in an intricate matter of heritable property, and had respected the clean edge of his mind and the rough vigour of his tongue. At that time he had cultivated the manners of a country laird, his deep pockets looked as if they might hold twine and pruning-knives and samples of grain, and he did not condescend to trim his Fife speech to the gentility of some of his colleagues. The Bench had made his appearance more decorous, for there was no fault to be found with his full-cut black coat and well-shaped trousers, and the white neckcloth which was voluminous in an elder fashion. But he had the heavy bent shoulders of a countryman who was much on horseback, and the ruddy cheeks of a man who was much in the east wind. Sixty years of age—seeming more, for his once raven locks were prematurely white, and his thick brows hung like the eaves of a snowdrift. The contrast of the venerable hair with a face the hue of a vintage port, in which were set two brilliant dark eyes, gave him an air of masterful vitality. His repute as a lawyer was high, but higher still as a man of affairs, for he was known to be Lord Snowdoun's chief adviser, and many believed him to be the real Minister for Scotland. In private he had a name for good talk, for he was a friend of Walter Scott, a light of the Friday Club, and, after Lord Newton, the best judge of claret in the New Town. A Tory of the old rock, there were no politics in his private life, for he was said to be happier pricking philosophic bubbles with John Playfair or Dugald Stewart, discussing the laws of taste with Francis Jeffrey, or arguing on antiquarian points with Thomas Thomson than in the company of the ponderous lairds and sleek Writers to the Signet who shared his own faith.

He greeted Mr. Lammas with a gusty friendliness. A servant was at his heels as if waiting for orders.

"You have left your mails at Ramage's, Professor? Away down with you, John, and have them moved to the Tappit Hen, which will be more convenient for the coach. It leaves precisely at ten o'clock, which does not allow you and me any too much time."

"I had bespoken a seat in tomorrow's Quicksilver," Mr. Lammas began, but a wave of his lordship's hand cut him short.

"I know, I know, but I have taken the liberty to dispose otherwise. You'll agree, when you have heard what I have to tell. You'll travel by His Majesty's Mail, the Fly-by-Night, and not cramp your legs and get your death of cold in Gibbie Robison's auld daily hearse. Away, John, and see that all is in order. Meantime we'll get to our meat. The owercome says that it's ill speaking between a full man and a fasting, but two fasting men are worse at a crack, and you and I have much to say to each other. Follow me, for dinner is on the table, and the cockie-leekie will be cooling. My cook is a famous hand at it."

Mr. Lammas descended to a gloomy apartment looking out on a strip of bleaching-green. The curtains were undrawn, though candles had been lit on the table and an oil-lamp on the sideboard. The walls were in shadow except the one opposite the window, where hung a picture of a fair-haired girl, one of Mr. Raeburn's happiest efforts, which Mr. Lammas took to be the long-dead Mrs. Kinloch. A small coal-fire burned in the grate, at which three uncorked bottles of claret were warming. The host sat himself in a chair with his back to the window, and the guest took the place adjacent to the fire.

His lordship said grace.

"A glass of sherry with the soup? It prepares the way for its nobler brother, Professor, even as Saul preceded the Psalmist. I hope you are a claret-drinker, which every true Scot should be. Once it was the beverage of our people—my father minded well when it was cried through the town of Stirling at six shillings Scots the chopin. Now, alack! there are gentlemen's boards where you never see it. Too many of this degenerate age confine themselves to port, like the French Navy when Lord Nelson was on the seas. . . . You took ship from Kirkcaldy? What like were the lambs as you came through the East Neuk? You would pass within two miles of the Kinloch gates. It is my grief that the sitting of the courts prevents me being with my herds at this season of the herds' harvest, for you must know, Professor, that I'm like Cato the Censor, *agricolarum voluptatibus incredibiliter delector.* I would sooner fill my mouth with hoggs and wedders than with sasines and cautioners.

"And how's my hopeful son?" he went on, when Mr. Lammas had exhausted his scanty agricultural knowledge. "You don't wheep at college? Pity that, for Jock, though he is eighteen years of age—no, he is past nineteen—would be often the better of a well-warmed backside."

"He is a young man for whom I profess an extreme partiality. His talents are considerable, his heart is warm, and he deports himself—"

"Ay, his deportment?"

"As decorously as can be expected from young blood."

"I am glad to hear you say so." His lordship cocked a sceptical eyebrow. "I wish the partiality you speak of may not blind you to Jock's failings. The lad's like a jack-o'-lanthorn. He's all I possess, and I would have him follow me and wear an advocate's gown, like four generations of Kinlochs. He'll aye have the kitchen-midden in Fife to fall back on if he finds the Parliament House thrawn. But his head is a wasp's byke for maggots. Now he would be a soldier, now he's for off abroad to see the world, and again he would be a fine gentleman and cock his beaver among his betters. There's still more yeast than wheaten flour in yon loaf. . . . But I did not bring you here to speak of son John. Till Dickson draws the cloth I have a word to say to you on the St. Andrews business that takes you south. I have prepared a small memorial to guide you, and I have sent a scart of the pen to Lord Snowdoun to advise him of my views."

For the rest of the meal Mr. Lammas listened to a cogent summary of the points in the University's case for presentation to the authorities of the Exchequer. Then the butler removed the tablecloth, placed two massive decanters, one of claret and one of brown sherry, a dish of nuts and a platter of biscuits on the shining mahogany, put coals on the fire, drew the curtains, lit two more candles on the mantelpiece, and left the room. Lord Mannour turned his chair towards the hearth.

"Now we'll go into the real business of this sederunt," he said. "What I brought you here for is no University concern. It's something a deal more important than that. It's nothing less than the credit of a noble family and the future of an unhappy youth. Have you folk in St. Andrews heard of a certain young lady who bides not a hundred miles from you—Miss Christian Evandale, of Balbarnit?"

"I saw her park wall this very morning. Yes, I have heard of her, though I have not seen her."

"She is a year younger than my Jock, and the two were bairns together. Old Balbarnit left me her sole trustee, and it's no light charge to have in trust youth and siller. For I would have you know that Miss Christian is the best dowered lass in the kingdom of Fife."

"She has beauty also, I gather. Your son has talked to me of her beauty."

"The devil he has!" His lordship gathered his brows. "I've had a notion that Jock was airting that way. The idiot will only burn his fingers, for it is not to be permitted. I would be indeed a faithless curator if I abused my position by seeking an advantage for my son. In this matter I will be the Roman father. Kirsty will make the brawest match in Scotland, and one that consorts with her looks and her fortune. Indeed, it is already made in all but name, and the fortunate man is one whom you are acquainted with, Professor—the young Lord Belses, no less."

"What does the lady say?"

"The lady is a wise woman, and by no means disinclined

to a high destiny. Why should she be averse to espouse rank and comeliness? I have seen the lad a dozen times and he's like Phœbus Apollo."

"Is he willing—my young lord?"

The brows unbent, and Lord Mannour's face was wrinkled in a wry smile.

"*Acu rem tetigisti.* In plain English, that's the devil of it. Dismiss Miss Kirsty from your mind, for I introduced her only that you should be fully seized of the whole matter. I have had a deal to do with my Lord Snowdoun over public affairs, for when he is invalided with the gout the Lord President takes over much of the conduct of Scots business, and I am his lordship's right hand. Likewise this affair of Kirsty brought me often, as her trustee, into consultation, for I may tell you the Snowdoun family ardently desires the match. Therefore I have heard much of Lord Belses, and had him much in my mind, and now his father has opened his heart to me. That's why I bade you here tonight. I would speak to you, not as Questor and Professor of St. Andrews, but as Anthony Lammas, umquhile governor to Lord Belses and, it may be presumed, with some influence over him. For, let me tell you, your young friend is ploughing a dangerous rig."

Lord Mannour held his glass so that the firelight made it a glowing ruby. He cocked his eye at it, sipped the wine for a moment in silence, and then swung round to his companion.

"He's riding a rough ford, and if you and I cannot help him across, then by God he is down the burn and away with it. . . . Fill your glass Professor, for it's with you that the heavy end of this job must rest. My Lord Snowdoun was here last week and we took counsel together, and the gist of our discussion was that the key to the perplexity was just yourself. It seems that the lad cherishes a liking for you, and a respect which unhappily he does not feel for his natural parent. We concluded that you were the only man alive that might correct his waywardness."

"It's more than three years since I saw him, and his letters lately have been few."

"Nevertheless, you are much in his mind. He quotes you—quotes you to the confusion of his mentors. Your tongue must whiles have wagged unwisely when you had the lad in charge."

Mr. Lammas blushed. "I was younger then, and I may have spoken sometimes with the thoughtlessness of youth. . . . But I beg you, my lord, to put me out of suspense. What ill has befallen my dear Harry?"

"Your dear Harry has been playing the muckle gowk. That's the plain Scots of it. I will read you the counts in the indictment. In fairness, let me say that from some foibles of youth he seems to be notably free. He does not gamble, which is so much the better for a family that has scarcely the means to support its rank and its deserts. He is temperate, and at no time is either *ebrius*, *eriolus* or *ebriosus*, as old Gardenstone used to put it. Maybe it would have been better for all concerned if he had birled the bottle and rattled the dice like the rest. No, but he has taken up with more dangerous pastimes. His father was ill-advised enough to let him travel abroad after Oxford, without a douce companion such as yourself. There's just the one capacity in which a man should cross the Channel in these days, and that's as an officer of Lord Wellington's. Well, it seems that in foreign parts he picked up some Jacobin nonsense, and now that he is back he has been airing his daft-like politics to the scandal of honest folk."

"I am amazed," Mr. Lammas cried. "Harry had a most sober and judicious mind."

"Well, he has lost it, and I think I can put my finger on the reason why. I care not a bodle if a young gentleman flings his heels and is a wee bit wild in his conversation. He is only blowing off the vapours of youth, and will soon settle down to be a 'sponsible citizen. But in this case there is more behind it. Lord Belses has found an aider and abetter. He is tied to the petticoat tails of a daft wife."

"A wife! He is married, then? . . ."

"No, no. There's no marriage. I used our vernacular term for the other sex when we would speak of it without respect. Wife, but not his. She may be a widow, for I cannot just recollect if her husband is still alive. His name is Cranmer, and he is—or was—an ill-conditioned Northumberland squire. Hungrygrain is his estate, in Yonderdale, on the backside of Cheviot. She is young, and by all accounts she is not ill-favoured, and she has bound the poor boy to her with hoops of iron."

"Is she his mistress?"

"God knows! I jalouse not, for it seems that she is an enthusiast in religion as she is a Jacobin in politics. There's no more dangerous creature on earth than a childless woman who takes up with matters too high for her. There's some modicum of sense left in the daftest man, but there's none in a daft hussy. It seems that poor Harry is fair besotted—will hear no word of ill about her—follows her like a shadow—sits at her feet to imbibe the worst heresies anent Church and State—an anxiety to his family and a disgrace to his rank. What do you think of your umquhile pupil, Professor?"

"I think—I do not know what to think—I am deeply distressed."

"And that is not the worst of it, and here I come to the gravamen of the business. The woman not unnaturally bears an ill name among decent folk. Things are said of her, gossip flies, evil is spoken which is maybe not always well-founded. The young bloods make free with her repute, for her drunken husband, if he is still in life, is no kind of a protector. So what does our brave Harry do? Out he comes as her champion. Whoever says one word against Mrs. Cranmer, or even cocks a critical eyebrow, will have to settle with him. That is his proclamation to the world. There is one young fellow—not so young, for they tell me he is a man of thirty—who is especially free with his tongue. It comes to my lord Harry's ear, who in a public place asks him to repeat it, and, when he is obliged, gives him the lie direct and gets a cartel for his pain. The man—I have his name—one Sir Turnour Wyse—is furious, and promises, as my father used to say, to knock the powder out of his lordship's wig. With that the fat is fairly in the fire. It seems that this Wyse is a truculent fellow, so there is no chance of a settlement. Further, he is a noted pistol-shot, and has already accounted for three men in the cool of the morning."

"They have not fought?" Mr. Lammas quavered.

"Not yet, for steps have been taken to prevent their meeting. Lord Belses has been impounded by his family and is under lock and key. Sir Turnour Wyse has posted him as a coward and is ranging the earth in quest of him. The belief is that Harry has come to Scotland, and the mad baronet is after him like a whippet after a hare. But, let me tell it in your ear, the lad is cannily in London under duress, and there he must remain till he is brought to a better mind. If he meets this Wyse he has not one chance in a thousand, and a young life must not be sacrificed to folly. So to London you must go, and this very night, for any hour may bring a tragedy."

"But what am I to do?"

"Reason with him. Free him from the toils of that accursed baggage. No doubt the trouble with Wyse can be settled without disgrace if the lad will only show a little sense. You are the last hope of his worthy father—and of me that has Kirsty's interests in charge. The credit of a great house is at stake, and, what is more important for you, the future of one you love."

"But if he will not be guided by me?"

"Then you must try other ways. You must conspire with Lord Snowdoun to achieve by force what cannot be won by argument. You must be the bait to entice the lad somewhere where he will be out of mischief. Have no fear, Professor. This is your supreme duty, and Lord Snowdoun and I will set it right with your Senatus, even though St. Andrews should not see you for many a day. Whatever money you need will be at your disposal. I have written down here the address in London to which you will go, and where Lord Snowdoun will give you full instructions. I place much on your wise tongue and the old kindness between the two of you. If these fail, there is the other way I have hinted at. There's plenty of wild country for hidy-holes between the Channel and the Pentland Firth. St. Kilda has not had a tenant since Lord Grange spirited away his thrawn auld wife."

Lord Mannour had talked himself into confidence and good temper.

"You'll be thinking it strange that I, a Senator of the College of Justice, should counsel violent doing to a minister of the Kirk. If that's in your mind, let me tell you that both in law and in religion there is a debatable land not subject to the common rules. I ask you to do nothing which can conceivably be against your conscience. For myself, as a student of the law of Rome, I am strong for the *patria potestas*, and that Jock knows to his cost."

"What is in my mind," said Mr. Lammas, whose countenance was troubled, "is that I am not the man for such a task. How can I, a humble scholar and provincial, hope to influence a dweller in the great world? I am not even familiar with its language."

"Maybe no. But when you get down to the bit, those discrepancies will count for little. Supposing it's a cadger's beast against a racehorse. As my father used to say, though one goes farther on the road in five minutes than the other does in an hour, they will commonly stable together at night. It's the end of the journey that matters."

Mr. Lammas passed a hand over his eyes.

"I am deeply distressed—and sore perplexed. My affection for Harry obliges me to do all that is in my power for his succour, but I am lamentably conscious that that all is but little."

"Tut, man! Why make such a poor mouth about it? You are over-modest. I tell you that I have for some time had my eye upon you, and Lord Snowdoun has had his eye upon you, and we are both convinced of your competence. Maybe you lack something, but you are the best available. You have years enough and learning enough to ballast you, and you are young enough to talk to youth in its own tongue. My ne'er-do-well Jock, if he were here, would no doubt bear me out on this latter point, for you are the one man he speaks of with decent respect. . . . Here's Grierson with the toddy-bowl. We'll drink a rummer to your success, and then you must take the road."

The butler set on the mahogany a mighty tray with the materials for punch—a china bowl, a potbellied flagon of whisky with a silver stopper, two tall glasses, a kettle of hot water, a bag of lemons and a dish of broken sugar-loaf. There was also a letter, which Lord Mannour, thinking it some ordinary missive on legal business, at first disregarded. He brewed the toddy to his taste, filled the two glasses, and handed one to his guest.

"Here's to you," he said. "The toast is success to honesty and confusion to folly."

But he set down his rummer untasted, for his eye had caught the superscription on the letter. With an exclamation he tore it open, and as he read it his black brows came together.

"God ha' mercy!" he cried. "This is from Lord Snowdoun—by special messenger—the man must have flown, for it's dated only two days back. Harry has broken bounds and disappeared, and they have no notion of his whereabouts. . . . Here' a bonny tangle to redd up!"

"Do my instructions still hold?" Mr. Lammas asked timidly, for his lordship's formidable face was very dark.

"More than ever," was the fierce answer. "But there's this differ, that you must find the lad first before you can reason with him. There's just the one duty before you, to get on to his scent like a hound with a tod. . . . Finish your glass, and be off with you. My man's waiting to lead you to the coach. Whatever wit and wisdom there is in your head you must bend to this grievous task. The day after the morn you'll be with Lord Snowdoun, and after that may God prosper you!"

Mr. Lammas rose, but not heavily or dispiritedly. This last piece of news had mysteriously altered his outlook. Youth had risen in him as it had risen the night before under the April sky. He felt himself called, not to a duty, but to an adventure.

CHAPTER III

TELLS OF A NIGHT JOURNEY

THE mood carried him with long strides to the hostelry of the Tappit Hen, Lord Mannour's man John being forced to trot at his side. The moon had scarcely risen, but the narrow street was bright with stable lanterns and the great headlights and tail-lights of a coach. The Fly-by-Night, carrying His Majesty's mails, seemed to Mr. Lammas's country eye but a frail vessel in which to embark on a long journey. Its crimson undercarriage and the panels which bore the royal arms glowed like jewels in the lantern light, for the polish was like that of a Dutch cabinet. The horses were being put to it, with a great clatter of hooves on the cobbles, but with none of the babble of stable-boys which attended the setting out of the St. Andrews diligence. This was a high ceremonial, performed with speed and silence.

Not more than three outside passengers were permitted on a royal mail, and Mr. Lammas, having seen his baggage stowed in the boot, climbed to the box seat. Thence he looked down upon a scene which filled him with romantic expectation. The coachman, who was in royal livery—so he must have had long service behind him—and had the best brushed boots and the best tied cravat that Mr. Lammas had ever seen, was a little rosy man with a hat nicely cocked on one side of a great head. He drank a glass of some cordial which a maid from the inn presented to him on a silver salver, chucked the girl under the chin, and then walked to the horses' heads, inspecting critically the curb chains and the coupling reins, and taking particular note that the tongues of the billet-buckles were secure in their holes. A second passenger arrived for the outside, also a little man, in a topcoat which enveloped his ears, and sat himself on one of the two roof seats. Then appeared the inside party, two ladies so shawled and scarfed that nothing could be seen of their faces, and with them what seemed to be their servant, who joined Mr. Lammas on the outside.

The coachman climbed to his box with the reins looped over one arm, settled himself comfortably, caught the thong of his whip three times round the stick, and cried a word to the ostlers. These stood back from the leaders, and the beautiful creatures, young beasts nearly thoroughbred, flung up their heads as they were given the office and plunged forward up to their bits, till the weight of the heavier wheelers steadied them and brought them back to their harness. The little crowd cheered, the guard played "Oh, dear, what can the matter be?" on a key bugle, and, almost before Mr. Lammas was aware, the cobbles of Edinburgh and its last faubourgs were behind him, and he was being carried briskly along the new south road.

The coachman attended strictly to his business till they were some miles from the city and moving between fresh-ploughed fields and a firth now silvered by moonlight. He then screwed his head and had a look at the two others behind. The prospect did not seem to please him. "Japanned! The whole dam lot of 'em!" he murmured. "And me that looked for the Baronet! Devilish poor lot to kick." After that he sank his head into his cravat, and his further conversation was addressed to his leaders.

"He means," said a voice from behind, "that we're all ministers of the Kirk, and are not likely to fee him well."

Mr. Lammas turned and observed his two companions. The one who had spoken was so small that his travelling coat made him look like a mole emerging from its burrow. The moon showed his face clearly—one of those faces in which an unnaturally square chin and unnaturally tight lips lose their effect from prominent goggle eyes. The other was a taller fellow with a lugubrious countenance and a thick white comforter round his throat. Since all three of them wore dark travelling coats the coachman's assumption was not unreasonable.

"Are you a minister, sir, if I may make bold to speir?" asked the man who had first spoken. He had a rich consequential voice, which put a spice of dignity into his inquisitiveness.

"I am a minister, but I have no charge." Mr. Lammas was in too friendly a mood to the world to resent questions.

"Stickit?"

"No, placed, but not in any parish. I am a professor."

"Keep us! On the divinity side?"

"No. My chair is philosophy. My name is Lammas."

The other repeated it with respect. "Lammas! And a philosopher! Had you been a theologian I would have kenned the name. Well, sir, since we're to be company for the livelong night we may as well be friends. My name is Dott, Duncan Dott, and I'm the town-clerk of the ancient and royal burgh of Waucht."

"A most honourable office," said Mr. Lammas cordially.

"You may say so. Honourable but laborious. If I were to tell you the battles I've had to fight on behalf of the common good—the burgh lands and the pontage over the Waucht water—the wrestling with oppressive lairds—the constant strife over cess and fess and market dues and the minister's teinds—gudesakes, Professor, you'd be content with your own canny lot. But it's not on burgh business that I'm now on the road, for I'm likewise a writer and have the factoring of two or three kittle estates."

He checked himself, as if he felt that discretion demanded no further revelations. But his curiosity was still active.

"I wonder who the two inside passengers may be—the two women rowed up like bolsters. . . . And can we have the favour of your name, friend?" he asked, turning to the third man.

The answer came in a melancholy voice out of the folds of the woollen muffler.

"Ye're welcome. My name is Pitten—Ebenezer Pitten—at least that is what I gang by. Properly it should be Pittendreich, like my father afore me and a' my kin Dunfermline way. But Miss Georgie will not hae it. 'Ye're a dreich enough body,' she says, 'without stickin' dreich at the end of your name. Forbye,' she says, 'it's ower long to cry about the house.' So Pitten I've been thae ten years, and I've near forgotten ony other. . . . Ye speir wha the two leddies are? Weel, I can tell ye, for I'm nae less than their butler. The younger—but ye'd not ken the difference, for, as ye justly observe, they are both rowed up like bolsters—the younger is my mistress, Miss Christian Evandale of Balbarnit, well kenned for the bonniest and best-tochered young leddy in the kingdom of Fife. And the other is just her auntie that bides with her, Miss Georgina Kinethmont, her that insists on calling me out o' my baptism name."

"I've heard tell of Miss Evandale," said Mr. Dott respectfully. "The clash is that all the lads in Fife and Angus and the feck of the Lothians are after her. She's bonny, you say?"

"Abundantly weel-favoured."

"And rich?"

"Fourteen thousand acres of guid farming land, and feus in a dozen burgh-towns, forbye a wecht o' siller in the bank."

"And an ancient family, no doubt?"

"No her. That is to say, no on her father's side, though her mother's folk the Kinethmonts are weel enough come. Her father was the son of auld Nicholas Ebbendaal, the Hollander that owned a' the Dundee whalers. He left his son awesome riches, and naething would serve that son but that he maun tak the siller out of ships and put it intil land, and set up as a laird. Ebbendaal wasna considered gentrice enough, so he changed it to Evandale, when he bought Balbarnit from the drucken lad that was the last o' the auld Metlands. 'Deed ye can see the Hollander in Miss Kirsty for a' her denty ways. I wadna put it by her to be a wee thing broad in the beam when she grows aulder, like a Rotterdam brig."

"You've an ill-scraped tongue," said Mr. Dott.

"No me. I'm an auld and tried servant o' the family, and I ken my place, but among friends I can open my mind. I've said naething against Miss Kirsty. She's mindfu' and mensefu' and as bonny as a simmer day."

"What like's her auntie, Miss what-d'ye-call-her?"

Mr. Pitten's voice sank, and he looked nervously round him. "Speak not evil of dignitaries," he answered, "lest the birds of the air carry it. But them inside will no hear me with the rummle o' this coach. Miss Georgie"—his voice sank lower—"is a braw manager and a grand heid for business, but she is like the upper and the nether millstone. She's a great woman, but an awfu' one, and she has a tongue in her heid that would deafen the solans. The best place for her would be wi' the sodgers, for I wager she'd fricht Bonyparte if she ever won near him."

They wore rolling along a flat road close to the shore, and the easy motion predisposed Mr. Lammas's companions to sleep. The first change of horses was accomplished with the precision of a military movement and in not more than sixty seconds. "Behold," said Mr. Lammas to himself, "how use creates skill, and skill habit." After that Mr. Dott seemed to sink inside his greatcoat, like a mole going back to earth, and his steady breathing, accompanied by an occasional gurgle, soon proclaimed that he was asleep. The Balbarnit butler presently followed suit, snoring portentously, with his mouth open and his head wagging over the coach's side. The noise caught the coachman's ear, and when he observed that Mr. Lammas was alone wakeful, he showed himself inclined to conversation.

"Let 'em snore," he said. "They'll be shook up and wakened right enough on Kitterston hill. Was I right? Are all three o' you japanned?"

"You were wrong. I am the only one in holy orders, and I am not a minister but a professor."

The other brooded over this information, and seemed to be puzzled.

"Professor," he said. "They 'ave 'em in Oxford, but you're not that breed. The only others I know of are the professors that cure corns and rheumatiz at the fairs. There was one at Barnet, I mind, that had a crown piece off me and left me lamer nor a duck. That your line o' country?"

"No," said Mr. Lammas. "I am a professor of philosophy."

The coachman grinned.

"I'll shake hands with you on that. A philosopher—that's what they calls me. 'George Tolley,' they says, 'you're a philosopher and no mistake. You always comes up smilin'. Never a grumble from you, George. And the philosophic way you handles your cattle is a fair treat to be'old.' So we're two of a trade, you and me, though we works different roads. How long have you been at it? Three years? It's thirty-seven years come Ladyday since I first took up the ribbons and started in on philosophy."

Mr. Lammas asked if he had always driven the Royal Mail.

"Lord bless you, no. They don't let any amateur serve His Majesty. The Mail, as you might say, is the last stage for a philosopher. I began when I was a nipper as stable-boy at Badminton with the old Dook. Then I was allowed to take a 'and with his Grace's private coach, and then for four years I drove the Beaufort back and forward from Gloucester to the Bull and Mouth. After that I come north, and took the York Express from Leeds to London. One hunner and ninety-six miles, and I have done it in sixteen hours. It's them north-country roads as larns you your job, for any ordinary tidy whip can push along the Brighton Age or the Bristol Triumph. It's nussin' horses that's the philosophy of coachin'—not, as young bloods think, the knack of flicking a fly off a leader's ear. Just you watch," said Mr. Tolley. "That off leader there is a bit too fresh. What does I do with him?"

The horse in question was fretting and fidgeting and suddenly broke into a canter which upset the balance of the team. Mr. Tolley promptly pulled in the wheelers, with the result that the leaders also were held back and made to feel the collar.

"A young spark," he said, "would have tried to pull him up by the bit, and would ha' made him wuss by bringin' him back on the bar. I pulls him up by his harness, all as sweet as sugar. That's what I means by philosophy."

Mr. Lammas was a willing pupil in this novel branch of his subject. He asked the inevitable question. There were many amateur drivers about, gentlemen who owned their own coaches or for a hobby drove a stage. How did such compare with the regulars?

It was a subject on which Mr. Tolley felt deeply, but, being a philosopher, he was a just man. With his whip hand he rubbed his smooth chin.

"That ain't easy to answer. The college boys that drives the Oxford and Cambridge stages are of no particular account, though some of 'em larns the job in time. And there's heaps o' gentlemen as can make a pretty show with four nicely matched tits past Hyde Park Corner that I wouldn't trust for ser'ous work. But there's no doubt that the gentleman when he sets his mind to it makes a fine whip, for he does for love what me and my likes does for hire, and love helps any game. Besides, he has eddication, and can think about things and find the reasons for 'em, while my philosophy is just what God Almighty has larned me by 'ard knocks. But Lord save us! some of 'em are terrible pernickety. They've mostly all got some fad, and I've 'ad gentlemen come lecturin' me about 'aving a short wheel rein, and fastening the buckles of my ribbons, and sich like. 'You may be right, my lord,' I says, very polite, but under my breath I says, 'Go and teach your grandma'.

"The best," Mr. Tolley continued reflectively. "Well, there was a Scotch gentleman, Captain Barclay, that drove this very Mail all the four hundred miles from Edinbro' to London. But I don't reckon 'im a finished whip, more what they calls a 'Ercules. But there's three—four—yes, five gentlemen I allows to be my equal, and the equal of any professional coachman that ever drew on gloves. There's Sir John Fagg in Kent. In Oxfordshire there's Sir Henry Peyton with his greys, and Mr. Harrison with his browns. There's Mr. Warde as works from Warwickshire into Shropshire, and Mr. John Walker down Sussex way. Them five I calls my equals, but there's one gentleman to whom I gives best every time. Whatever stakes he enters for George Tolley withdraws, for he knows his master. And that gent is Sir Turnour Wyse, Baronet, of Wood Rising 'All, in the county o' Norfolk. Well I knows the name, for he sends my missus a brace of pheasants every Christmas."

Mr. Lammas started.

"Sir Turnour Wyse! I did not know that he was a famous whip."

"Well, you know now. The famousest! A pink! An out-and-outer," cried Mr. Tolley enthusiastically. "He sometimes travels with me, and then I keeps my ears open to pick up what I can. Not that he 'asn't his fads. Short wheel reins—that's the worst of 'em. I saw him this very day in Edinbro', and I was hopin' to have him sittin' tonight where you're sittin'. But if he's comin' south it'll likely be in his own chaise."

Mr. Lammas's eyes were growing heavy, and this the coachman observed. "We'll dry up now," he said, "and you'd best have a nap. We're comin' into hilly ground, and will have to slacken down a bit. In three hours we'll be at Berwick, where you'll get a glass of summat, and at Newcastle you'll have your bellyful of breakfast."

So Mr. Lammas dozed uneasily, and woke up to find the Mail halted at an inn for a change of horses. The little cold wind which precedes the dawn was blowing, and he drew the collar of his coat about his ears. A light fog, too, was rolling up from the sea, which blanketed the ground, but left the inn gables and a tall tree sticking out in a dim grey half-light. He found Mr. Tolley in a bad temper.

"This cussed fog," he grumbled. "Wuss than black

darkness, for the lights don't show. I wouldn't mind it if we 'ad decent narrow roads atween 'edges, but this stage is mostly in the open and what's to hinder us from bumpin' into loose cattle. Likewise these new quads ain't up to the mark, and I'll be shot if I don't report Mackutcheon for bad hosses. It ain't the first time he's done it. Them wheelers is too small and weak for Kitterston hill, and we can't slow down, for we're behind time already. And I'll be shot if that near leader 'asn't 'ad the megrims. I don't like the stiff neck of him, and the way he's snatchin' at his collar."

Sunrise was not far off, but the mist dimmed the first premonition of it from the east, and though the nostrils smelt dawn the eyes were still in night. The morning was windless, except for tiny salt airs that rose like exhalations from the abyss on the left which was the sea. The road had become a sort of switchback among shallow glens, and the befogged lamps showed that it was bounded by no paling or hedge or dry-stone dyke, but marched directly with bent and heather. Curlews were beginning to call like souls lost in the brume. They reminded Mr. Lammas of spring days at Snowdoun under the Ochils and at Catlaw in Tweeddale; they also reminded him of his former pupil and his difficult errand, and so drove out the last dregs of sleep. He observed that his companions were also awake. Mr. Dott's head had emerged like a turtle from his overcoat, and he was blinking and sniffing the raw air, while the Balbarnit butler, yawning extravagantly, was searching in some inner pocket for snuff.

The easy motion of the earlier hours had gone, and Mr. Tolley seemed to have his hands full with his horses, and to be disinclined for conversation. As compared with the ordinary stagecoach the Mail was lightly laden; nevertheless, with five passengers and much baggage, it carried a full burden for its make. The horsing at the last halt had not been good—even Mr. Lammas's unpractised eye could see that. The wheelers were small and light and moved badly together, and the off one, when he felt the weight behind pressing on him, was inclined to break into a canter. The near leader, a weedy bay with poor shoulders, seemed to be only half broken, for it kept its head jerked away from its partner, and was perpetually shouldering the pole. In these circumstances the driver's tactics were to force the pace, taking most of the short descents at a gallop and thereby acquiring momentum for the next hill. The speed was exhilarating, but it was also nerve-shaking, for the coach swayed ominously, and at one hill with a crook in it Mr. Lammas was convinced that they were over.

Mr. Dott was nervous.

"I don't like it," he muttered between his clenched teeth. "These are awesome hills if that fog would let us see them—I've travelled this road before—and it would have been wiser-like to have had a lock-wheel or a drag chain instead of taking each brae as if it was the finish of Musselburgh races. What the—!" His words were jerked out of him like squeaks from a bladder. "Forgive me, but this will betray me into profane swearing. Hey, coachman—driver—are you determined to break all our necks?"

Mr. Tolley disdained to answer, but after the fourth or fifth appeal he condescended to address Mr. Lammas.

"Best way with this raw stuff is to sweat it, and in five minutes we'll have Kitterston hill behind us. Keep an easy mind, sir, for I've 'andled wuss cattle on wuss roads. We'd 'ave daylight if only this blasted fog would lift."

Presently they topped a rise, and after a hundred yards on the flat the road seemed to tilt forward into an immense trough of shadow. It did not take Mr. Dott's fervent "It's Kitterston—God be kind to us" to tell Mr. Lammas that they were descending no ordinary hill. Close to the top there was a patch of special steepness which brought the coach's weight down upon the wheelers and set them cantering. Mr. Tolley whipped the canter into a gallop, and, swaying sickeningly at the corners, they rocketed down into the abyss. Mr. Lammas felt an awful exhilaration, for never had he known movement so swift and so mysterious. He sat tight, clutching the handrail, his feet braced against the footboard, while from his companions behind came little noises that may have been prayers. Mr. Tolley knew his job, for even in what seemed a reckless gallop he steered a course. The surface of the road was hard hill gravel on which the wheels scarcely bit, but on the left side was a rut of softer ground, and by keeping the coach's near wheels there he made it act like a brake.

The fog thinned as they descended. Presently Mr. Lammas realized that they were over the worst, for he felt the gradient lessen and saw the road sweep before them in a gentler slope. They must be nearing the bottom, and at the bottom there would be a stream, and either a ford or a bridge. Once they were past the water hazard they could breathe freely. . . . Then, as the vapour thinned he realized that it was actually daylight. The sun was showing through the cotton-wool layers, and the smell of the sea came with a pungent freshness. His spirits rose, his mouth shaped itself to whistling, and he was embarking on "Dunbarton's Drums" when he saw something which froze the music on his lips. For in the vanishing fog the road had cleared right to the valley bottom, and there, not ten yards off, was a flock of sheep, which had drifted down from the moor and were taking their ease on the King's highway.

Mr. Tolley saw it too, for he rose in his seat and endeavoured to pull up his team. It was too late, for the galloping leaders were into the flock. They both fell, the main bar unhooked, and the wheelers were on the top of them. The coach lurched, slewed round as the wheelers swung sharp to the right, and then with a violent grating and creaking bowed forward into a shallow ditch. Mr. Tolley did not lose his seat, and Mr. Dott and the butler kept theirs by a desperate clutch on the rail, but Mr. Lammas, who had got to his feet in readiness to jump clear, was catapulted by the shock into a bush of heather.

He picked himself up, shaken but with unbroken bones, and hurried back to the place of disaster. There he was the witness of a wild spectacle. The leaders were wallowing under the splinter-bar and Mr. Tolley was struggling to disengage them, while the guard dealt with the half-frantic wheelers. Barring cut knees the horses seemed to have taken no harm, but the pole of the coach had snapped. Mr. Dott, still on the roof, was investigating a brown leather satchel to see that his papers were safe, and the butler was descending with difficulty to resume his duties. For his two ladies had emerged from the coach's interior, and one, who was still masked and shawled like a highwayman, was filling the morning air with her complaints. The other, who had rid herself of her cloak, revealed a very pretty face under a green travelling hat. "Hold your tongue, Aunt Georgie," she was saying. "There is no harm done. You're screaming like a seagull over nothing."

Suddenly beside the wrecked Mail there drew up another vehicle, also coming from the north. It was a curious make of chaise, very broad, with a dicky behind it; it had a pole instead of the usual shafts, and it was drawn by two cobs who seemed to have come fast and far. In the dicky sat a servant in a dark livery, and the driver was a tall man, who wore a white beaver and one of the massive frieze coats called dreadnoughts. He was on the ground in a second, and strode to the struggling Mr. Tolley at the coach's head. He seemed to know his work, for he unbuckled certain straps and helped to get the leaders on to their feet, quieting the near one with curious pattings and strokings. Then he cast an eye over the broken pole and the panting wheelers.

"You've made a pretty mess of it, George," he said. "I always warned you what would happen."

The driver raised a furious red face, but one glance at the speaker was enough to compose his features into respect. He touched the rim of his hat.

" 'Twas bad hosses as done it, your honour," he grumbled. "Bad hosses and them bloody sheeps."

"Bad horses be hanged and bloody sheep be crucified," was the answer. "You hadn't control of your team or you could have pulled up in time. The fog has been lightening for twenty minutes—I watched it coming down the hill. It's the old story. If you had had short wheel reins and breechings to your harness, this need never have happened. How often have I told you that?"

Mr. Tolley would no doubt have made answer, but the tall man gave him no chance. "Bustle along George," he said, "for His Majesty's business can't wait. Let the guard—who is it?—Ribston?—take one of the wheelers and ride the four miles to Berwick, for the mails must be in time for the morning Highflyer. Take you the other wheeler and go hunt for a smith—that pole is smith's work—and put up the leaders at the inn here. They won' be fit for much for a week. Ribston will bring out fresh beasts, and you should be in Berwick by midday. . . . As for these gentlemen, my advice is that they look for breakfast and then take a chaise to Berwick. Ah, you have ladies?" he added, as he caught sight of the two figures who were striving with the shaken Mr. Pitten. He advanced with hat in hand, and addressed the elder.

"Madam," he said, "I have the good fortune to be travelling the same road. Can I have the felicity of serving you? I can offer you two seats in my humble chariot, and my servant can assist yours in bringing on the baggage. I can promise you that in half an hour I will turn you over to the chambermaids at the Red Lion."

Miss Georgie seemed about to raise difficulties and Miss Kirsty to make polite protests, but he smilingly ignored them. This was a man of action, for in three minutes the elder woman was sitting at his side and the younger in the seat behind, he had taken the reins, lifted his whip, and the cobs were trotting Berwick-wards. His orders about the coach, too, were being exactly fulfilled. The leaders were limping to the inn stables in the charge of Mr. Tolley, and the guard, laden with mail bags, had set forth on one of the wheelers. The other passengers, having secured their valises, were making shift to carry them to the inn, and the two servants were struggling with the ladies' baggage. As they reached the door, Mr. Tolley was leaving on his quest for a smith, and he shook hands ruefully with Mr. Lammas.

"That was an accident as no mortal man could prevent," he declared. "He's wrong—you take my word for it—clean wrong. It 'ad nothing to do with long wheel-reins or breechin' to the 'arness. It was bad hosses and bloody sheeps. For all his wisdom he 'as his megrims, just like that cussed near leader."

"Who was the gentleman?" Mr. Lammas asked.

"Why, Sir Turnour Wyse, Baronet—him I was tellin' you about."

CHAPTER IV

IN WHICH A YOUNG LOVER IS SLIGHTED

WITH a preoccupied mind Mr. Lammas entered the lobby of the little inn with its homely fragrance of new-kindled fires, oil-lamps and morning cooking, bowed to the smiling and flustered landlady, and heard Mr. Dott order a generous breakfast. That commanding figure in the dreadnought had strongly impressed him, and he marvelled at the way in which fate was speeding up his experience. Ten hours ago he had heard from Lord Mannour the name of Sir Turnour Wyse as the main peril which threatened the young man whom it was his mission to save; Mr. Tolley on the coach had spoken of him in worshipping accents; and now the man himself had appeared, a god from a machine, looking, like some Homeric hero, larger than human in the morning fog. Most clearly destiny was taking a hand in the game.

Horses could be provided, said the landlady. The gig had been already bespoken to carry the ladies' baggage and the servants, but the sociable was at the gentlemen's disposal and would be ready as soon as Rob Dickson had had his brose and had caught the young mare. Again Mr. Lammas had a delicious sense of being drawn into a new world. The short walk to the inn had been like a bath in cold water, for the mist was furling into airy corridors which revealed at their end the bluest of skies, and a great salty freshness was coming up from the sea. The bustle of the inn and the demand for horses was like a sudden resurrection of his boyhood. Also he was furiously hungry, and Mr. Dott's command for fresh haddocks, eggs, and a brandered collop to follow had amply interpreted his desires.

Out from the parlour came the sound of lusty singing.

> "Katie Beardie had a coo,
> A' black about the moo,—
> Wasna yon a denty coo?—
> Dance, Katie Beardie."

He recognized both the voice and the song. He opened the door to find Jock Kinloch taking his ease before the remnants of a mutton ham.

There was nothing of the St. Andrews secondar about Jock's appearance. He wore a coarse, knitted woollen jersey, and much-stained nether garments, of which the ends were stuffed into heavy sea-boots. His head was more tousled than ever, and the weather had given his complexion the ripeness of his father's.

"God be kind to us!" he cried. "Nanty!" And then he stopped, for he saw that a stranger was present and changed his address to "Professor." "You're a sight for sore eyes, but I never looked to meet you here. I thought that at this moment you would be at Ramage's taking your seat in the Quicksilver."

"I left last night with the Mail, and half an hour back we had a breakdown at the hill foot. May I present to you Mr. Duncan Dott, the town-clerk of the burgh of Waucht? This is Mr. John Kinloch, Mr. Dott. You are no doubt familiar with his father's name."

"Not Lord Mannour's son?" said Mr. Dott, relaxing his tight jaws into a grin, and holding out a cordial hand. "Indeed I know of your father, young sir, and what is more, in the old days I have often fee'd him, for he was the burgh's favourite counsel in their bits of law business. Ay, and three months back he did us a great service. The burgh had a plea against Dalitho the tanner anent his stink-pots on Waucht

Green. We lost before the Lord Ordinary—a most inequitable decision, but old Curlywee is long past his best—but the Upper House gave it in our favour, and your worthy father, sir, delivered a judgment which will long be remembered as the pure milk of the legal word. I'm honoured to meet his son. . . . You'll take another bite of breakfast with us, for it's a snell morning."

"I'll have a cup of tea with you when the wife brings it, but I must get back to the boat. You say the Mail has spilt itself? That would be the clatter of horses I heard at the stable door and took for the gaugers from Berwick."

"You haven't told me what brought you here," said Mr. Lammas. "I got a request from you on the Kirkcaldy packet, and I need not tell you that I obeyed it. But I thought you were at Kinloch."

Jock winked mysteriously.

"I'm on a bit of a jaunt," he said. "I came down the coast yesterday with some friends of mine—friends of yours too, Professor."

"Where are you bound?"

Again Jock winked.

"That's telling. Maybe just to see the world, and get the fine fresh air, and see the solans on the Bass.

"Who are your companions?"

"The best. Who but Bob Muschat, your old crony, and Eben Garnock himself."

Mr. Lammas started. What took the Chief Fisher in such haste down the Berwick shore, for Eben Garnock was a great man who did not stir himself except for a good purpose. It could not be fishing business, for the herrings were gone north towards the Tay. And how came a new member of the brotherhood like Jock Kinloch to be taken thus early into the inner circle?

Jock's face had an unwonted gravity. "I would like a word with you, Professor, before you go. Maybe I can do something for you and you for me."

At that moment an untidy kitchen-maid brought in the

breakfast and plumped it on the table, and the landlady followed more ceremoniously with the tea-urn and a great jug of creamy milk. The travellers fell greedily upon the food, but Jock contented himself with a cup of tea and a new-baked scone. Conversation ceased while the first pangs of hunger were being quieted.

But the peace was suddenly broken. A melancholy countenance poked itself round a half-opened door. "We're for off"—it said, addressing Mr. Lammas. "Is there onything I can do for you in Berwick? We'll be there long or you."

Jock Kinloch sprang to his feet.

"Pitten!" he cried. "Where on earth have you sprung from?"

The head came a little farther into the room.

"I've been delivered by the mercy of God from the miry pit. Have ye not heard, Mr. Kinloch? The Mail coupit—or came near to coupin'—at the foot o' Kitterston hill, and left the hale clanjamphry o' us on our flat feet. Nae blood spilt, the Lord be thankit, but such a stramash I never beheld."

"But *you*—what brought *you* here?"

"I was with my leddies—Miss Christian Evandale of Balbarnit, and her auntie, Miss Georgina Kinethmont. Well ye ken them, Mr. Kinloch. We're off to London, and we have startit unco ill."

"The ladies! They took no hurt?"

"Not a bodle. They sat snug as mice in the inside o' the coach, though Miss Georgie was wantin' somebody hangit for the breakdown. Syne by comes a braw gentleman in a chaise, and he whups the twasome awa' wi' him to Berwick. They're at the Red Lion, and I'm followin' wi' their mails. I maun haste, or I'll get the ill-scrapit side o' Miss Georgie's tongue."

The head withdrew and Jock flung himself from the room in pursuit. Sounds of whispering and then of loud command were heard from the lobby. Jock returned with a fiery face and a stern purpose in his eye.

"I'm off, Nanty," he said, forgetting the presence of Mr.

Dott. "The wind's right, and I'll get Eben to slip down in the boat, and I'll be there before Pitten in his old hearse of a gig. Kirsty in trouble and me not beside her—the thing's not thinkable! You're certain she wasn't hurt? Tell me, did you speak to her? Did you hear her plans?"

"Not I," said Mr. Lammas. "She and her aunt were swathed like mummies in the inside, while I took the air on the box. All I saw of her was for three minutes this morning, and all I learned was that she had a pretty face."

"Never mind her looks. What like was the man who picked them up in his curricle?"

Mr. Dott answered. "Well-favoured and well set-up and everything handsome about him. A young Corinthian, I doubt, for he seemed to know more about horseflesh than is becoming in a man who does not make his living by it."

Jock groaned.

"I'll be obliged, Nanty, if you lose no time in getting to Berwick. I may be glad of your company there. If they and that fellow are at the Red Lion, you had better go to the other shop—the King's Arms—about the middle of Hide Hill as you go down to the Sand Gate. Whether they take the Highflyer or a post-chaise, I must catch them before they leave. Meet me there in an hour's time."

Mr. Dott looked after the departing figure with a reflective smile.

"A stirring lad," he decided, "with much of his father's spunk. Love, I suppose. Calf-love."

"They were children together."

"All the more dangerous, and the more hopeless. The affection of bairns is a poor foundation for a wooing, for the light female mind wants something new. I would not give a groat for Mr. Jock's chances, for they tell me that Miss Kirsty is like the lassie in the song—wooers pulling at her from every airt. We'd better stir our shanks, Professor, for, besides our proper business, I would like you to keep tryst with that young man."

Rob Dickson had eaten his brose and caught the mare,

and the two embarked in an ancient vehicle which must have carried goods as well as passengers, for it was floury with pease-meal and smelt strongly of wool and tar. It was a cumbrous concern, and Rob was a poor charioteer; also the young mare, just off the grass, was both sluggish and capricious. She bored into the left side of the road, took the hills at a dragging walk, and shied furiously at every stirk that put its head over the adjacent dykes. So their progress was erratic and slow, and both grew impatient.

"This donnered animal will have you late for your tryst," said Mr. Dott.

"It will make me miss the Highflyer," said Mr. Lammas, "and that I cannot afford to do."

"We're in too great a hurry nowadays," said Mr. Dott. "It's an awful thing the speed of this modern world. When my father took the road it was on the outside of a beast, not in a varnished contrivance on wheels, and little it mattered to him, honest man, whether he was an hour late or a day late. But nowadays we must scour the country as if the devil were behind us, and if there's a crack in our perjink plans the whole edifice goes blaff. Bethankit that I go no farther than Berwick, so I'm near my goal."

Mr. Lammas, watching bitterly the stagnant rump of the young mare, asked if Mr. Dott's business would be concluded there.

"Not precisely, but Berwick will be my headquarters. I have a journey to make into the adjacent hills. A queer bit, Professor. Heard you ever such a name as Hungrygrain in Yonderdale?"

Mr. Lammas was stirred to attention. Where had he met these uncouth syllables? He searched his memory and recollected. Last night Lord Mannour had named the place as the home of the Delilah who had enchanted Lord Belses. Here was one who could give him valuable news.

"Strangely enough I have heard the name before. Isn't it the property of a Mrs. Cranmer?" He spoke with a studied negligence, for the topic might be uncongenial to his companion.

But Mr. Dott showed no embarrassment.

"Not precisely. Hungrygrain is the property of Justin Cranmer, Esquire, a justice of the peace and a deputy-lieutenant for the county of Northumberland, and formerly of His Majesty's 8th Regiment of Foot. Of him I know nothing, but report says that he is another than a good one. My business is with his lady, Gabriel Cornelia Lucy Perceval or Cranmer—it's surely a daft-like thing to christen a woman after an archangel—in her own right mistress of Overy Hall in the county of Norfolk, a far better estate than Hungrygrain."

"You know this Mrs. Cranmer—you have seen her?" Mr. Lammas asked eagerly.

"Never set eyes on her, but numerous letters have passed atween us. You'll be wondering, maybe, what a country writer in Scotland has to do with a great English lady. The matter is simple. Mrs. Cranmer, through her mother, who was a Hamilton of Mells, heired some sheep-farms at the head of Waucht water, which I have the factoring of, as my father had before me. The rental's good enough, but there has aye been some factious dispute about the marches, and I've long had her instructions to sell if I could get a good bid. I've got the bid, but the deil's in her to clinch it, for the lady is like a bog-blitter, here the day and gone the morn. So when I heard she was at Hungrygrain I sent her a letter saying I proposed to wait on her in person, got the papers together, packed my pockmanty, and here I am. A chaise to Yonderdale, which is somewhere up in the Cheviot hills, an hour with her ladyship, and then I can birl home with an easy mind."

The dreariest journey has its end, and the sociable was now on high ground, looking down on a plain where a broad river twined among meadows. Suddenly they found themselves on the edge of the town of Berwick, walled and ramparted like a fortress, with red roofs shining agreeably in the morning sun. They entered by the Scotch Gate and came into a broad street which was full of bustle, for a fish market was being held along one side, and from it rose the voices of vendors accustomed at sea to shout against the wind, a babble punctuated oddly by a bugle blown from the adjacent barracks. They passed the Red Lion with its flapping sign, admired the Town Hall with its elegant piazza, turned into Hide Hill, and drew up before the broad entry of the King's Arms.

"So this is Berwick," remarked Mr. Dott. "A burgh-town that cost Scotland muckle good blood. It's waesome to think that our old enemies of England have got it safe in their pouch at last."

They were the first at the tryst, for, as they were giving their bags to the boots, who had informed them that there were rooms at their disposal, Jock Kinloch's fiery face appeared on the kerb. He had changed his fisherman's clothes for the kind of thing he wore at Kinloch—corduroy pantaloons and stout shoes, an ill-cut grass-green coat, and a white hunting stock. "Nothing but my old duds," he lamented, "and me with a new suit from McKimmies lying in camphor. Come on, Nanty, for we've no time to lose—the south coach will be starting in half an hour. I had a job to persuade Eben to set me here, for he doesn't like Berwick—that was why we put in for water this morning up the coast. He says the Meadow Haven is like hell—you can get in fine and easy, but it's damned hard to get out."

While Mr. Dott entered the inn, Jock took Mr. Lammas at a round pace to the Red Lion, cleaving his way through the market frequenters like the forefoot of a ship through yeasty seas. In the yard of that hostelry stood the Highflyer ready for its horses, with the baggage already strapped in its place. Mr. Lammas noted the chaise which he had seen that morning on Kitterston hill, and which an ostler was washing under the instructions of a gentleman's servant. Jock, a little flustered, led the way in by a side door, and the two found themselves in a low-ceilinged hall from which a broad staircase led to the upper floors. It was empty, and he was just about to dive into a pantry in search of some servant to conduct him to the ladies, when he saw something which made him straighten his back and pull off his hat. A party was descending the stairs.

Miss Georgie had swathed herself again for the road in clothes like a polar explorer's, but Miss Kirsty had donned a lighter travelling cloak in the shape of a long pelisse of brown velvet, which was open in front and gave a glimpse of a pale-yellow muslin gown. Round her throat she wore a muslin kerchief like a small ruff which made a fitting base for her handsome head. Amazingly handsome she was, all ripe and golden, with her exquisite skin and bright hair and merry, commanding blue eyes. There was a flush on her face, and she was smiling, and the glimpse of white teeth between red lips increased her brilliance. Mr. Lammas was impressed, but he was not dazzled, for he remembered Pitten's words about her ancestry. There was in her beauty a promise of coming heaviness. Some day this radiant creature might be too fair of flesh, when the girlish lines had coarsened, and the peach-bloom of the complexion had gone. Even now there was just a hint of over-ripeness.

She had been given the arm of a very splendid creature. Sir Turnour Wyse, having shed his dreadnought and submitted to the attentions of his valet, shone like Phœbus in his strength. He had a strong square face, a thought too full in the cheeks, but most wholesomely browned by weather. There was nothing flamboyant in his appearance. His dark hair, cut short in the sportsman's style, was innocent of pomatum; his fine white hands had but the one ring; he had a plain bunch of seals at his fob. And yet everything about him breathed an air of extreme fashion, the finest and most workmanlike fashion. His coat, cut full about the pockets and of some tint between plum and claret, fitted his broad shoulders like a glove. His plain neckcloth was perfectly tied, and his long hunting waistcoat had not a crease in it. His breeches were elegantly shaped, his boots seemed moulded to his legs, and his tops had the bloom of a horse-chestnut. But the man's clothes, even his figure and face, were the least of him; what made him impressive was his air of arrogant, well-bred security. Here was one whom none of life's checks would find wanting.

There followed, in those few minutes before the horses were put to the Highflyer, a scene which made Mr. Lammas's spine cold with misery.

Jock Kinloch stepped forward, and it was at once apparent to his friend that he could not meet the situation. He looked shabby, flustered, provincial.

"Kirsty," he cried, and his voice faltered. "Are you all right, my dear? I heard of your mishap, and I'm here to offer my services."

It was Miss Georgie who replied, and she was clearly no friend of Jock's. "Thank you kindly, Mr. John," she said with acid in her voice, "but we have no need of your services. Miss Evandale is on the road to the metropolis, and she has made all arrangements. What, may I make bold to speir, are *you* doing in Berwick when you should be at your books?"

She had reduced him to the undergraduate, the hobbledehoy who had intruded himself upon his elders. Jock flushed and looked piteously at Miss Kirsty. But that young lady was under the glamour of a new and prodigious experience, and she had no eyes for him. Or rather she had eyes only to dazzle, not to welcome, and for this purpose Jock was poor game. He was a slave whom she had long ago mastered and who might now be sent back to the servants' quarters. But her voice was friendly, with the casual friendliness with which one addresses a faithful but officious dog.

"I am obliged," she said, "but I have no call to make on your good nature. My aunt and I are about to take coach for the south. We are London-bound. We intend to pay a visit on the way. We shall meet, no doubt, come October at the fox-cubbing."

Then, feeling something strained in the air, she made a hasty introduction. "Mr. Kinloch—Sir Turnour. The son of a country neighbour."

Had she said "a country neighbour" it would have been

less hard, but the words "son of" seemed to rank the boy far down in the degrees of the negligible.

Sir Turnour was no fop with a quizzing eyeglass. He regarded Jock with the fresh critical eyes which he would have turned upon a horse or a dog. Those eyes took in every detail of the ill-made clothes, the ungainly posture, the nervous lips. They were not hostile. They were not disparaging. But they seemed to look from a great height upon something very lowly.

He bowed curtly.

"The gentleman addressed you familiarly," he said. "Is he perhaps a Scotch cousin?"

"Oh no. Only a childhood's friend. Long ago we played together."

Sir Turnour smiled with infinite tolerance.

"I see. As your Scotch poet sings,

" 'We two have paddled in the burn.'

It is a claim to acquaintance which should not be denied. Your servant, Mr. Kinloch," and he made him a second bow. "I fear," he added, turning to his companions, "that there is no time to exchange youthful reminiscences, for I hear the horses on the cobbles. I must see you comfortably bestowed, and would to Heaven I could be your fellow-traveller! But I have your promise, Miss Evandale, that you will sit by me when I drive my blue roans next to Richmond, and I shall not fail to exact its fulfilment."

He swept the ladies with him, and no one of the three had another glance for the melancholy Jock. Miss Kirsty, blushing divinely, clung closer to Sir Turnour's arm, and Miss Georgie tossed her towering head-dress. Clearly the girl was powerfully attracted by this new cavalier, and it was not less plain that he was smitten, for the eyes with which he looked down on her face were suddenly drained of arrogance.

This Jock saw, and it left him white and gaping—not wrathful, but stricken, as one who finds the foundations of life destroyed. It was the bereavement he suffered from, not the insult. But Mr. Lammas was furiously angry, and had an unregenerate impulse to run after the stately gentleman and buffet his ears. For the scene he had witnessed had outraged his innermost decencies. The man had not been uncivil, nor had he been contemptuous—far better if he had, for it would have been proof of jealousy, vanity, or some other respectable human emotion. He had scarcely even been condescending. He had simply by his manner blotted out Jock from the world, ignored him as a thing too trivial for a thought. This god-like aloofness was the cruellest insolence that he had ever witnessed, and his heart ached for the boy. The great world had shown itself to the humble provinces and withered them with its stare. Mr. Lammas for the moment was a hot Jacobin. He longed to take that world by the scruff, with its wealth and brave clothes and fine, well-fed, well-tended bodies, and rub its nose in something mighty unpleasant.

Jock still stood limply, like a man who has been struck between the eyes. Mr. Lammas dragged him to a chair, and fetched a mug of strong ale from the adjacent taproom.

"Drink that," he said fiercely, "and pull yourself together. Don't stand mooning there like a dying duck."

Jock drank, and presently he raised his head.

"You saw that? I've got my *congé* with a vengeance. . . . 'Son of a country neighbour!' . . . Did you ever hear the like? And yon old Jezebel of an aunt girning at me! And Kirsty smiling up at yon fatted calf!"

His temper rose. "What did she call the fellow?" he shouted. "Sir Something Somebody? Two yards of haberdashery and buxom flesh and a red face atop of them—that's a woman's fancy. The devil fly away with the whole sex. . . ." He repented. "No, I won't ban little Kirsty. She's still a baby and easy glamoured. But by God I'll be even with the man." Then in sheer misery he dropped his head on his arms and wept.

A horn blew loud in the yard. Mr. Lammas jumped to his feet in consternation. "I should go with the coach," he cried.

"And my mails are at the King's Arms and I have no place bespoken.". . .

Jock clutched his arm, and turned on him a distraught face.

"You can't leave me, Nanty. For God's sake stay with me. I beg you in the name of common humanity. I summon you by the Fishers' Oath. I'm in hell, and if you leave me alone I swear I'll cut my throat or drop into the harbour."

Mr. Lammas was in a sad quandary. In two minutes the coach would be gone, and he would have failed in his duty of urgent speed. But could he forsake this white-faced boy whose eyes had the pleading pathos of a dog's?

"What's your hurry, man?" Jock moaned. "Your snuffy old college business can surely wait a day."

"I have a private mission as well, and that is of extreme urgency."

"Well, you've a private mission here in Berwick that's just as urgent."

Mr. Lammas came to a sudden resolution. He would take Jock into his confidence, for one of the actors in the play had five minutes back wounded him cruelly, and he would sympathize with Mr. Lammas's errand.

"That man with Miss Evandale," he said, "was Sir Turnour Wyse. He is the best whip in England and reputed to be one of the best shots. He has challenged Lord Belses in a private quarrel, and is seeking him to force him to fight. At Lord Snowdoun's request I go to London to find my dear Harry, and, please God, to save his life."

These words wrought a miraculous change in Jock Kinloch. He rose violently and sent the ale-mug crashing to the floor. He seized Mr. Lammas's coat by the lapels and thrust his face close to his. His sorrows seemed to be forgotten in a strong excitement.

"Wyse!" he exclaimed. "That fellow was Sir Turnour Wyse? And he is after Belses to pistol him. By God, this time I'm on the side of the hare. . . . And you're for London seeking Belses? You're in luck, Nanty, for you have come to the right bit and the right man. Would it surprise you to hear that at this moment Belses is a long sight nearer Berwick than London? . . . There's the filthy coach starting. Let it go and good speed to it, for I've done with the whole concern. We're for a bigger game, Nanty, my lad. I'll have Eben Garnock at the King's Arms in half an hour. Back with you there, and get us a room to ourselves. A room, mind you, with a key to the door."

CHAPTER V

KING'S BUSINESS

JOCK KINLOCH flung himself out by the entrance which gave on the High Street, while Mr. Lammas remained seated till he heard the toot of the guard's horn which proclaimed that the Highflyer had started on its southward journey. Then he sought the courtyard, from which ostlers, grooms, and idle spectators were slowly clearing. There was no sign of Sir Turnour, but his broad chaise was there, and his servant was superintending the last cleaning and polishing operations. Bright as a new pin it shone in the morning sun.

At this point it behoves the chronicler to get on more easy terms with his hero. The titular dignities of Mr. Lammas must be dropped, for they are now out of place in a world in which they have no meaning. To us he shall be Nanty, as he already was to Jock Kinloch and to the humblest bejant of St. Andrews.

Certainly there was nothing of the professor in the young man who jostled his way among the market folk in the High Street and swung into Hide Hill, from which he looked over the shining river to the red roofs of Tweedmouth, and the green pastures which were England. His sober black clothes did not rank him among the sedentary, for his long strides were like those of a hill shepherd, and there was an odd light in his eyes. His feelings were a compound of anger and excitement. The scene at the Red Lion had stirred in him what he had scarcely looked for, a most unphilosophic wrath. That assured baronet represented a world which he had hitherto admired and cultivated, for it was to it he looked for the fulfilling of his ambitions; but now he found that it roused in him the liveliest antagonism, for it had treated a friend like dirt. Was it some Jacobinical strain in him, he wondered, that made his soul revolt against such arrogant condescension? He clenched a fist with which he would joyfully have assaulted Sir Turnour's comeliness. . . . But, steadying and cooling his indignation, came the reflection that he had heard news of high practical import.

In the last twelve hours he had thought of his task as meaning a visit to London, a conference with Lord Snowdoun, and a search for the missing lad in some far quarter of England. Now, if Jock spoke the truth, Lord Belses was somewhere close at hand, and at any moment he might be facing the purpose of his mission. A sudden thought made him quicken his pace. Sir Turnour was dallying in Berwick. Why? The man had come north looking for Belses, to force him to fight, or to make him eat humble pie. Sir Turnour also might be aware of Jock's news. Some time in the next day or two, somewhere in this neighbourhood, it was his business to rescue the boy from this intolerable bravo. The thought sent little shivers down Nanty's spine, for the man had looked immensely formidable, but he was conscious, too, that it stiffened his resolution. If he was to go into battle, let it be against this baronet, and all the cruel, glittering world for which he stood.

He mounted to his bedroom in the massive stone hostelry of the King's Arms. There was no sign of Mr. Dott, but he found the landlord, and arranged for privacy in a little chamber on the first floor, which was a withdrawing-room used by the Whitader Club at their monthly dinners. Then he descended to the street, where three minutes later Jock appeared in company with Eben Garnock. The Chief Fisher was a man a year or two on the wrong side of fifty, huge in frame, at once massive and spare, with a great grizzled beard which almost covered his broad chest. His eyebrows, too, were thick and grizzled, and from the caves beneath them eyes of an intense blue looked out upon the world. They were notable eyes, for they were at once calm and vigilant. Nothing would either escape or perturb them. His forehead was a full round dome, and when he removed his cap it combined with the baldness of his head to give him an air of solemn, brooding sagacity. But Nanty knew that that mountainous face could quicken readily into a mountainous humour, and he could picture Eben wrestling with North Sea gales, his beard tossing on the wind, taming the elements to domesticity, half elder of the Kirk and half pirate from a Norway wick.

When the three were seated in the little room, with the door looked and the key on the table, Nanty felt a sudden shyness which he had never known at Senatus meetings. His boyish upbringing told, and he realized that he looked upon Eben Garnock with a respect which he did not feel for any of his learned colleagues. These belonged to his familiar life, and he met them on equal terms; but Eben ruled in a strange world in which he was the merest novice—a world, moreover, in which for a time he must now dwell. So he left it to the Chief Fisher to begin. But Eben was a man of sparing speech, and he was occupied in filling and lighting a deep-bowled pipe. So there was a short silence, while Jock looked out from the window on the main courtyard.

"There's the man who was at breakfast," he reported. "The town-clerk, I mean. I wonder where he is bound for."

Nanty looked out, and saw Mr. Dott seated in a high yellow gig with red wheels. In the shaft was an animal, one of whose near progenitors must have been a carthorse. His brown satchel was under his arm, and his air was that of a country doctor suddenly called in ill weather to visit a distant patient, a combination of distaste and dutiful resolution.

"I know, for he told me. He is going on legal business to a house called Hungrygrain in the Cheviot hills."

Jock cried out, and Eben, having got his pipe going, looked sharply at Jock.

"He'll find some wild things there," said the latter.

"Hungrygrain! If that isn't the queerest chance! Yonderdale's no place just now for a poking lawyer, and he has as much hope of doing business as a snowball of rolling through hell. He'll likely take some mischief. A decent soul, too. I wish it had been possible to warn him."

"What is wrong with Hungrygrain besides the name?" Nanty asked.

Jock laughed. "If you could tell us that you would tell us something that Eben would like very greatly to know. Ay, and His Majesty's Government, too. . . . We'd better get to work, for there is no time to waste. All the cards go on to the table, Nanty Lammas—for Nanty, you are in this ploy, and St. Salvator's and the logic classroom are at the other side of the moon. There are no secrets between us, for we are all Free Fishers. Eben has empowered me to speak, for I have more of the gift of the gab than him. Well, the first thing I have to say to you is that this is King's business, and devilish high business. Three days back Eben was closeted with the Lord Advocate and with other folk that shall be nameless, and he got his orders. It's not the first job he has done for His Majesty, though it may be the kittlest, and he did me the honour to pick me along with Bob Muschat, for he wanted somebody who had some pretension to gentility. Ay, gentility," he added bitterly, "though yon cedar of Lebanon up at the Red Lion might not allow the claim."

The broken-hearted lover seemed to have disappeared. Jock spoke with assurance and a crisp vigour.

"And you're in it too, Nanty, as Providence has ordained, and your St. Andrews business must go hang. You saw my father last night, and I'll warrant your talk wasn't only about college property. Was it about Belses?"

The other nodded.

"I guessed as much. Now let us have your story, and then you'll hear ours. I have a notion they'll fit together like the squares on a dambrod."

Nanty repeated the gist of what Lord Mannour had told

him, while Jock listened with sundry exclamations, and Eben silently with eyes on the floor.

"And I thought the fellow was my enemy," was Jock's comment. "And I had worked myself into a fine glow of hatred, as I told you on the Pittenweem road. Now I could love him like a brother. The man's a victim to be pitied."

"And to be rescued."

"Ay, please God, to be rescued. You say that that red-faced baronet is seeking his blood? Well, I'm seeking his, or my name is not John Kinloch, and that simplifies my purpose, though it complicates the job. He is still in Berwick?"

"I saw his chaise twenty minutes ago in the Red Lion yard."

"Then it's possible that he knows what we know—that he is close on his quarry. God, there'll soon be rough work at Hungrygrain."

"Hungrygrain?"

"Just Hungrygrain. That is where my Lord Belses is at the moment. It's a bleak, God-forgotten spot among whaups and peesweeps and peat-mosses. But there have been queer ongoings there for many a day, and at this very hour there are queerer still. And now there's converging upon that moorland bit a dour country writer, who'll likely get his throat cut, and a fine gentleman in buckskins who seeks satisfaction for his wounded honour. He'll maybe get more satisfaction than he likes. It's a bonny kettle of fish, and it will soon come to the boil."

"We must get the poor boy out of the place before his pursuer gets there." Nanty was on his feet, for his immediate duty seemed plain.

"Sit you down," said Jock. "The thing is not so simple as that. You have still to hear our side of the business—the King's side. My father told you that Belses was being made a fool of by a woman. Well, that woman is the pivot of the thing. Mrs. Cranmer they call her."

"Mr. Dott's client."

"A bonny client! Now what takes a woman like Mrs.

Cranmer to have for her doer a Scots writer from a forsaken hole like Waucht?"

"Mr. Dott said she was kin to the Hamiltons of Mells and had some farms on Waucht side."

"So? If there's Scots blood in her, that makes her the more dangerous. But, whether or not, there's no question of her power for ill, and it would seem that she comes between Ministers and their sleep. What kind of a character did my father give her?"

"He said she was young and handsome, and a religious enthusiast, and tainted with Jacobinical views."

"Ay. That's the character she has with most people, and that's the kind of candle that attracts a poor moth like Belses. I wonder if my father knows more, or my Lord Snowdoun. Maybe not, for the Cranmer case is not yet a Cabinet matter, I understand—still in the stage of proof, and not ripe for judgment. Maybe it is still secret between the Advocate and the military and the Free Fishers." He looked towards Eben, who gravely nodded.

"Rid your mind of that picture, Nanty, my man," he went on; "the innocent sweet lady, a thought high-flying in her politics, the kind of siren to capture a young man of sensibility. Put something very different in its place. Put a woman who hates this land of Britain with a cold hatred—who will stick at nothing to get her ends—who can play a desperate game with the patience of Job and the subtlety of Monsieur Talleyrand and the courage of Lucifer—who does not know the meaning of love or honour or friendship—who will use every gift of mind and body for a black purpose. Have you got that clear, for it's gospel truth? Eben has seen some of the proofs of it, and they damn her to the lowest hell."

Nanty shuddered. "My poor Harry!" he muttered.

"Well may you say your poor Harry. He is nothing more than a cat's-paw. To have the son of my Lord Snowdoun, the manager of Scotland, dangling at her petticoat tails is a sort of evidence of respectability, you see, and she misses no point in the game."

"That game—what is it?" Nanty asked.

"It's easy told. Britain, as I have often heard you say, is fighting for her life and for the liberties of Europe. We have plenty of ill-wishers at home to stir up trouble, and the more trouble here the weaker our stroke will be on the battlefield. That's an axiom, as you logicians say. We are fighting the greatest military genius of all history, and that does not leave us much margin. Whatever happens, it will be a damned near thing. So any knowledge of our plans that may get to the enemy is worth a hundredfold more than in an ordinary war, the margin, as I say, being so close. That is what this beldame is doing. She has spun her web up and down the land, even in high places, and the silly flies walk in. She has made a great bureau of treason to foster revolution at home and to send damning confidences abroad."

"An incendiary and a spy!"

"You've hit the mark, Nanty. Arch-incendiary and master-spy. Now that web has to be swept down and the spider destroyed."

Jock's face had an earnest passion which made him suddenly an older and shrewder man. For the first time he reminded Nanty of his father.

"This is a shocking tale," he said. "This woman—is she wife or widow?"

"She has a husband, and that is one of her chief assets. The other is the reputation she has built up for sentimental innocence. Her husband, Justin Cranmer, is a trumpery body, another cat's-paw. Eben can tell you of him."

"A long, blackavised man," said the Chief Fisher, "wi' a skin like a candle-dowp. I've seen him twa-three times. When he's at home he is either hunting the hills wi' his dowgs, or lying as fou' as the Baltic—at least that's what they tell me. But the feck o' the time he's ranging the land at cockings and horse-racings."

"Ay," said Jock, "but he's the laird of Hungrygrain, and Hungrygrain is a Godsend to his lady wife. She has estates of her own in Norfolk, so she is well-dowered, besides what her paymasters give her. But Norfolk is too conspicuous a place for her game, so her headquarters are shifted to the North. The devil might have made Hungrygrain for her purpose. It lies at the back end of a moorland glen called Yonderdale, and there's no road but a drove-road within five miles. There's a bit of a clachan, but the inhabitants are all Squire Cranmer's folk, and a savage pack of heathens by all tales. There are no neighbours except a few drunken bonnet-lairds, and Cheviot hems it in like a dyke. Above all, it is not ten miles from the sea—take note of that, Nanty—a lonely bit of coast with a snug little harbour at a burn mouth. She is a noble spirit, her friends say, unequally yoked to a boor, but her wifely duty and her care for the poor tenant-bodies take her often to Hungrygrain. But when she is there this Methody fine lady queens it among poachers and black-fishers and tinklers who do her biddings and know fine that they would lose their tongues if they blabbed. . . . What do you think of my picture? It's wilder than anything in Walter Scott or Lord Byron, but Eben will bear me out that it's God's truth."

"If Harry has gone there, surely he will learn the facts and be disillusioned."

"That is just what puzzles me. This morning we heard, never mind how, that he had arrived there yesterday. We had heard, too, some rumour of his quarrel with Wyse. He was looking for sanctuary no doubt, and Hungrygrain struck him as remote and secret. Very likely the woman knew nothing of his coming till he appeared, and may not have welcomed him. If she connived at it, then it looks as if she had made him a partner in her infamy."

"That I will never believe," said Nanty firmly.

"Well, put that question aside, for we shall soon be enlightened. Now you must hear more of Hungrygrain. Eben, you take up the tale."

"In the auld days afore the Union," said the Chief Fisher, "there was a brisk smuggling trade across the Border. Ye'll maybe have heard o' that, Mr. Lammas. Every second man in Jeddart, they say, was a free-trader. Well, Yonderdale was the hame o' the business, and the laird o' Hungrygrain the chief manager o't, and the cotter-folk o' Hungrygrain deep to their necks in it. They were a wild clan wi' an ill name—the warst fighters at ilka fair from Stagshawbank to St. Boswells, a thrawn lot that stuck thegither and made ony man's quarrel the quarrel o' a'. Weel, the Union came, but Yonderdale didna change its trade. It turned its eyes to the sea, and found a howff where it could land its bits o' contraband and send them along the Border. Yondermouth is nae use, for the Water o' Yonder taks a long bend to the south afore it wins to the sea, and besides, Yondermouth is a well-kenned fisher toun where lawless doings wad be bridled—a toun like our ain Leven or Anster. So they found what they wanted up north along the shore at a place they ca' Hopcraw, where a burn comes in frae the hills. There's deep water there for them that ken where to look for it, and there's not a cothouse within three mile. Mair, by a straight road ower the muir it's no above ten mile frae Hungrygrain. The place is well kenned by us fishers, but it's no our business to speak o't. The gaugers, too, have a notion o't, but they never seem to hit the right hour and the right corner, and mony a weary traivel they've had for small purpose. There's nae better mart for the free trade on the east shore, and a' the lairds frae Liddel to Till, ay and ower the Border too, get their tea and brandy and tobacco from the guid folk o' Hopcraw."

"And that's the channel through which this woman communicates with France?"

"One o' them. Nae doubt there's others—one maybe down in the Norfolk sands near her ain estates—but Hopcraw is the chief."

"What are your orders from Government?"

"Just to watch—and report. We have word that one of her ploys is comin' to a heid, and we hope to nip it, and bring to justice them that's 'sponsible."

"That will mean violence and fighting."

"Na, na. The Free Fishers are men o' peace. Nae fechtin' for us except in our ain canny way o' business. There's King's ships that'll dae what fechtin' is needit, and there's a plan by which we can get word to them."

"Then your purpose is to go to Hopcraw?"

"No me," said Eben with a slow smile which brought his brows down over his eyes. "To steer for Hopcraw wad be like kindling a beacon on the hilltops. We maun gang warily in this business, for Hungrygrain has plenty sharp een on the watch. That's why I was sweir to come into this river o' Tweed. I wadna trust the Berwick boats that carry the frostit saumons to London, for some o' them are chief wi' Hungrygrain and wad signal news o' us if they suspected our job. Na, we're for Yondermouth, where I'm well-kenned. Some o' our Fife lads are out east at the Banks at the white-fishing, and what mair natural than that we should join them? We'll hae some sma' trouble wi' a yaird that'll take us in there for twa-three days to Davie Dimmock, the boat-builder's, and while we're lying snug we'll send out spies like the auld Israelites."

Jock burst in.

"Eben will keep the *Merry Mouth* in Yondermouth, and find some way of slipping up to Hopcraw and seeing what goes on there. Meantime Bob Muschat and I take a quiet step Yonderdale way. Ay, and you too, Nanty, for we need you to deal with Belses. There's a ticklish job there for somebody."

"I cannot. I must be off at once to Hungrygrain by the shortest road. I tell you, there's not a moment to lose, for Sir Turnour Wyse may get to him this very day."

"Remember your calling, Nanty," said Jock. "Logic, my brave boy! The baronet is not going to pistol your Harry like a common cut-throat. Whatever mischief is on foot, we have a day or two of grace to prevent it. What good would you do if you posted off to Hungrygrain and hammered at the front door? They would only set the dogs on you, for you have no *locus*, as my father would say. You would find the folk there in an ill key, pestered by a bumptious lawyer, and maybe on the top of it the baronet damning their eyes and telling them they are dirt. What would you do in such a collieshangie? No, no, our way's the best. The wind's fair, and we'll drop down the coast, and be in Yondermouth in the afternoon. There's a grand moon, and at the darkening you and me and Bob will slip off up the water, and see what's to be seen. They that work with Hungrygrain must take the tinkler's road—the deep wood and the thick bracken and the long heather."

"Then for Heaven's sake let us be off."

"You're coming?"

"I'm coming. And I warn you I'll press the pace."

"God, Nanty, you're a man after my heart," Jock cried. "We're in luck, Eben. We have the Law on our side, and now we've got the Gospel. The expeditionary force is complete, chaplain and all."

In the street they looked down Hide Hill towards the Sand Gate; it dropped steeply to a quay, beyond which the river lay like a broad band of light. The passers-by on the kerb had come to a halt, for over the cobbles rattled a striking equipage. It was a broad chaise, drawn by two stout galloways, with a dicky behind in which a servant sat with folded arms. Sir Turnour had shed his dreadnought in the warm spring sunshine, and his shoulders showed trim and square on the box-seat. Rarely had Berwick seen a better-shaped coat, or a smarter beaver, or so complete a mastery of whip and ribbons, as he steered the pair at a good pace down the uneven street amid the fish carts and country wagons.

The three watched him as he reached the Sand Gate and turned west along the dock side.

"He's a comely body, your baronet," said Eben, "and he can manage a horse. He's for the English Gate and the Tweed brig."

"I wish I knew his purpose," said Nanty. "For all we can tell he may be on his way to London."

Two of the onlookers were commenting on the sight, horsy-looking gentry in tight breeches and battered leggings.

"Whae is the gentleman?" one asked. "I never saw beasts better guidit."

"I dinna ken," was the answer. "He doesna belong hereways."

"For Newcastle, think ye?"

"No him. He has gotten the pair that Davidson hires out for the Yetholm coursin'. Slugs on the highroad but graund on the braes. That ane's no for Newcastle. He's for the hills."

CHAPTER VI

IN WHICH A TOWN-CLERK IS ILL-RECEIVED

MR. DUNCAN DOTT, perched atop of the narrow gig of the King's Arms, prepared to enjoy himself. His valise was left behind at the inn, for he proposed to return there in the evening and had indeed bespoken for himself a snug little supper. His only baggage was his brown leather satchel of papers, which was securely wedged between him and the driver. The morning was fresh, what wind there was blew from the north-west, and the ascending sun promised before noon the mellow warmth of spring. Only in the west, where at a great distance the valley was closed by a line of little hills, a thin cloudbank broke the even blue of the sky.

"It'll be a grand day," he observed to his companion. "The wind's in a dry airt."

The other pursed his lips.

"Ye'll maybe need your topcoat or night. I dinna like yon wee cluds, and it was ower bright this mornin' when I was washin' my face."

As they crossed the bridge of Tweed the tide was running and the salmon cobles were straining at their moorings. Thereafter they entered a shining world, fields of bent noisy with young lambs, cothouses snowy with fresh harling, hawthorns bursting into green, and on their left the sea, which had no colour but shone like a vast crystal with essential light. Mr. Dott's spirits soared, and he unbuttoned his greatcoat so that the air could play about his throat.

"England's a fine country," he remarked. "It's the first time I've crossed the Border, and if it's all like this I don't blame our forebears for raiding it whiles to see what they could find. There's sour bits in Scotland."

"There's sour bits in England," said the driver, a morose man called Niven. "Ye're for Yonderdale? Wait till ye see it afore ye mak up your mind about England."

"What sort of a place is Yonderdale?" Mr. Dott inquired.

"Sour," said the driver, and spat. "Sour I would ca' it. A lang dreich glen—naething but burns and hill-faces—perishin' cauld in winter, for the drifts at the top o't dinna melt till May, and no that cheery in the best o' weather. It's ower high up in Cheviot for human habitation. What takes ye to Yonderdale, sir?"

"Business. A small matter of business."

The other laughed.

"It's no muckle business gangs up Yonder water, except its ain kind o' business, and I'll wager that's no your kind. Ye're a lawyer, I take it? Well there's just the one sort o' law in Yonderdale and that's the stout arm and the holly cudgel. Ay, and waur. There's sudden deaths up thereaways that nae coroner sits on. Ye'll no ken what a coroner is, maybe?—he's a kind of a procurator fiscal."

"Dearie me," said Mr. Dott. "That's a bad account. Does your job take you often there?"

"No above twice a year—wi' a dealer in the back-end after the hogg lambs, or a farmer seekin' store cattle. And Yonderdale doesna come muckle our way, neither. They're queer folk and keep themselves to themselves, nae doubt wi' good cause. What part o' Yonderdale are ye for?"

Mr. Dott's answer induced a whistle, a lugubrious sound which expressed something more than surprise.

"Hungrygrain! Keep us, but what seek ye at Hungrygrain? Are ye acquaint wi' the folks there? Are ye expectit?"

"I have given notice of my coming," said Mr. Dott primly.

The driver seemed to ponder. His taciturnity had given place to curiosity, for he proceeded to ply Mr. Dott with questions, which that gentleman answered in monosyllables. He had become suddenly the confidential man of business. One question only he asked in return—had Niven ever seen or spoken to Squire Cranmer?

"Spoken to him? No likely. But I've seen him a score o' times, and I've heard enough about him to fill a book."

But what he had heard he showed no wish to communicate. "There's an owercome in the hills, 'queer like the folk o' Hungrygrain,' and if a' tales be true the squire's the queerest o' the batch. If your business is wi' him I wish ye weel, for he's a kittle customer, and if ye're servin' a writ or onything unpleasant ye'll be lucky to get awa' wi' hale banes. Dinna count on me, for I meddle not wi' Hungrygrain. I'll take ye there, which is my lawful calling, and syne ye maun fend for yoursel'."

Mr. Dott's spirits were a little dashed, especially as Niven with a fateful countenance continued to ingeminate the word "Hungrygrain." They had left the shore road and were in a land of sheep-walks, fields of grass bounded by drystone dykes, and now and then a common bright with furze and the young sprouts of heather. It was no longer the gleaming country of the morning, for though the sun still shone, colour seemed to have gone out of the landscape, which now wore an air of bleakness and melancholy. Presently they topped a ridge, and looked across a shallow trough of bog and bent to the lift of a mountain range. On their left was the loom of woodlands with the sea beyond, and to their right a glimpse of a habitable farming country, but the immediate prospect was strangely wild and desolate. The mountains had a thick veil of cloud on their summits, a veil which seemed to be steadily dropping lower.

"Cheviot," said Niven, pointing with his whip. "And ill weather on its road. We'll be drookit or we win hame. That's the water o' Yonder ye see in the howe, and Yonderdale begins where the twae hills hurkle thegither. Hungrygrain is at the backside o' the bigger yin."

As they were about to descend into a hollow, there came

a sound of wheels behind them, and Niven drew sharply into the roadside to allow another conveyance to pass. This was a broad chaise with a dicky behind in which a servant sat. In the driver's seat was a figure more in keeping with Hyde Park or the Brighton road than with that moorland solitude. He acknowledged Niven's courtesy by raising his whip, and the pair of horses, handled by a master, took the hill at a steady trot.

"Now, whae the deevil is that?" Niven enquired. Thoughts of Hungrygrain seemed to have laid on him a spell of depression which was broken by the spectacle of this splendid gentleman. "He's drivin' the Red Lion galloways, and Davidson doesna lend them to a'body. Man, he's a provost at the job. Did ye see the way he managed the near beast when he was for shyin' at the bog aik?"

"I know who the gentleman is," said Mr. Dott. "He made himself useful this morning at the accident to the Edinburgh coach of which I told you. He is a sporting baronet—one Sir Turnour Wyse. What puzzles me is what he can want in Yonderdale."

"He's no for Yonderdale. The Yonderdale turn is twae miles on, and this road gangs to mony places. Alnwick, for yin. Ay, he'll be for the Duke's at Alnwick. He's no the breed that frequents Yonderdale."

The rain began before they reached the hills, a thin spring rain with little wind behind it. It blanketed the view except for a few hundred yards of moor. Niven turned to his right up a stony rut like the track to a farm-town. Presently a knuckle of hill loomed through the mist, and the road descended through a coppice of wildwood to the edge of a stream which was running low in the spring drought.

"The Water o' Yonder," said Niven. "Aye when I've been here afore it has been running frae bank to brae. This is a dooms ill road, but Yonderdale doesna work muckle wi' wheeled carriages. Pack-horses and shanks's pony is mair its way o't. We'll draw up and eat our piece, sir, if ye're agreeable, for we're no above three miles frae Hungrygrain."

"Is there no inn?" asked Mr. Dott, who had hoped for a dram with his bread and cheese.

"There's an inn, but it's the other side o' the water, and we'll no trouble it the day. Purdey is the man that keeps it, and he's not just precisely a friend o' mine. If ye ca'd him an ill-tongued sauvage ye wadna be far wrong."

They ate their snack in the lee of a clump of rowans, a cold meal to which the weather made indifferent kitchen. Soon the drizzle became a downpour, and in that funnel of a glen the wind gathered force, and drove the rain in spouts and sheets which searched out every corner of the travellers' persons.

"Let's get on," said Mr. Dott, shaking a deluge from his hat. "My business will not take long, and then I'm for dry breeks and the fireside."

Niven, a sodden pillar of depression, whipped up his beast and the gig jolted out of the trees up a long incline.

Even in the thick weather Mr. Dott realized that he was coming into a different kind of country. He was conscious of open spaces around him instead of coverts. They passed a cottage or two, and the smell of peat-reek tantalized him with a hint of unattainable comfort. It had become colder, and he shivered a little inside his greatcoat. Three miles, Niven had said; then half an hour's talk, a scart or two of the pen, and his face was set for his native Waucht.

A heavy gate of axe-hewn bars shut the road, and he had to descend and open it with cramped fingers. It looked as if they were entering some sort of neglected policies. Stunted evergreens dotted the roadside, and a burn was crossed by what had once been an ornamental bridge with a broken stucco coping. Mr. Dott peered into the gloom to detect the first sign of a dwelling.

Suddenly at a turn of the road a man stepped from a clump of hollies.

He was a long man in a frieze coat, and on his head was a leather cap with the flaps tied under his chin—a cross between keeper and earth-topper. He held up a hand and whistled, and at the sound two men appeared from the opposite side of the road, smaller men, but cut to the same pattern. He roughly seized the horse's bridle and forced him back.

"Who are you that make so free with Hungrygrain?" he asked in a voice as harsh as a crow's. Mr. Dott observed that his accent was not that of a peasant.

"Canny, friend," said Niven. "We're frae the King's Arms in Berwick. This gentleman is seekin' a word wi' the laird."

Mr. Dott spoke up.

"I have announced my coming by letter to her ladyship. It's with her that my business lies, for I'm the factor of her lands in Scotland."

The tall man did not take his hand from the bridle.

"Are you so! A responsible job. But you have come on a fool's errand, for we have no use for factors in Hungrygrain. Turn you about and back with you before you get a belt on your hinderlands."

Mr. Dott's temper rose. "What the devil have you to do with your mistress's affairs? I tell you this is an important matter in which good money is involved. Take your hand from the beast's head or I'll report you for insolence."

The man laughed, showing broken teeth.

"You're a brisk little bantam, but you are crowing on the wrong dungheap. There is no mistress here."

"But I had it from her own pen that she was to be here in this week of April. Stand out of the way. I will see the lady."

"There is no lady here."

"Where is she?"

"Where indeed?" The man had a disquieting gap-toothed grin. "Where can she be? Maybe

" 'Up the mossy mountain
And down the dowie glen?'

Anyway, she is not here."

"Then I will speak with Squire Cranmer."

The other's grin vanished, and his face became suddenly fierce and malevolent.

"You will not speak with the Squire. You'll be out of here in ten seconds. You're not wanted."

"I protest," Mr. Dott began, but his words were cut short, for the tall man swung the horse round so violently that it almost fell, and the wheels crashed into a tangle of young birches. One of the others struck the animal over the rump with a cutting switch, and the next the travellers knew they were being borne at a gallop back the road they had come.

Niven after five minutes succeeded in pulling up on a little hill. He wiped his brow with a damp sleeve.

"So that's that," he observed. "Did I no tell you there were queer folk in Hungrygrain?"

Mr. Dott was in a furious temper. "Heard you ever the like of such impudence? You'll turn this moment and go back."

"No me. I'm no for a slit weazand, and that's what we'll get if we gang contrar to Gibbie Winfortune."

"Winfortune?"

"Ay, that's the name o' the lang chiel."

"You know him?"

"Muckle o' him and naething that's guid. I'm bauld enough in my day, but the bauldest will keep a quiet tongue if Winfortune is on the road. He's kenned for the wildest deevil atween Tyne and Till."

The rain had stopped and the wind had blown clear a space in the clouds which suddenly revealed the sun. What had been an enclave in the fog expanded for a moment into a wide landscape. Mr. Dott looked back, and got his first view of Hungrygrain.

The glen above the gorge became a valley a mile broad between steep grey-green hills. To Mr. Dott, accustomed to Waucht side, where the lairds vied with each other in lining their fields with strips of woodland and crowning the tops with acres of feathery larch, the place seemed indecently bare.

There appeared to be no cultivation, no plough-land. He was on an eminence and could see the house itself in its shabby policies, and the upper course of the stream. The Yonder ran in a deep-cut green trench well below the valley level, so that it showed no friendly pools and shallows, but had the secret air of a river underground. The containing walls of the hills seemed so sheer that only a goat could graze on them. Mr. Dott had been wont to look on a pastoral upland as a thing homely and kindly, but this place had a horrid savagery, a chill sharper than the April rain.

But it was the sight of the house of Hungrygrain that sent a shiver down his spine. He had never been so unpleasantly affected by any human habitation. It stood in what may once have been a lawn, but was now a rough field. Part was a ruinous peel-tower, to which wings had been added of good whinstone with some pretensions to elegance; likewise there was a small square building connected with the rest by a kind of arcade. The whole place was of an extreme shabbiness, but, except for the peel, it was not in decay; it was lived in, used, misused, a place not of death and emptiness, but crowded with a maleficent life. Secret, too, as secret as the deep-trenched stream. The blink of sun only made it more eerie. It would have been more decent, he felt, had it been perpetually shrouded in mist, for no sunshine could make it other than menacing and furtive.

"An ugly bit," said the philosophic Niven. "Weel, the sooner we're ower Tweed the better."

"I'm not going back," said Mr. Dott.

"Are ye clean daft?"

Mr. Dott felt that he was, but the behaviour of the man Winfortune had roused in his soul a desperate obstinacy which mystified and slightly scared him.

"I do not leave till I have done my business. I did not travel all these miles from Waucht to be turned away by an impudent dog of a gamekeeper. You will turn and go back."

"I'll do naething of the kind. I'm not meeting my Maker afore my time. Bethink ye, sir. If ye go back to Hungrygrain ye'll be flung out and get rougher usage than afore. One man canna force a door that a dozen are haudin' against him."

"Nevertheless, I must try. And if you will not take me, my feet will." Suiting his action to his words Mr. Dott attempted to descend from the gig.

Niven rubbed his chin in dire perplexity.

"If I did my duty I would carry ye back to Berwick, though I had to fell ye first. . . . Bide a wee, sir. There's maybe another way. Ye canna get into Hungrygrain wi' Winfortune on the rampage, but he'll no aye be there. Half his time they tell me is spent ryngin' the country. What for should ye no sit ye down somewhere in Yonderdale and wait your chance? Ye'd maybe find the leddy walkin' her lane. Or get a word wi' the maister whae's mair ceevil-spoken than the man."

"You're right," said Mr. Dott. "I'll go to the inn."

"Ye maunna do that. Purdey's ower thick wi' Winfortune. Na, na, but I'll tell ye what. I'll tak ye to the manse."

"The manse? We're not in Scotland."

"No, but Yonderdale has a minister. Oh, a rector o' the parish likewise that bides in the low country, but up here there's a kirk, manse, and minister. Ye see, sir, in the auld days the folk came to Yonderdale maistly frae the other side o' the Border—frae Rule Water and Jeddart way—in the early days o' the lang sheep. And they brought their kirk wi' them, and built a manse and had their placed minister and twae screeds ilka Sabbath day. Things is sore changed now, and I doubt there's few darkens the kirk door, forbye a wheen wives and weans. But there's a minister still, whae baptizes them and buries them, and marries them when they've the decency to think o' lawfu' marriage. His name's Blackstocks, Richie Blackstocks, frae Ettrick or Yarrow, I mindna which. He's an auld man that bides alane wi' nae wife, and by a' accounts a quiet mensefu' body and wise enough to let sleepin' tykes lie. He'll gie ye a bed for the nicht, and tell ye the lie o' the land. I'll drive ye to the manse. It's down in the wuds they ca' Yonder Dene."

They jogged downhill back to the narrow part of the glen and the thick coverts, Mr. Dott's mind in a sad ferment. He was at once resolved and miserably afraid. The training of a lifetime forbade him to give up a piece of business before it was completed, but in Waucht there were peaceable folk who treated him with respect, and never before had he encountered naked savagery. His world was disrupted, he had lost his bearings, and it was necessary that he should find again the points of his mental compass.

The brief sunlight passed, and once again the rain descended, this time with a steadiness which promised a wet evening. Niven turned down a woodland track which seemed to lead towards the stream. In a few hundred yards it opened upon a clearing in the trees, a shelf of level ground beyond and behind which, even in the wild weather, could be heard the churning of the Yonder. A low privet hedge bounded a little garden.

"Here's the manse," said Niven. "Ye've nae baggage? Weel, I'll wait till I see ye inside."

Mr. Dott pushed open a white gate and very stiffly advanced up a path gravelled with rough pebbles from the stream. The house was scarcely more than a cottage, but it had been newly whitewashed, the garden was tidy and bright with daffodil and primrose, and from the smoking chimney came the comforting smell of peat-reek.

He knocked at the door, but there was no answer. Again he knocked, and then with the head of his stick he beat a loud tattoo. By and by steps were heard approaching, the latch was lifted, and before him stood a little old man. Behind this figure a moment later appeared a second, a stalwart old woman in a mutch with her skirts kilted as if she had been tramping the fields. It was she who spoke.

"Whae is it? If ye're frae Hedderwick's at Yondermouth ye can gang back, for there's nae mair dealings atween him and huz. The last seed tatties ye sent us were a black disgrace."

"I am a traveller from Scotland," said Mr. Dott, "with

business at Hungrygrain, on which I would fain as a fellow Scot consult the minister."

The woman's face changed.

"Come inbye, sir," she said. "There's no mony travellers seek the manse o' Yonderdale. Come your ways in, for ye canna stand there in this uncovenantit weather. And you, sir," this to the old man, "ye'll get your death o' cauld standin' there in your hosen feet. Where's your bauchles?"

As he entered Mr. Dott heard wheels move on the road. Niven, seeing him safely bestowed, had departed for Berwick.

He was ushered into a little low-ceilinged room with books everywhere, lining the walls in home-made shelves, stacked in corners, and piled on chairs and on most of the table. A peat-fire glowed dully, and a little clock on the mantelpiece as they entered chimed very sweetly the hour of five.

"Ye'll hae to change your clothes," said the woman, "for ye're as wat as a flowe-moss. Ye'll put on a sark o' the minister's and an auld pair o' his breeks, and his chamber-robe, till your ain things are dried. I'll mak up a bed for ye, and get ye ane o' his nightgowns, though it'll maybe be jimp your size. . . . Ye're frae Scotland, sir? Whatna pairt?

"Waucht!" she cried. "Man, I was bred within five miles o't, though we flittit to Caddonside when I was a young lassie. Brydon, they ca' me, and we bode at the Black-cleuchfoot. It's heartsome to see a body frae Waucht. Quick wi' your changin', sir, for ye'll be wantin' meat. The minister has his supper at six."

The old man had not spoken, but had made little sounds of welcome, and now he patted Mr. Dott's arm. He had thin silvery hair which hung almost to his shoulders, and a fine-drawn face the colour of old ivory. His dress was knee-breeches of homespun, homespun stockings, and a very shabby black coat. He looked old, but hale, and there was still vigour in his movements. Mr. Dott, as he got rid of his drenched garments, began to think less evilly of Yonderdale.

Half an hour later he sat warm and dry before a fire which had been enlivened with birch billets. Presently came the housekeeper with a summons to meat, and in the other living-room, which looked towards the stream, he listened to a lengthy grace. Then the three fell to a meal of burn trout, oatcakes, scones, cloudberry jam, and thick creamy milk, after which the host concocted a modest bowl of toddy.

"Awa' into the study," the housekeeper told them, "and hae your crack. The weather's clearin' and you'll maybe get your nightcap after a'. The minister," she turned to Mr. Dott, "is fond o' a breath o' caller air afore he gangs to his bed. He ca's it his nightcap, and, certes, it maun be guid for his health, for there was never a man o' his age less troubled wi' his perishin' body."

The conversation at the meal had been of the most formal kind, chiefly, on Mr. Dott's part, replies to the housekeeper's questions about Waucht and its people. But when the two men sat by the study fire they seemed to enter suddenly into intimacy. Mr. Dott's voice may have been one reason, the soft singsong very different from the Northumbrian burr, and the sight of the minister's face was another, for from every line of it shone a kindly simplicity. But it was simplicity that did not exclude shrewdness, for he had already guessed Mr. Dott's predicament.

"You went to Hungrygrain on an honest errand, and got a surly answer? That, I regret to say, is nothing uncommon. . . . No, I have no dealings with the squire or his people. I cannot tell you if Mrs. Cranmer is there now. I see none of the family. Three years ago when she was a bride she visited me, but since then I have heard little of her and have seen nothing. I fear that it may be an ill-assorted marriage. and I do not think it can be the lady's fault, for she seemed to me as kind as she was beautiful. . . . The squire I can hardly claim even as an acquaintance. There is a small endowment from which my stipend is paid by a firm of Newcastle lawyers, so I have no cause to meet Squire Cranmer on worldly affairs, and he does not frequent the house of God."

Mr. Blackstocks drew a strange picture of the valley. "A

hundred years ago," he said, "Yonderdale was a pleasant little haven by a burnside. The Squire Cranmer of that day had lands in Teviotdale through his wife, and was a leader in the new ways of sheep-farming. So he brought many Scots folk to Yonderdale, and with them their Presbyterian faith. Since then there has been a sad decline, both in the lairds and in the people. The place had always a certain repute for lawlessness, but then it was no worse than shifting from glen to glen merchandise which had not paid the King his dues. But soon the thing took a darker colour. Our men became known as hard drinkers and desperate fighters, and got an ill name over all the Border. When I came here forty years ago I lifted up my testimony against the iniquity, and for ten years I was a voice crying in the wilderness. It was as useless, Mr. Dott, as the bleating of a snipe. But I loved the place and some of the folk and I resolved to stay here. I could still lead a sheep or two into the fold, and if Ephraim was joined to his idols I might be of use to Ephraim's wife and bairns. I had failed as an iconoclast, but I believed that I might still be a comforter. So I stayed on, and shall doubtless lay my bones here."

The old man's conversation was as soothing to Mr. Dott as the warm fire and the excellent supper. His errand and the mischances of the day slipped from his mind, and he was content to explore the soul of this philosopher, for he had a lively interest in his fellows. He asked his host how he filled his time.

"Too pleasantly, I fear," was the answer. "I have the duties of my calling—my diets of worship on the Sabbath, and such pastoral visitation as I am permitted. But for the rest I have a noble leisure, and I am fortunate enough to have the tastes to fill it. I am a devout lover of nature and something of a naturalist. I derive much happiness from cultivating my little garden, and I am a noted beekeeper. But I have two occupations which lie next my heart. *Imprimis*, I am a fisherman, and I think I have cast a fly in every burn in Cheviot, for I used to be a famous walker, Mr. Dott, and these ageing shanks of mine can still do their twenty miles in a day over heather. Yonder is a great stream for fish—the trouts you ate at supper were taken from it by myself. It is a sport in which I have no competitor save the little boys who guddle the stones, for the folk of the glen follow less innocent pursuits. *Secundo*, I have my books. You see them round you, and soon they will drive me out of house and home. A new volume from Newcastle or Edinburgh is my chief indulgence. You are college-bred, Mr. Dott?"

"Glasgow," was the answer.

"Ah, I was at the college of Edinburgh, and I fear I give more time to pagan lore than to the Scriptures. I fell in love with the classics and the classical philosophers. I mind how my worthy father would reprehend me when I quoted Plato or Seneca. He was a divine of the old Scottish stamp and would shake his head woefully. 'I am not concerned,' he would say, 'to hear what the heathen have thought. What did Mr. Alexander Henderson think, or Mr. George Gillespie, or Mr. Samuel Rutherford?' But he lived to see me a placed minister, though he never held me quite sound in the fundamentals. . . . Dearie me! As we grow old we see that there are many roads to Jerusalem. *Uno itinere non potest pervenire ad tam grande secretum*. The classics have ever since been my delight, and I amuse myself by little ventures in translation—in emendation, too—the idle pleasures of an idle old man. So with that and angling I fill my days contentedly."

"You're the first true philosopher I have ever met," said Mr. Dott. "Man, you've discovered the secret of a happy life."

The minister smiled and held up a deprecatory hand.

"No, no," he said. "Only of an idle one. Yet I hope I do not let these trifling joys come between me and my duty God-wards. I try to sit loose to my pleasant idols, for soon I must bid them goodbye. This very morning, reading in Epictetus, I found a word for myself."

He rose and fetched a book from the table.

"Here is what the *Enchiridion* says. I will roughly translate the passage. Listen, Mr. Dott. 'As on a voyage, when your ship has moored offshore, if you go on land to get fresh water, you may pick up as an extra on your way a small mussel or a little fish; but you have to keep your attention fixed on the ship and turn round frequently for fear lest the captain should call. So it is also in life. If there is given you, instead of a little fish or a small mussel, a little wife or a small child, there is no harm in it. But if the captain calls, give up all that and run to the ship without even turning to look back. And if you are an old man, never even get far away from the ship, for fear that when he calls you may be missing.' That is a word in season for me. I have no wife and child, and my little fish and small mussel are my rod and my books. But I must sit loose to them, for my call will not be long in coming."

An hour later the housekeeper looked in. "It's a braw nicht now and a fine mune. Haste and get your nightcap, sir, for it's near time for your bed."

"Marget must be obeyed," said the minister, and, having clapped an ancient hat on his head, he led his guest out of the back-door to the shelf of garden above the Yonder. After the rain the stream was loud, but the wind had sunk, and there was no other sound but an occasional owl and the soft rustle of homing beasts. On the other bank the trees ceased at the gorge's edge, and the bare breast of a hill rose to the pale sky. It was the colour of ripe corn in the moonlight and dotted with the white forms of sheep.

The old man filled his lungs with the soft air.

"That is a sight I love," he said. "The sheep look like white tombstones in some ancient graveyard of the gods."

Mr. Dott did not love it. The peace of the minister's study had gone from him, and he knew again the curious disquiet that he had felt at the sight of Hungrygrain. It was not the loneliness but the secrecy which oppressed him, an unpleasing sense of anticipation.

"What's that moving among the sheep?" he asked sharply.

Something was making the animals scatter. Something

stirred at the far side of the Yonder. Mr. Dott waited tensely, for he realized that whatever it was it was coming towards them. He glanced back to the house where the open door made an oblong of light. Mr. Blackstocks was quoting Greek, but he did not listen, for his eyes were strained upon the near lip of the ravine.

Suddenly a figure appeared on it and stumbled towards them. Mr. Dott caught the minister's arm and would have drawn him towards the house, till he saw that there was no menace in the figure. It was that of a young man, whose clothes were dripping wet and much disordered, and whose face was white and weary. Blood from a wound on his forehead was blinding his eyes.

CHAPTER VII

IN WHICH A BARONET IS DISCOMPOSED

THE young man's face was ghastly in the light of the moon. He clutched at Mr. Dott, who retreated in alarm, but who came forward when he realized the truth. This was a sick man with no purpose of hostility; his clothes were stained, and one coat-sleeve was torn, but they had once been fashionable; his cravat was wildly disordered, but it was of fine cambric; his countenance was dirty and blood-smeared, but the features showed breeding. Mr. Dott was reassured.

"Hold up, sir," he said, giving him his arm. Then to the minister, "We must get him inbye, for this garden is no place for a dwam. Your study sofa is the bit for him."

He was a tall youth and leaned heavily on his small companion. They were met in the passage by the housekeeper, who exclaimed shrilly, "Is't the minister? Is't himsel'? Whae in the warld? . . . Tuts, gie me a haud o' him. The chiel's sick, and, gudesakes, he's gotten an unco clour on the heid. . . . Losh, he's awa' wi' it." Sure enough the young man fainted and was carried by sturdy female arms to the lamplit study.

The minister stood by twittering gently, while the housekeeper laid the youth on the sofa, undid his neckcloth, unstrapped his pantaloons, and drew off big boots. She fetched a basin of hot water and bathed his brow, felt his pulse in the most professional manner, and shook a disapproving head.

"Nae wound to speak o'," she announced. "Just a wheen scarts on the scalp as if a gled had pikit at him. But the lad's sair forfochen—fair foundered. There's been ill wark somewhere this nicht."

"A drop of brandy is what he needs," said Mr. Dott.

"And whaur am I to get brandy, think ye? There's no the savour o't in this house. There's whisky in plenty, but whisky's nae guid, for it wad only fever him."

There was something ominous about the dead-white face, and the wet hair streaked over the still bleeding forehead. The sick man gave no appearance of coming to himself, but lay with his head limp and his pale lips open, and his breath seemed to be faint and difficult.

"We must get a doctor," said Mr. Dott.

"There's nae doctor nearer than Yondermouth, and he wadna be muckle use if ye got him. He's yin that's no often sober. But there's nae surgeon's wark needit. Thae wounds are just scarts and scrapes, and the bleedin' is near stoppit. I've skill enough o' medicine to ken that. If I could get a cup o' brandy and het milk down his throat, I'se warrant he'd sleep like a bairn and be a weel man in the mornin'."

"Then brandy must be found," said Mr. Dott. "Is there no Christian house nearby where we could beg a bottle?"

"Nane but Hungrygrain, and he'd be a bauld man that went seekin' favours at yon door."

"But there is an inn. I've heard tell of an inn."

The housekeeper raised her head.

"Ay, there's an inn. It's a queer kind o' hostel, but ye'd maybe get what ye socht."

"Is it near?"

"Ayont the water. No abune a mile. Ye'd hae to cross the plank brig at Ritterford."

"Then I'm off to the inn. There's a grand moon to light me, if you'll set me on the road."

"Ye canna miss it. There's a path doun this side o' the Yonder till ye come to the brig, and ayont it there's the inn on the tap o' the brae. Ye'll hae to speak the landlord fair, sir, for he's a thrawn body. I've kenned better men than Purdey, but I've kenned waur. Haste ye, for there's nae time to loss. I'll get the puir lad out o' his clothes and inside one o' the minister's nightgowns, and into the spare bed. See, he's comin' to. . . . But I daurna let him sleep till he has gotten his cordial."

The figure on the sofa stirred, its eyes opened, and a strong shudder overtook it. As Mr. Dott set out on his errand it seemed to be trying to speak.

Sir Turnour Wyse did not turn his chaise up the hill track which Mr. Dott had followed. His goal was the inn, and he had been advised in Berwick to cross the Yonder by what was known as the Roman Brig, and then to bend right through a firwood, to cross a strip of moor, to traverse the village of Yonder, and so find the inn a mile beyond on the hill above the stream. The directions had been given him with curious covert looks, which Sir Turnour had remarked but heeded little. He felt himself to be too far north for the manners of civilization.

The road, once he had left the highway, proved to be vile in the extreme, and the steady downpour of rain which had begun did not add to its cheerfulness. He buttoned the high collar of his dreadnought, but the deluge trickled down his neck, and made great pools on his leather driving apron. Sir Turnour was not commonly sensitive to landscape or weather, but this place struck him as wholly abominable. The ragged fir trees looked like gibbets. When he emerged on the moor he was met by such a blast of wind and water that he could scarcely see the track, and his galloways stumbled among ruts and potholes. The clachan, through which he presently passed, was sodden, shabby, and tumble-down, like a city slum transported to a sour upland. There was no sign of life in its street, not even a wandering dog, but he was conscious of unfriendly eyes watching him from behind dirty windows.

Sir Turnour, who that morning had been an easy master

of his world, began to feel at a disadvantage, and the novel sensation affected his temper. He had come north on an errand which bored him, but which he could not shirk. No man had ever insulted him with impunity, and at whatever trouble to himself he must bring this young whippersnapper to instant account. It was not his reputation that moved him, for that he believed to be impregnable: it was his own self-respect. He could not be comfortable in his mind while one walked unpunished who had questioned his breeding or his courage. . . . But the enterprise, which had hitherto worn the guise of a majestic punitive expedition, was now losing its dignity. He had hoped to find Belses in his own home and to bring him to book with all the decencies of good society. He had learned by secret channels that he had gone to his mistress's Northumbrian home, and that had seemed a not unfitting venue for a settlement. But to seek him in this howling wilderness was another matter. What code of manners could obtain in such a desert? His purpose was to meet one of his own class in the environment of that class, and not to dig out a wretched fugitive like a fox from a hole. He felt that his grand, rock-like self-sufficiency, his complete competence in life, was being imperilled. He might even be in danger of becoming ridiculous. It was an irritated and discomposed baronet that pulled up at the inn.

The place was in the last degree forbidding. It may once have been the mansion of a small laird, for its high-pitched roof and crow-step gables seemed ancient, there was a little courtyard before it, and a ruinous dovecot crowned the slope behind it. But its visage was inhospitable as seen in the driving rain. The small casements were uncurtained, there was no sign above the door, and the door did not stand wide, as a good inn-door should, to welcome the traveller. The forecourt was dirty and cumbered with rubbish, and there was at least one broken pane in each window. One detail alone was satisfactory. Flanking the house were roomy stables, which seemed to be well-cared for, and from which came the stirring of horses. A place could not be wholly comfortless where horseflesh was respected.

The first fury of the rain had ceased, and there was a break in the mist which, from the high vantage-ground of the inn, opened the upper valley. The tree-filled gorge of the stream gave place to a bare glen flanked by hills, which to Sir Turnour's lowland eyes seemed monstrous precipices. In the middle distance a house was apparent, a gaunt rambling erection set among starveling evergreens and ill-nourished firs. A gleam of sun caught its walls, but gave them no cheerfulness, and the end of a broken rainbow on the hillside gave it no colour. The place was ugly as a brickyard and cold as a tomb, and it had a character, too, which Sir Turnour was conscious of but could not define. It was ominous, and stared at him with malign eyes; on that he was clear enough, for he was accustomed to trust his intuitions and back his fancy.

The water from a gutter gathered in the eaves above the inn door and descended thence in a steady cascade, so that any one entering ran the risk of a wetting. So Sir Turnour sat in his chaise and shouted for the landlord.

At first there was no answer. There was a fresh stamping of hooves from the stables, and what sounded like the voice of an angry man. A cow routed in some outhouse, and a clatter of pails was heard in the direction of the steading. But the weatherworn door behind its curtain of water did not open.

Again and yet again Sir Turnour shouted, and each time his voice became angrier. He was just about to descend, with his whip ready for action, when a voice spoke behind him. Some one had come up from the direction of the stream.

It was a big man, who wore corduroy breeches and a homespun coat with huge pockets. Thick blue worsted stockings enveloped his enormous calves and bulged over his stout country shoes. His rounded shoulders and the downward thrust of his shaggy head gave him the air of a dangerous bull.

"What's the steer, mannie?" he asked.

Sir Turnour did not understand the question, but realized that it was not friendly.

"Are there no men about this Godforsaken hole?" he thundered.

"There's me."

"Are you the innkeeper?"

"Ye've said it."

"Then what the devil do you mean by not attending to your duties? I want a stable for my horse, and rooms and fire and food for myself and my servant. Look sharp about it." He flung back his driving apron, and descended from the chaise.

The man did not move. "Ye can get back into your coachie, and turn your beasts' heads, and return the road ye came. There's no place for ye here."

Sir Turnour was at his ease again. Here was a surly ruffian to be brought to heel, and that was a task with which he was familiar. He divested himself of his dreadnought and his gloves, and handed them to his servant, who was standing at the galloways' heads. Then he strolled round the chaise and confronted the innkeeper.

The latter had menace in every line of him. He advanced a step with his head thrust forward and his long arms loose for defence or attack. But when he raised his eyes and saw the other clearly, the resolution seemed to go out of his air. For what he saw was no fleshy, dandified traveller, as he had judged from the voice and the figure as it had appeared on the box seat. Sir Turnour stood on his toes as lightly as a runner, his strong clenched hands white at the knuckles, his poise easy but as charged with swift power as a thundercloud is charged with fire. The innkeeper marked the square shoulders, the corded muscles of the shapely neck, the slim flanks—above all, he marked the vigilant and scornful eye. He was himself a noted wrestler, but he knew that he could not give this man a fall, for he would never get to grips with him. The other would dance round him on those light feet, and an arm like a flail would smite him into unconsciousness.

He was a bold man but no fool, and he recognized the trained fighter, no genteel amateur, but one bred in a tough school. So he surrendered at discretion and touched a damp forelock.

"No offence," he grunted. "Ye take up a man too short, sir. What's your honour's will?"

Sir Turnour smiled.

"Jarvis," he cried to his servant. "Take my baggage indoors. Kick open that door, if it is locked." Then to the innkeeper. "My will? That you should be a little more active in your public duties, friend. I want rooms, fire and food, and civility—civility observe, for I am particular on that point. Quick with you, for your accursed sky is beginning to drip again."

The innkeeper showed a surprising activity. He was at the door before Jarvis could assault it, opened it with a clumsy bow, and himself carried in the larger of Sir Turnour's two valises. The travellers found themselves in a stone-flagged hall which smelt half of stable and half of taproom. Tables and settles were littered with crops, rusty and broken spurs, hawks' jesses, medicines for hawks, hounds, and horses, powder-flasks, shot-pouches and a miscellany of other litter. The landlord led them up an oaken stair, with many broken treads, to an upper hall which was chiefly remarkable for possessing a huge rug of woven rushes into which the feet sank. He flung open a door.

"There's your parlour, my denty sir, and ayont it lies your bedchamber. Your servant will have to bed in the garret. I'll get a fire going in a jiffy, but it's a dry house, this o' mine, and the roof's tight, and it's no ill to warm. Meat ye'll want. What time will ye be pleased to dine?"

"Your cursed roads have given me a twist. Let us say six o'clock, sharp to the minute. What can you give me?"

He listened gravely to the landlord's inventory of his larder, for he was one that took his meals seriously. "Faith, we shall not do so dustily. A grilled salmon steak, a cut of hill mutton, and a welsh rarebit—I have dined more scurvily in my day. Claret, no. I have no stomach for your north-country claret.

If your ale is sound I will have a tankard of it, and a bottle of your best port for the good of the house. But first I must have a message sent to the house of Hungrygrain. The place is close at hand, I think?"

At the mention of Hungrygrain the landlord who had drifted into a complaisance which was almost servility, bristled like a terrier.

"What do ye want with Hungrygrain?" he asked surlily.

"What the devil is your business what I want with Hungrygrain? Civility, my friend." Sir Turnour's eyes had a frosty gleam in them. "You will take a message to Squire Cranmer—that, I think, is the name—and you will say that—"

"I will take no message. No message will gang out of this place the day."

"Oho! So that is the way the wind's set! Listen, my man. You will take, or procure the taking of, my message, and that instantly. If you do not, I shall take it myself. But in that event I shall first of all have had the felicity to thrash you soundly and to fling you down these steep stairs of yours. Make your choice, friend. I am stiff with sitting in my chaise, and I should not be averse to a little exercise."

Once again the two men measured each other with their eyes, and once again the landlord's conclusion was pessimistic about his chances.

"What's your errand?" he growled.

"You will make my compliments to Squire Cranmer—the compliments of Sir Turnour Wyse, Baronet, of Wood Rising Hall in the county of Norfolk, and of White's Club—you will present my *carte de visite*—and you will inform him that I propose to do myself the honour of waiting upon him tomorrow morning at ten o'clock. You will add that, as the matter is somewhat private, I would beg of him to say nothing of it, and not to mention my name till after our meeting. Do you follow?"

"I follow. What if the Squire will not see ye?"

"Now, what do you know of the courtesies due between gentlemen? You take too much upon you, my man." Sir

Turnour extracted a slip of pasteboard from an ivory case, and placed it in an envelope which he took from his valise.

"See that the rain does not make it pulp," he said. "Off with you or send your trustiest man. Let me have an answer by six, and the dinner you have promised me, and we shall yet be good friends. . . . God, man what is the trouble? The Squire is your master, and a good one by all I hear, but you seem as shy of approaching him as if he were the Devil with his tongs! Did you never take a message before from one gentleman to another?"

The landlord departed, a slovenly maid appeared with a pailful of red peats and another of birch billets; the valet Jarvis, who had been busy in the bedchamber, assisted Sir Turnour to his toilet before the fire. His boots were drawn off, and his legs adorned with fine silk stockings, and a pair of handsome monogrammed velvet slippers. He exchanged his coat for a *néglīgé* jacket of a loud-patterned tweed, and a quilted silk dressing-gown. Water was boiled somewhere downstairs, and a basin provided wherein Sir Turnour delicately washed his hands and face. Then he lay back in a much-rubbed leather armchair, trimmed his nails with a penknife, and proposed to enjoy a siesta before dinner.

But, though he was a little stiff and the fire was gracious after the stormy out-of-doors, Sir Turnour did not doze. Instead he indulged in daydreams. The shining form of Miss Kirsty Evandale tripped through the corridors of his fancy. He had never had the name of a woman-fancier—more stirring occupations had filled his time. On the whole women had bored him with their airs and graces, their extravagant demands, their exigent charms. He did not even greatly admire the female form—too full of meaningless curves and cushions, too bottle-shouldered and heavy-hipped—a well-made man seemed to him a far finer creation of God. He could talk to them, banter them, take his pleasure with them, but none had ever touched his heart. But the girl that morning—she differed from any other woman he had ever known! She walked like a free creature, she was ripe and vital and yet fresh as a spring flower, a dainty being yet wholesome as a blood-horse, and she had the most darling laughing eyes! Sir Turnour found himself moved to poetry, and strove to dig Latin tags out of his Harrow memories.

Suddenly his dream was broken. The door had opened and a stranger had entered.

Sir Turnour saw a tall man, booted and spurred and much splashed with mire, who brought into the warm room the tang of sharp weather. His shoulders were a little bent as if he were much in the saddle, and his hair, like Sir Turnour's, was cut as short as a groom's. But his dress, though plain, was not rustic, and he bore himself with dignity and assurance. His face was a fine oval, a little heavy perhaps at the chin; he had a small mouth and full lips, which were parted as if he were perpetually on the brink of a smile. But the notable feature was his pallor, a dead white which accentuated the darkness of his hair and eyes. It was a surprising face, for it had a beauty rare in his sex, the delicacy of a woman combined with a most masculine authority.

"Childe Harold," thought Sir Turnour, as he hove himself out of his chair. "Or his creator?" He had stripped the young Lord Byron of many a guinea at the Cocoa Tree.

The two men bowed, and the newcomer held out his hand.

"Sir Turnour Wyse?" he said. "I am honoured to make your acquaintance, sir. Your fame has travelled even to these moorland solitudes. Your message was delivered to me, and I hastened to wait upon you to receive your commands. Would to Heaven I could offer you the hospitality of Hungrygrain, but alas, at the moment my household is in confusion and no fit lodging for a gentleman." He shrugged his shoulders as if to imply a host of petty disasters needless to recount. "In what way can I serve you, sir?"

"I am deeply obliged, Mr. Cranmer. My errand is simple and should be short. I desire an interview on a strictly private matter with one whom I believe to be at present your guest. But since the affair has a certain unpleasantness, I thought it common courtesy first of all to acquaint you with my purpose and to desire your assent to it."

Mr. Cranmer looked puzzled.

"A guest? Hungrygrain has few guests."

"I will be explicit. The gentleman I seek is my lord Belses."

The other frowned and seemed to meditate. Then the nascent smile on his lips broadened into a laugh.

"Belses! The Snowdoun hopeful! My dear sir, you have come on a curious errand. Now I think of it I have heard some tale of a quarrel between you and his callow lordship—I returned only the other day from town—it was common gossip in the clubs. But what whim possessed you to think that you would find the cub here?"

"I had information in Scotland that he was at your house." Sir Turnour was trying to decide just how much he disliked this dark Adonis.

Mr. Cranmer bent his brows so that they made a straight line beneath his pale forehead.

"Sir Turnour," he said, "we are two men of the world and can speak frankly. You have heard rumours of some connection between this Lord Belses and my family? I will not particularize, for the topic, as you will understand, is painful to me. But I ask you, is it likely that I would receive in my house one to whom such gossip attaches? Do I look like a man who would tamely consent to be cuckolded under his own roof-tree?"

Mr. Cranmer drew himself up, and his pose was that of indignant virtue, a chivalrous and noble wrath. Sir Turnour had seen just that same pose in admired actors on the London stage. But all the time there was that lurking smile at his lips. He realized that he disliked him exceedingly.

"You can assure me that Lord Belses is not at Hungrygrain?"

"After what I have said another man might take your question as an insult, but I can make allowance for your natural irritation. You have been shamelessly misled, Sir Turnour. Lord Belses is not now in my house and never has been. Were he in my power, I should be the first to deliver him to you for just punishment. . . . That is my answer, and I rejoice that it will save you a longer stay in these poor quarters in this doleful weather."

He held out his hand. Sir Turnour took it ungraciously, but did not forget his manners.

"I am about to dine," he said. "Will you join me?"

"I thank you, but I have already dined—at our unfashionable Northumbrian hour. I bid you good-day, Sir Turnour, and I wish you speedily better luck in your mission."

A minute later there was the sound of departing hooves on the cobbles of the inn yard. Sir Turnour did not resume his armchair, for he was profoundly discomposed. His information about Belses had come to him from a sure source, he had implicitly believed it, and had looked forward to bringing a tiresome affair to a proper close. But now he must resume his quest—after a snubbing. For this damned play-actor had snubbed him, had taken a high line with him, had proved him deficient in the finer feelings of a gentleman. . . . What had he heard about Cranmer? A complaisant husband. A bumpkin whose heart was in some provincial hunt. Had there not been a story, too, of heavy drinking? Yet the man's appearance had not suggested these things. He looked active, shrewd, formidable. He had the air of one accustomed to good society. His pallor could scarcely come from a disordered liver, for his physique was vigorous, a point on which the baronet was no small authority.

Dinner was served, but Sir Turnour did scant justice to the meal. His appetite had mysteriously gone, and even the excellent port did not improve his spirits. The memory rankled of an interview in which he felt that he had shown at some disadvantage. . . . This Cranmer, could he trust him? Was he lying? But why should he lie? He could have no reason to protect Belses. . . . The one thing clear in his mind was that he detested Cranmer as vigorously as he had ever detested a fellow mortal, the more vigorously because he had no just cause for his dislike. Sir Turnour was a good-humoured man, and a hatred so irrational and intense made him uncomfortable.

The table was cleared, and he sat sipping his port in the armchair by the fire. His confused thoughts and the heat of the lamplit, shuttered room presently made him drowsy, and he thought of ringing for Jarvis to put him to bed.

Then came a small knock at the door. It opened to admit the hesitating form of a little man in a greatcoat, a man with a nutcracker jaw and prominent goggle eyes.

CHAPTER VIII

IN WHICH THE HUNTER MEETS THE HUNTED

SIR TURNOUR stared at the singular figure which was now inside the room and busy with apologetic shuffles and bows. He seemed to be a small man of the professional class, a country doctor maybe, for sober black apparel was revealed under the lapping greatcoat.

"Your pardon, sir," said the figure. "I'm sure I beg your pardon for intruding on you. But I'm seeking the landlord, and this hostel is as short of folk as a kirk on Monday."

Sir Turnour did not rise from his chair. He had no mind to have his private chamber treated as a taproom.

"I know nothing of the landlord's whereabouts," he said coldly. "I have the honour to wish you good-night, sir."

"But I cannot find him," the little man wailed. "No, nor a Jock or Jenny to do my business. The place is as deserted as the grave. And find somebody I must, for I cannot wait."

Sir Turnour grew cross. "What concern have I with your business? What do you want?"

"Brandy," was the answer.

"Confound your impudence. Do you take me for a drawer?"

"No, no, your honour." The little man shrank back as if he feared that the formidable presence in the chair would do him a mischief. "I was just seeking help from a fellow-Christian. The brandy is not for myself, but for a young gentleman that has gotten a sore clout on the head and now lies in a dwam."

"Where is he?" In spite of himself Sir Turnour's interest was awakened.

"He's bedded at the manse."

"The what?"

"The manse. The minister's house. They have a manse here, though it's not Scotland. And the wife there, who seems to have some skill of medicine, says the lad must have a cordial if he is to sleep off his weakness."

A fantastic suspicion entered Sir Turnour's mind.

"Who is this young man? Describe him."

Mr. Dott came a step farther into the room as he saw the baronet's severity relax.

"That's just what we don't know. He came out of the wood an hour syne stottering like a palsied man, and all bloody about the forehead, and before we could speir who he was he spins round like a peery and goes off into a dwam. He's just a laddie, your honour, and a gentleman, if I'm any judge of gentility."

"Describe his appearance."

"Very dirty and dishevelled, for he had been among the sheughs and craigs of the burnside. But let me see. . . . Yellow hair—I think it would be yellow, under the blood and mire. A small whitish face, and a kind of thin gentry nose. He had on him a good stand of clothes, though they had had rough usage, and his hands were as fine as a lassie's."

"His height?"

"About the same as your own, but he's a lath of a lad, and not buirdly like your honour."

Mr. Dott was gaining confidence. He had now recognized the man before him as the god from the machine who had intervened on Kitterston hill, and he had resolved to appeal for aid to one who was such a master of circumstance. Sir Turnour's suspicion was growing into a certainty. His dislike of Justin Cranmer had made him violently distrustful of every word that gentleman had spoken. The man had lied to him, and he was not wont to let a lie go unpunished. For the moment he saw in Cranmer a more fitting object of his wrath than the youth who had been the purpose of his journey.

But Sir Turnour's face was schooled to impassivity, and Mr. Dott read in it none of these changing emotions. He saw in it only reflection, and it gave him hope.

"I have already seen your honour twice this day," he said. "I was in the Mail when it coupit on Kitterston hill, and your honour came birling up like Jehu. And you passed me on the road about midday when yon ne'er-do-well from the King's Arms was driving me here. It's a sore time of night to disturb a gentleman, but if you could find it in your heart to do a Christian act by the poor lad . . . help me to get some brandy in this house . . . or maybe—"

Sir Turnour was on his feet, shouting for his servant, who appeared at once from the bedroom.

"Where is this manse, or whatever you call it?"

"Oh, just a step—less than a mile—a wee bit ayont the burn."

"My boots," he told his valet. "And get me the flask of eau-de-vie from my dressing-case. I am going out for an hour. See that the fire is kept bright, and have a glass of punch ready for my return. . . . I have not the favour of your name, sir. Dott? Well, Mr. Dott, I will accompany you to the parsonage, and have a look at the sick man. I may know something about him. And since broken heads are going in these parts, we will take precautions."

When he had been assisted into his boots, Sir Turnour buckled under his coat a brace of pistols.

There was little talk between the two as they threaded a track through the dene much clogged with tree-roots. The baronet was occupied in nursing his wrath against Justin Cranmer, his dislike of whom was fast growing to a passion. He had never felt in this way towards Belses, whom he had considered a puppy that must taste the whip, but otherwise a mere unpleasing accident like the toothache. But Cranmer was grown man and formidable man; no mistake about that, for he had the wary eye of the duellist and the face of one not accustomed to refusal. He had been polite but arrogant, that confounded hedge-squire. Sir Turnour had longed at the time to fasten some quarrel on him, and if he had been lied to, here was ample cause for quarrel. Also the track was infernal. Mr. Dott in stout high-lows, well nailed by the Waucht cobbler, made good going, but Sir Turnour's smooth-soled riding boots were perpetually slipping on the sodden earth.

At the manse door they were met by the housekeeper.

"Ha'e ye brocht the brandy?" she demanded of Mr. Dott.

"Aye, and I've brought a gentleman to give us a hand."

The woman cast one look at Sir Turnour's massive figure in the moonlight, and then bobbed a curtsy. She recognized some one of a type not often seen in Yonderdale.

"He's come to himsel'," she whispered. "The minister's wi' him. He's snug in the best bed, and I hae the milk for his cordial on the boil. Whaur's the brandy?"

Sir Turnour drew from the pocket of his greatcoat a silver flask. "It is eau-de-vie I'll warrant," he said, "such as rarely visits Northumberland. Has the sick man spoken and told who he is?"

"Not yet. He has gotten his speech but nae freedom wi't. He cried out something about an angel—Gabriel, I think it was—and then he seemed to be feared for what he had said. But his een are gettin' mair world-like, and the minister is guidin' him back to sense. I heard the crack o' the twae through the door. Yince he has had his cordial he'll be a new man."

"Will you lead me to him at once, my good woman?"

"When I've gotten his draught prepared, and that'll no be a minute. Bide ye here, sir."

The housekeeper retreated into her tiny kitchen, and a few moments later appeared with a steaming posset-cup which sent forth an agreeable odour of good brandy. She led the way up the steep staircase and opened a bedroom door. There was a sound of talk coming through the door, which ceased when it opened.

Sir Turnour and Mr. Dott, following close on her heels,

saw a little square room almost filled by a great uncurtained four-poster. Beside it sat the minister, and four candles guttered in the draught of the open window. Their light showed a young man in a flannel nightgown, whose face was paler than the bleached linen of the pillowslips. His forehead was bandaged, and surmounted by an incongruous red nightcap. At first his figure was blocked by the housekeeper, who was feeding him from the posset-cup. When he had drained it he lay back again upon his pillow, and a faint colour returned to his cheeks.

Sir Turnour at the bottom of the bed was gazing earnestly at the face, which was now a little in dusk, since the table with the candles had been pushed aside. Doubt, recognition, and doubt again were in the baronet's eyes. But the sick man put an end to all uncertainty. The baronet stood out clear in the candlelight, and the patient became suddenly conscious of his gaze. He pulled himself up in bed with such vigour as to displace his nightcap and set the candles rocking.

"Wyse, by all that's lucky!" he cried. "Speak, man. Are you Wyse, or am I raving mad?"

"My name is Turnour Wyse," was the answer. "We shall have something to say to each other, my lord, when you are fit for speech."

The young man let his head drop back, and his newly revealed hair was, as Mr. Dott had said, as yellow as a girl's. He laughed, but not pleasantly; his laugh had discomfort in it, and fear, and a sharp anxiety.

"Have you come here for my sake?" he asked.

Sir Turnour bowed.

"I have requested satisfaction for an insult," he said, "and that satisfaction has been withheld. I am not in the habit of letting such requests go unanswered. So since you chose to seclude yourself from me, I have been forced to come in search of you."

He spoke firmly, and a little pompously, for these were the words with which he had long proposed to open this particular conversation. But to his surprise, and indeed to his alarm, he felt, as he spoke, something of a fool. This pallid youth in the flannel nightgown seemed a poor quarry for so noted a hunter. He had set out to draw a badger and found a rabbit, and he discovered that he had no fury against the rabbit. Belses, trim and handsome and point-devise, with a coterie of affected youths behind him, had annoyed him extremely; but had he been the same being as this rag of a boy?

The housekeeper intervened.

"Ye maun let him sleep, sir. The posset will dae him nae guid if ye keep him conversin'."

But the lad in the bed seemed to have got a new vigour which could not be due only to the milk and brandy. He raised himself on the pillows, and brought a slim boyish arm outside the blankets.

"I have that to say to this gentleman which cannot wait. . . . Sir Turnour, will you believe me when I tell you that I did not hide myself from you? I was not my own master. My family intervened. . . . When I could free myself I found an urgent duty laid on me, a matter of life and death. I would beg of you to let our affair lie over till my road is clear. Be assured that when the time comes I will give you all the satisfaction you desire."

"A matter of honour does not permit of delay," was the answer, very stiffly spoken.

"Then, if you refuse postponement, I must take the other way. You shall have your apology, as grovelling as you please. I will eat humble pie."

Sir Turnour was scandalized. This rabbit was even poorer game than he had thought. He shrugged his fine shoulders, and on his comely face came an expression of surprised disgust.

"I had thought that I was dealing with a gentleman," he said.

The young man laughed miserably.

"A gentleman! Yes, I fancied myself one, but God knows what the word means! There are some that claim it who most foully profane it.". . . He stopped, for there was that in the other's face, its confidence and simplicity and large honesty, which switched his thoughts on to a new track. It was as if he was for the first time seeing clearly the man before him.

"Listen to me, sir," he said. "I respect the punctilios of honour and would observe them. But if I am faced with a desperate crisis I will discard these punctilios like an old coat and still claim the title of gentleman. . . . If I could secure not your forbearance only, but your active help in this crisis, there is no humility to which I would not bow. I would lick your boots, sir, and think I did honourably."

Sir Turnour was in no way mollified. He had heard this kind of talk before, and did not like it; it savoured of poets and Jacobins and creatures of sentiment who had no place in his robust world. But the earnestness of the young man's voice impressed him in spite of himself.

"What is this crisis?" he asked. "I must hear more about it before I answer you."

The young man looked round the room.

"I am among friends, I believe—friends, and one honourable enemy. My host is a servant of God and this woman is a ministering angel. The fourth I do not know," and he looked at Mr. Dott, "but he has an honest face. I fling myself upon your mercy. Tonight I have been near death, but that is a small affair. There is worse than death in the house of Hungrygrain. There is an incarnate devil, and torture, and despair."

"Large words," said Sir Turnour. "Condescend to explain yourself." But he was not wholly sceptical, for he had a notion that he had recently met the devil referred to.

Colour had come back to the young man's face. He addressed the housekeeper. "I am perishingly hungry, for I have scarcely eaten today. Can you give me some bread and cheese?"

The woman expostulated. "Na, na, sir, it's sleep ye need. Ye should hae naething on your stomach but the het milk."

"But I am too hungry to sleep—and too hungry to speak—and speak I must. Already I feel a new man, but an empty one."

Sir Turnour intervened.

"You were struck on the head—how long ago?"

"Four hours, perhaps."

"And since then?"

"I have been chased."

"And you fainted when you came here, and were senseless for half an hour? Your case is plain, sir. You have had a small concussion, which took some hours to affect you. I have suffered the same thing myself in the ring and in the hunting field. Once I went for three days with a concussion on me, pursuing my ordinary life, and then suddenly fainted dead away on the bench at Quarter Sessions, and it was an hour before I came to myself. Food will do you no harm, provided your meal is light."

"There's a mutton ham in the house, Marget," said the minister. "Bring it, and some of your new scones. It's far past bedtime, but I think I could take a bite myself."

Ten minutes later four pairs of jaws were busy in the little room, for even Sir Turnour had accepted a slice of mutton ham and a glass of ale. Belses, propped up on his pillows, looked wholesome enough except for his anxious eyes.

"Cranmer is at Hungrygrain—and his wife," he said.

"I came here to see her on business," said the aggrieved Mr. Dott. "They said she was not here. There's some unholy liars in this glen."

"There is devilry afoot there," Belses went on, "and she is being tortured to make her comply with it. I speak of your Squire." He turned to the minister. "Have you anything to say in his favour?"

The old man shook his head. "I have not spoken to him for years," he said. The housekeeper pursed her lips. "I'll speak nae ill, but I ken nae guid o' him."

"You know nothing of him? No one does. He goes through the world with a mask on his face, which he removes only in this valley. Tell me, Sir Turnour, what repute has Justin Cranmer in your world?"

The baronet shrugged his shoulders. "He has the name of a rustic booby. At Mortimer's they say he is too fond of lifting his elbow."

"I have heard that—that is the repute he wants—but it is a lie, a monstrous lie. The man is cold and temperate and a deep schemer, but what his schemes are I cannot tell. . . . But I must go back in my tale." The boy pressed a hand on his bandaged forehead as if to clear his recollections.

"I met Cranmer first eighteen months ago in Italy, and for a little we travelled together. He had some kind of business, I do not know what, but he was often absent from his lodgings and he had dealings with a strange medley of people. He was civil and not ill-educated, and he made a great parade of attention to his wife. The lady—but I will not speak of her," he added as he saw Sir Turnour's face harden. "For the moment, I am content to be neutral on the matter. It is enough to say that she has no single quality in common with her husband.

"We parted, and met again in Bruges. There Mr. Cranmer's activities were increased, and among the company he kept were some who were not fit associates for his wife. He seemed to cultivate my acquaintance and make public parade of it as if it were some sort of protection. There was one man who was much with him—Aymer was the name he went by there—an evil fellow who stank of a false bonhomie. And there were others who roused my gorge and from whom Mrs. Cranmer seemed to shrink. Yet she was deep in her husband's business, whatever it was—they often consulted together—I have seen her head bent beside his over papers. I could make nothing of it, for he is common flawed earthenware at the best, and she—she, by your leave, sir, is saint and angel."

Sir Turnour frowned. "On that point let us keep our neutrality—it is your own word. I would hear more of the husband."

"In London I renewed my acquaintance with the Cranmers at their house in Great George Street. The man was much away from home, and I understood that he was visiting his properties in the north, but when we met he was uncommonly civil and seemed to have the design of throwing me much into the company of his wife. At first I did not actively dislike him. My feeling was rather distrust and lack of comprehension, for I could not reconcile the repute he seemed to cultivate as a *bon-vivant* and simple sportsman with the glimpses I had of the man in undress. In these latter I detected a subtle brain and some mysterious consuming purpose. Also there were moments when his affection for the lady seemed to ring hollow, and I have found her often with the mark of tears on her face and with terror in her eyes. You must understand that she was all kindness and innocence—"

"We will let her innocence be."

"No, sir, but you must hear me on that, for it is most germane to my story. I formed the opinion that, just as he was intent on making a particular public repute for himself, so he was busy making one for his wife. He would twit her with Jacobinical opinions and quote her sayings in company—sometimes jocularly, sometimes ruefully, for he himself posed as a staunch Government man. Sometimes he would carry her with him to the north, and from those visits she would return a pale ghost, like one who has been in a torture-chamber. Or they would visit her own house in Norfolk, to which she professed a deep attachment, but, judging from the effect on her, these journeys were not in the nature of holidays. I was driven to conclude that Mr. Cranmer was engaged in affairs in which he forced his wife to take part, and that that part was hateful to her. And I could not think that these affairs were honest."

"You have evidence on that point?"

"None fit for a court of law. Only suspicions. I had inquiries made, but the tracks were well concealed. Twice I have seen in Great George Street the man I knew in Bruges as Aymer—stumbled upon him as it were by an accident, which Cranmer did not regard as fortunate. But I found out one thing. His name in London is not Aymer."

Sir Turnour laughed. "You are clearly no great success as a spy, sir."

The other shook his head mournfully. "I am not. I know little of the underworld of the town, and the thing was too delicate to permit me to call in helpers. But day by day my conviction grew. I was assured that the lady was in deep unhappiness, and that it was her husband's doing. I burned with indignation at the character he was getting her. But I was like a man striving with a feather bed, for there was nothing hard at which I could strike. . . . Then came certain incidents with which you are familiar. I will cut my story short, for it is only the conclusion that matters. My family laid hold on me with private *lettres de cachet*, and I was consigned to the family bastille. There word reached me that the Cranmers had gone to Northumberland. My mind was in a fever. I cannot tell why, but I had a fixed belief that with this journey northward some tragedy was approaching its climax, and that the lady was in desperate danger. . . . I broke from my prison. The house in Great George Street was shuttered, and tenanted only by the old man Cottle, who acted as steward. From him I had confirmation of the journey. . . . Also I found at my lodgings a letter from Mrs. Cranmer."

"She begged you to follow her?" Sir Turnour's tone was cynical.

"She begged me to forget her and never think of her more. It was the completest *congé* a man ever had. But between the lines I read that her heart was broken and that she was in some deadly peril. From Cottle I had directions for the road, so without an hour's delay I posted north."

"From spy you became Bow Street runner?" Sir Turnour, himself a truthful man, bowed to veracity in another. Cottle had been, at various times, his own informant. "What, in God's name, did you hope to accomplish by rushing blindly upon the seclusion of husband and wife?"

" 'Pon my soul, I don't know." There was a flush now on the young man's face. "I was distraught. I could not think. I had no plan. I only knew that I must act or go mad. I rode the north road like Dick Turpin, and left some weary cattle behind me. Three days ago—it was Sunday night—I reached Hungrygrain as the dark was falling, having lost my way in those ultimate moorlands. I was alone, without a servant. The place was so silent that it seemed deserted, but I was aware that my approach had not been unobserved, and that the neighbourhood was full of eyes. And now, sir, I became an actor in an extravagant play—God send it be not a tragedy!"

Belses stopped and again put his hand to his forehead. "Let me get the stages clear, for it still seems a sort of whirligig. . . . I was admitted after a long parley by a shaggy serving-man, who looked to be apter at cutting throats than at waiting table. The house was bare and in confusion, as if its occupants were about to start on a journey. I asked for the master, and had to kick my heels for an hour in an ill-lit chamber as cold as a tomb. By and by Cranmer came to me, and he was no longer the suave gentleman I had known. His face was black with suspicion and his tone was a menace. Why in hell had I come uninvited, poking my nose into another's affairs? I was amazed, for an unexpected visit of one gentleman to another is not commonly construed as a threat, yet that was how Mr. Cranmer took my arrival. I felt that I had had good warrant for my forebodings. I made a story of a hasty journey into Scotland, the road missed, and a recollection that he dwelt in the vicinity, but I could see that I was not believed. I inquired for his lady, and was told that she was not there, but had gone to her house in Norfolk. Then I thought he would have put me to the door and left me to find a lodging in the dark. But he seemed to change his mind, though with no access of graciousness. I was bidden stay the night, and conducted by the same bear of a servant to a little room up many cold stone stairs. I had a solitary meal—and was left to my own devices. I found the door locked and myself a prisoner."

Sir Turnour had awakened to a lively interest. He had sat himself on a corner of the bed, and now leaned forward that he might not miss a word.

"In the morning I was given breakfast, but when I bade the man leave the door unlocked he only grinned. He was obeying Squire's orders. He added in a guttural dialect, far coarser than our Scots, that I must bide till Squire came for me. All that day I looked out of a narrow window on the bare green face of a hill. Below was a stream and a path beside it, and some ruinous sheepfolds. People passed—not many—rough countryfolk—and the house with its massive walls was utterly silent. Yet I was conscious that a fierce life was going on in it somewhere, and that something was preparing which concerned me most urgently. When my evening meal was brought—like a dog I was given but the two meals a day—I tried to force my way past the servant. But I was no match for him in strength. His great arms plucked me back and set me in a corner like a naughty child.

"By the second morning I was desperate. I professed to be ill, and demanded an interview with the Squire. Cranmer did not come, but instead a tall surly fellow who spoke the King's English and seemed to be something of a doctor. When he saw that my trouble was of the mind rather than of the body, he laughed and turned his back on me. But he knew who I was, for he called me 'my lord.' 'Keep quiet for a day or two,' he said, 'and no harm will come to you. A few nights in Hungrygrain will cool your blood, which in a young man is apt to be hottest in the spring.'

"There was no hope of escape by the door, which was solid as a rock. I turned to the window, and at first I saw no better chance there. It was flush with the wall, and had no ledge; when I craned my neck upward I found that the coping of the roof was at least twenty feet above me. The ground was perhaps thirty feet beneath—no great distance, but I had nothing with which to make a rope, for I was not a storybook hero to fashion cords out of bedclothes with no tool but my teeth and fingers. I had a thought of trying the drop, but the landing seemed hard, and a broken leg I thought would not better my position.

"So the second night came and I was still without hope. The next morning a strange thing happened. In the ground floor, or in the cellar beneath it, there must have been some storehouse for fuel, for in the forenoon three country carts arrived laden with peats and proceeded to unload underneath my window. The shovelling of the stuff into the storehouse was left for a later day, and in the meantime they merely decanted their loads in a great heap and went away. In that heap I saw my chance, for it made an irregular mound some ten feet high. I had now not more than twenty feet to drop, and something soft to fall on. The weather had changed, and violent flurries of rain swept down the glen, which would be nearly as good a concealment as the dark of night. I waited till the air was thick with drizzle, so that a man could not see a yard, and then ventured. The falling was not as soft as I had hoped, and I jarred every bone, but broke none. I got the peat dust out of my eyes, and started out to reconnoitre.

"My first impulse was to find my horse, or somebody's horse, and put many miles between myself and that accursed dwelling. . . . And then a doubt struck me. Cranmer had said that his wife was in Norfolk, but he might have lied. I could not leave the place without an effort to make certain, for if his doings there were so sinister that he thought it necessary to make me prisoner, the lady, if she was in Hungrygrain, might be in an evil case. I remembered the tears I had seen in her eyes, and the shadow of terror. I could not leave till I was certain of her absence.

"So in the screen of the rain and mist I crept along the house wall. First I came to a great ruinous tower which I took to be the old peel, and which was certainly not lived in. My passage was difficult, for I had to climb into and out of a cabbage garden which lay beneath the tower. Then I found myself on the other side of the building at what I took to be the front. Rough pasture came up to the walls, but there were signs that once there had been some kind of a pleasance. Then, as ill-luck would have it, the rain storm passed and the sun came out. I dared not go farther, so I dropped down in a tuft of evergreens to wait for the next shower.

"As I sat there, two figures crossed the grass. One was the tall man who had visited me the previous day. He wore a leather cap with the flaps tied down over his ears, and under his arm he carried a gun like a gamekeeper. The other was the man I had known at Bruges as Aymer, and whose name in London had been Vallance. He was bareheaded, dressed roughly in country style, and he had a pen stuck behind his ear. He seemed to have come out of doors for a breath of air in the blink of fine weather. I could not mistake the large mottled face and the thick, grey, tufted eyebrows.

"Then the sky clouded and the rain began more fiercely than ever. Now was my chance, so in the cover of it I approached the house again. I calculated that I must be near the entrance—or one entrance—so I moved with caution. Most of the ground floor windows were shuttered. The first unshuttered one opened on a kind of gun-room, for it was full of old saddlery and poles for otter hunting, and on the walls were guns and fishing rods. In the next I saw a glint of fire, and, as I raised my head above the sill, the profile of a human face.

"There were several people in the room, but in the thick weather they showed very dim, for the glass of the window was foul, and the fire was only a glow of peats. Then some one called for a light, and a lamp was set on the table. I saw Cranmer plain. He was seated in a big armchair with a long pipe in his hand, and a glass of wine at his elbow. There was a decanter on the table, and the others had glasses. One I think was Aymer, but I am not clear, and I did not consider the rest, for my eyes were held by a figure at the back, who sat pen in hand as if waiting for instructions. It was Mrs. Cranmer, and if ever a human countenance revealed a soul in torment it was hers. Her eyes had a blindish look as if she were trying to divert her mind from some fear by nursing a hope or a memory. But she was not succeeding. She was on the rack, and at any moment nerves and will might crack in an agony of panic.

"I lay crouched on the ground trying to think. It would be no good to enter the house, for I should only be again a prisoner. I must get away and find succour. But where? And how? Who would believe me? What friends had the lady other than myself? I could think of none, but her helplessness filled me with such fury that I was determined that if need be I would save her alone, though I should have to do murder, and though it cost me my life. My resolution was so white-hot that it made me calm. Not a minute could be wasted, for I had a sense that whatever evil was coming would come soon. I must get away from this glen to some place where Christians dwelt. I knew nothing of the countryside, but I remembered that the Yonder flowed east to the sea, and by the sea there must be towns and civilization. Being a Scotsman I had the points of the compass in my head, so I turned east and doubled across the grass to the cover of a wood.

"The rain had abated a little, and I could see perhaps fifty yards around me. So alas, could other people. Suddenly I realized that Cranmer had his sentinels posted, for before I reached the wood a whistle was blown and answered by another, and I saw a man leap out of a clump of evergreens to intercept me. My passion had made me calm, as I have said, and also vigilant. I am light on my feet and a good runner, and I have stalked the red deer with my cousins of Breadalbane, and can hold my own with any ghillie. At that game I was not afraid of a loutish Northumbrian. . . . But I had not allowed for my ignorance of the ground. I easily gave the slip to my first pursuer, and entered the wood, which was carpeted with blaeberries and young heather. I reached a stream which I crossed by a plank bridge, and was just stopping to get my breath when I almost fell into the arms of a fellow who was running up the left bank. With the enemy also behind me, I was compelled to re-cross the water. The flood was rising and I was all but swept down into an ugly cataract, but I caught a birch root on the far bank and pulled myself up to a rocky shelf, above which I saw the steep lift of the hill.

"It was there that I nearly met my end. For a man was waiting for me, a man with a great iron-shod staff. I swerved, and he struck at me—struck to kill, for if I had fallen I should have gone over the cataract. By the mercy of God his blow did not hit me squarely, but sidelong on the edge of the forehead, tearing my scalp and blinding me with blood. But the sting of it steadied me, for it was more sting than shock. I slipped from him, staggered along the shelf till I found open ground, and then breasted the hill. He was a heavy fellow, and, shaken though I was, I had the pace of him.

"By that time the darkness had come. I laboured upwards, very sick in the pit of my belly, but when I had rested for a little and got the blood out of my eyes, I had some accession of strength. Near the summit of the hill I found a shelter among rocks, where I lay till the moon rose, for I was afraid of returning blindly on my tracks. After that I had a glimpse of the lie of the valley, and moved downstream, hoping soon to come upon a path. But presently I realized that the blow had been severer than I had thought, for I had a cruel pain in my eyes and began to stumble giddily. It was borne in on me that I must find a shelter, or I would swoon upon the hillside and be taken, for I was certain that Cranmer would have his hounds out after me and beat every covert in the glen. . . . There was a light beyond the stream which must come from a dwelling, and I decided that I would risk all and make for it and throw myself upon the charity of the householder."

The young man smiled wanly.

"The rest of the tale you know. My instinct was true, for I have found friends. Friends—and one enemy, but all honest folk. I have had food and care, and now I must sleep, but I cannot close my eyes till I have made a plan. Am I safe here for the night? For be sure they will follow me."

The housekeeper answered. "For the nicht, nae doubt. But after that I daurna say. Squire Cranmer has a lang airm."

The minister shook his head. "This place is as open as an inn parlour, and there is no corner where you could be concealed. Somehow you must be off before dawn and make for Yondermouth, where you will be safe. They will not suspect your presence here for some hours. Beyond that I cannot advise you. You, sir," and he looked towards Sir Turnour, "you are a man of the world, which I am not. Can you offer no counsel to this young man in his perplexity?"

The baronet had recovered his composure, which had been momentarily disturbed by Belses' story. He did not disbelieve it, for the voice had rung true, but he distrusted the narrator's interpretation. He would have nothing to do with the whimsies of a romantic hobbledehoy.

"You have lived long in this place," he addressed the minister. "Have you any warrant for thinking the squire a villain?"

"I am loath to suggest evil," was the old man's answer, "when I have no certain knowledge."

"Tut, sir," broke in the housekeeper, who had been strongly moved by Belses' tale. "Ye needna be sae mim-mouthed. Naebody kens muckle o' Squire's works, but a'body kens that he's anither than a gude yin. The fear o' him lies like a cloud on Yonderdale. If ye stood in his road he'd thraw your neck like a hen's."

"Marget may be right," said the old man. "If he has a failing, it perhaps leans in that direction."

"Nevertheless, my lord, I think you are the victim of your own heated fancies." Sir Turnour's hard precise tones fell on the company like a blast of cold air. "You have chosen to idolize this lady, and you have imagined her a martyr to add to her charm. Since you are in love with her you must needs make a rogue of her husband."

"He canna be in love wi' her," the housekeeper protested.

"He's a dacent young lad and she's a married woman."

"I do not question your facts, but your reading of them is a fairy-tale. You have offended somehow a boor, and, since he is a tyrant in this outlandish place, he has taken the ancient way of showing his displeasure. My advice to you is to make your best speed homewards, and put this Cranmer family for ever out of your mind. When we meet again in town I shall be ready to receive your apologies on the matter between us—or some better form of satisfaction. Meantime, since I see you are recovered, I shall return to bed. . . . You," he turned to Mr. Dott, "will have the goodness to show me the path to the bridge by which you brought me here."

Sir Turnour rose to go. The boy in the bed made a last appeal.

"You are a gentleman, sir. You believe my word. Can you leave things in this posture? Will you not help me to—to save innocence from wrong?"

"No, my lord, I am too old and too wise to interfere in domestic brawls. For all I care Cranmer may be the death of his wife and swing for it—it is a result I should not deplore. I bid you goodnight, and you, Mr. Parson, and I advise you to bustle this youth out of a neighbourhood which has become unhealthy."

"Do you go too?" Belses cried after the retreating Mr. Dott.

"No me. I'm coming back when I've set this gentleman on the road. Some time the morn I've got to see Mrs. Cranmer on a small matter of business."

Sir Turnour smiled, not unkindly. " 'Pon my honour, you're a well-plucked attorney," he said.

But the baronet, as he made his way, when his convoy had left him, up the steep track beyond the stream, was by no means in that mood of sceptical composure which his last words at the manse had suggested. The irritation against Belses, which had been for some days a thorn to his spirit, was now changed to a vigorous distaste for the Hungrygrain household. He disliked the woman from all he had heard of her, one of those emotional hussies who brought poor fools like Belses to grief. And for the husband he had acquired a strong detestation. The man was bully and tyrant, a disgusting fellow who ruled at his pleasure in this filthy solitude. That was perhaps no concern of his, for he was not a *censor morum* for rustic louts. But he had lied to him, lied grossly and insolently. That was to say, he had tried to bully him, him, Turnour Wyse, for whom the rest of the world had a wholesome respect. Could the thing be permitted to pass unchallenged? He thought not. It was borne in on him that before he left Yonderdale his dignity required that he should have some further speech with the master of Hungrygrain.

Sir Turnour threaded his way among the scrub in a very ugly temper. As he came out into a clearer patch of ground a branch caught his coat and pulled it apart, and three pairs of eyes, watching him with interest from the undergrowth, saw about his waist the belted pistols.

CHAPTER IX

TELLS OF A DARK WOOD AND A DARK LADY

THE first lamps were beginning to twinkle in the Yondermouth cottages, and the riding-lights were lit in its little harbour when Nanty and his two companions took the road up the left bank of the Yonder, where in a marshy haugh it had become a tidal water noted for sea-trout. Behind them in the *Merry Mouth*, Eben Garnock was in conference with Davie Dimmock, the boat-builder, anent the damaged yard; it was his intention later in the night to slip up the coast in the cutter's boat to Hopcraw and prospect that secret haven.

Nanty wore his second-best pantaloons and his frieze gaiters, but in place of coat and waistcoat he had a knitted jersey strangely patterned in greys and browns which Eben had brought from the northern islands. Jock Kinloch was in the fisher's clothes which he had worn that morning at the Kitterston inn, and Bob Muschat, a tawny young giant with arms like a gorilla's, chose to travel barefoot—the soles of his feet, he said, being tougher than any shoe leather.

The cutter had stood well out from the land, and had escaped all but the fringe of the rain which cloaked the hills. Most of the voyage had been in blue weather, with a light wind on the starboard beam, and Nanty, sprawling on a heap of tarpaulin in the bows, had experienced the same lift of the heart that he had got the day before on the Kirkcaldy packet. He dozed a little, but in spite of the night journey he did not crave sleep. The leagues of dancing water around him were a sufficient refreshment. This was very unlike the journey he had planned, a backbreaking coach ride from which he would have stiffly descended for grave conferences with Lord Snowdoun. It was something far better, for he had been whirled into the caprices of a boy's dream. He was not neglecting duty, for he had Lord Mannour's instructions, but he wondered what his colleagues in the Senatus would say if they could see his present quarters and company. Eben was splicing a rope, looking like a patriarch from a lost world, Jock Kinloch was peeling potatoes and singing snatches of dubious songs, and Bob Muschat at the tiller was the eternal seafarer who has not changed since the first hollowed log first adventured on the water. Nanty had the feeling that he had slipped back through a crack in time to a life which he had tried a hundred years ago. It was comforting and familiar and yet desperately exciting. He had a small quiver of fear somewhere in his blood, for his three companions, even Jock, were of a tougher breed than his own. "I've read too many books," he told himself, "and spoken too many idle words. God help me, but I mustn't shame them."

They had their evening meal riding at anchor behind the small breakwater of Yondermouth, and as the dark fell Eben set the three ashore a little way up the Yonder estuary. It was now that there descended upon Nanty an afflatus of which he was half ashamed. When he stretched his legs over the first miles of furzy common he could have sung; when before moonrise the darkness closed in thicker upon them and they all stumbled over ditches and tussocks, he wanted to roar with laughter. The others plodded stolidly on, but he strode with a shepherd's heather-step, and there were moments when he longed to run, so compelling did he feel the vitality in blood and sinew.

They reached a track, a faint marking in the bent, and swung to the left. "The road frae Hopcraw," said Bob, who acted as guide. A mile or two farther and they crossed a highway. "The Alnwick road," said Bob. A little way on the first flush of the moon lit up the sky. Beyond them the lift of the hills was plain, and a dark cleft which was the opening of Yonderdale. The bracken was wet, for they were now within the orbit of the day's rain. "There's been a deluge," said Bob, "and the burns will be up. Yonder can be whiles as dry as the Well Wynd at Pittenweem, and whiles it's a fair ocean and ill to ford. Bide a wee, sir, and let's straighten out our plans."

Eben had had a rough chart of Yonderdale which Nanty and Jock had studied in the afternoon, and Bob, who had more than once prospected the ground, had it clear in his head. It was he who gave the orders.

"The mune will set or three, and by that time we maun be far up the glen. Ye mind where the village lies? We maunna gang near it, for the folk there never gang to their beds, and if a craw flew up the street the hale town wad ken o't. But we maun tak that side of the water, the south side, for the north's ower dangerous, and we maun be at Tam Nickson's afore it's light, for deil a body maun see us enter Tam's hoose."

"Nickson's is our military base," Jock explained. "We can't go ferreting about this glen without a hidy-hole. Nickson's our friend. He came here from Annandale a donkey's years ago, and his skill of sheep is so great that he has been kept on at high wages, though he's not exactly popular in the place. He's a pack-shepherd—you know what that means?—and they say he has a pack of ten-score ewes. He must have done well for himself. He's an old man, isn't he, Bob?"

"Auld as the Three Trees o' Dysart. He'll never see four-score again, but he's a soople body for his years."

"Well, Nickson keeps himself to himself, and since he is the chief support of the Hungrygrain flocks, the folk leave him alone, as he leaves them alone. There's not much happens in the glen that he doesn't know, but he lives by himself by a burnside, so his house is our natural headquarters. He's a friend of Eben's, and Bob stayed with him when he was here before, and he manages now and then to send us word when there's trouble in the wind. It's likely Nickson's doing that we're here today."

"If he hates Hungrygrain, why does he stay on there at his age?" Nanty asked.

"Ower auld to shift," Bob answered. "Besides, he doesna hate Hungrygrain. He telled me it was the bonniest bit God ever made, but sair defiled by man. He has a terrible ill-will to the Squire—some auld bicker—and he's no that fond o' Winfortune, and Hartshorn, and Meek, and the ither birkies. But he delves his yaird and reads his Bible—he's a godly man, Tam—and shapes tup horns into staff-handles, and cannily lets the world gang by—except at clippin's and speanin's, when they tell me he's fiercer than a twa-edged sword."

"Are the Hungrygrain people ill to work with?" Nanty asked.

" 'Some say the Deil's deid and buried in Kirkcaldy,' " Bob quoted oracularly. "But he's no in the Lang Toun, and he's no deid. He's live and weel and rangin' the earth, and if there's one bit he's chosen for his special habitation it's just Yonderdale. . . . We maun haste, sir, for we've nae time to dally. The highroad's no for us, for there's folk on it at a' hours, and there'll be mair the night, if, as Eben thinks, there's some special traffic wi' Hopcraw. When we're past the brig we'll tak a path I ken o' up the burnside. Afore the night's out we may hae to scatter, so we maun be clear about the rondyvoo. Tam Nickson's house afore daylight—at a' costs afore daylight. If ony o' us is late he maun just lie out in the shaw till the morn's night, for it's death and damnation to us if we're seen, beside destruction to Tam himsel'. Are ye clear, sir," this to Nanty, "how ye win to Tam's? It's a mile abune the house of Hungrygrain where a burn comes down frae the north to Yonder—the one house on a' the hillside, cockit up amang rowan trees on a shelf like the poop o' a Hamburg smack. A man's unco kenspeckle gaun up till't, but once he's there he can spy out a' Hungrygrain. . . . We maun haste if we're to sup Tam's sowens for breakfast."

Bob led them at a round pace across the drove road, which Mr. Dott had travelled earlier that day into the dene of the Yonder. The stream was in spate, but not too high to forbid a passage, which was effected at the narrows between two boulders where Nanty pleased himself by jumping more cleanly and surely than Jock, and not less well than Bob with his prehensile naked feet. After that progress was slower. Bob's alleged path was a thing of faith rather than of sight. Where the trees were pines and the ground a carpet of needles and young whortleberries the going was good, but when whins intervened or burnt heather or the matted stumps of fallen oaks, and the moon was shut out by thick undergrowth, it was necessary to walk as delicately as Agag. Moreover, Bob was taking no chances. He never turned a corner till he had reconnoitred in advance on his belly. A sound which he could not at once identify sent him flat on his face.

"It wants a lang spoon to sup kale wi' the Deil," he whispered apologetically to Nanty. "I've been here afore, and seen Hungrygrain guardit like Edinbro' Castle, and by folk that you never saw unless you went seekin' them. Besides, we're just fornent the inn. There's a brig nearby, and after that we'll tak a slype up the hill, for we maun be high up to pass Hungrygrain policies and come in by the backside o' Tam's house. . . . Wheesht! What's that?"

All three lay prone among the whortleberries. There was a gap in the trees just ahead where the moon shone, and in that gap was the figure of a man. It was a tall man in a greatcoat, and he seemed to be having difficulty in keeping his footing on the slippery path. A branch pulled his coat apart, and a brace of pistols were revealed at his waist.

All three recognized him. Bob's hand went automatically to cover Nanty's mouth, and it was not till the figure had passed out of sight that the latter was permitted to speak.

"It's Wyse," Nanty groaned. "Good God. I may be too late! He is armed. . . . Can he have met Harry? Or be on his way to meet him?"

"Not at this time of night," said Jock. "Comfort yourself, Nanty, you're still in time. But what in the devil's name takes the man wandering at midnight in a black wood? Where does that path lead to?"

"It runs frae the inn to the Hungrygrain road," said Bob. "It's no muckle o' a road, just a path ower a plank brig. . . . Wait on, sirs. It's the shortest way frae the manse to the village. The man had maybe some business wi' the minister."

"The minister? What's he like? And what could he want with him?"

"He's a dacent auld body that gangs his ain gait like Tam Nickson and meddles little wi' Hungrygrain. . . ."

Nanty's anxiety made him take the lead.

"We must follow him," he whispered fiercely. "And one of us must go to the manse and see what is there. Yon proud gentleman does not stroll out by night with pistols at his waist for nothing. You, Bob, must try the manse, for you know the road and you know the minister. Come on, Jock, for there's not a moment to lose. There's light enough to fight by. Any minute my poor Harry may come by his death."

Bob nodded, and with no more ado turned down the path towards the stream, with a final injunction of "Tam Nickson's, mind ye, afore it's light." Nanty seized Jock's arm and dragged him up the steep bank of the dene, where their nailed shoes gripped better than Sir Turnour's riding boots.

"Canny, Nanty, my man," Jock grumbled. "I wish you would practise the logic you teach. Belses is in Hungrygrain House—we know that. Wyse cannot have arrived many hours ago. Is it likely they would have arranged a meeting at midnight several miles away? Be reasonable, man. Yon baronet's a stickler for all the forms, and a tried hand at the game. What about seconds and the other decencies? I hate the fellow like poison, but he's no hedge-murderer."

"God knows what he is. Our business is to follow him, and not take our eyes off him till we know his purpose."

"I've got it," said Jock. "He's staying at the inn and is on his way back after a breath of fresh air. He's a wise man to go armed in a den of thieves like Yonderdale. . . . But maybe Belses is at the manse? No, it's not possible. What would a spark like him be doing with a country minister? Or he's at the inn? Maybe Cranmer turned him away from his door."

The mention of the manse caused Nanty to halt in his tracks with a momentary thought of following Bob. It was a fortunate impulse, for it prevented him from blundering into a party of four men who had begun to descend the track from the edge of the dene. They were moving fast, with heads down like hounds on a trail. The ground was open, with little cover, and there was only one chance of concealment. Jock darted to the left up the hill, and Nanty, obeying a different instinct, slipped downward to the shelter of a clump of elders.

Things happened fast. Jock was seen, a man shouted, and the four fanned out to cut him off. Out of the tail of his eye Nanty saw this before he reached the elders. Some ancient impulse, born of boyish games of hide-and-seek, made him attempt a diversion. He too shouted and waved his arms; he saw that he was observed, and that the pursuers had turned towards him. He saw nothing more, for he dared not turn his head. Some of the hounds were on his trail, and his sole purpose was to outdistance them. He raced up the stream side, with only his ears to tell him of the pursuit.

Spare living had kept his body lean and hard, and he had always been notably light on his feet. But never in his life had he been in danger from other human beings, and at first his heart fluttered in his throat. He had no doubt about the danger; his instinct told him that these men behind him, whoever they were, were bent on evil. He had broken on purpose into an unhallowed sanctuary, and its custodians would not forgive him. At first he choked as he ran, and his fear seemed to clog his breathing. . . . And then suddenly the suppleness of his limbs gave him confidence. The sounds behind him came no nearer. His stride lengthened, for the ground was firm and open, and he found that he leaped a tributary gully like a deer. . . . Something else heartened him. He was conscious of being in a new world, a world which he had always revered and dreaded, where his duty was not with books and papers, but with primitive hazards and crude human passions. It was a professor of logic who was thus pitchforked into the primeval, and it lay with him to prove that a scholar could also be a man.

But where was he running? The mischief was that he knew nothing of the ground, and at any moment might land in a cul-de-sac. The dene had begun to narrow ominously and might soon be a chasm. Was that why the pursuit was so sluggish? Was it shepherding him into a fatal corner? He had been running near the water's edge, and now he began to draw farther uphill. In a gap lit by the moon he thought he saw his enemies behind, stumbling and slow but resolute as weasels. The undergrowth was growing thicker, and would cripple his speed. At all costs he must find a place less encumbered, or his youth and swiftness would be of no account. Or better still, could he put the hounds at fault?

He was now on a little knuckle of rock well above the stream, and in front it appeared as if crags were beginning to crowd in upon it. There was some sort of path by the water's edge and the pursuit was still on it. They must be confident that that way there lay no escape, that they had him in front of them penned on a single narrow track. Could he increase that confidence? He picked up a stone and flung it far ahead so that it seemed to have been loosened by his feet. He heard it plash in deep water. Twenty yards on he did the same, and then dropped in the fern, looking down upon the waterside path. He was staking all upon his theory of the mind of his pursuers. Suddenly forty feet below him they came into sight, two men running steadily by the stream's edge. They must believe that in a few hundred yards they would have him cornered in some nook of cliff. . . . He let them pass, crawled upward through the bracken, and made for a patch of light which was the open hill.

There was a broken-down dyke which separated the dene from the moor, and as soon as Nanty had crossed it his spirits rose. He had no fear now, no nervousness; these heavy-footed countrymen could never come up with him; he had the whole world before him and legs that could not tire. The moon was nearing its setting, but the land was still bright, and all Yonderdale was clear below him. He halted for a second to get his bearings. Behind him was a tree-choked glen, with very far away the dimness of seaward plains. In front was the great hollow of the upper Yonder, the hills steep around it as if sliced by a knife, but from the altitude at which he stood, revealing further round-shouldered tops huddled towards the north. And almost at his feet he made out the demesne of Hungrygrain, with one light burning low in the house, perhaps from an open door.

Nanty prospected his road, for it would be very dark after moonfall. He must make a circuit round the glen head, and come back on the north side to Tam Nickson's cottage—he saw the gash in the hill where it must lie. He must reach it before dawn and that meant three or four miles in black darkness but he could not miss it so long as he followed the crest of the hill, for the burn which ran by its door was the only tributary of the Yonder from the north. He was in a mood of high exhilaration, for these uplands, sweet with spring herbs, intoxicated him like that sunlit sea over which he had sailed in the afternoon. He was in a clean world, the world of youth and spring, and his heart shouted to it. He wanted to declaim poetry:

> "Rumoresque senum severiorum
> Omnes unius aestimemus assis. . . ."

What he did was to canter like a colt over the flats of grass and heather which sloped upward before him to the west. Another tumbledown wall checked him, and he dipped into a tiny hollow through which a trickle of cold water slipped among yellow mosses. He drank from the spring and stood up to clear the drops from his eyes, and as he did so he was aware that he was not alone.

Had the pursuit circumvented him? The thing moved, whatever it was. Was it human, or a stray ewe or roebuck? It had seen him and feared him—it was trying to escape. The slope made a patch of darkness in which he could discern movement but not form, but the thing emerged from the patch, stumbled, and came to a sudden standstill, as if its strength had failed it. Then came a sound from it, a small miserable sound of weakness or fear.

Nanty took three steps across the moss and stood beside a recumbent figure. It was a woman, and in the last ebbing of moonlight he saw that she was staring at him with terrified eyes.

"What ails you?" he said, and his voice was gruff in the extremity of his surprise. "Can I help you? How came you here?"

His words wrought a miracle, for it seemed that they were not what she had expected. She rose to her feet; very slim she was, and her head was higher than his shoulder. She peered into his face and saw something there which both comforted and perplexed her, for her voice lost its tension.

"Who are you? Oh, tell me who you are that travels the Green Dod at midnight? You are a stranger? You do not belong to Yonderdale? Your voice is kind."

"I am a stranger," said Nanty. "But a midnight hill is fitter for a man than a woman. It is you that should explain your presence here."

"Alas, I cannot. It is too long and cruel a story. I am in trouble . . . in danger. By your speech, sir, you are from Scotland, and I am part Scotch. I think you are a gentleman. Let me come with you till we are beyond the hills. I will be no drag on you—"

She started, for a fox barked in a neighbouring cairn, and her movement told Nanty that she had been lately through some extreme terror.

"Where do you wish to go?" he asked.

"Out of Yonderdale," she stammered. "Out of Yonderdale, even if it means out of the world."

"I can escort you to the hills at the head of the glen," said Nanty. "I must beg you to hasten, madam, for I have myself a long road to go."

She obeyed like a docile child. She wore the rough country shoes and stockings of a dairymaid, and round her shoulders was a plaid of checked shepherd's tartan. Nanty observed that she walked like a free woman, not mincing or shuffling, but with firm steps that did not falter as the slope steepened. Once or twice he offered to assist her, but she needed no help, and presently the moon went down, and in the darkness he was aware of her only by the rustle of her movement at his left side.

His mind was in a not unpleasing confusion. In two days he had stepped out of order and routine into a world of preposterous chances. He had been hunted by those who sought to do him a mischief; he was endeavouring to wrest a malign secret from a moorland fortress; he was trying to save a friend from death; and now in the dark of the moon he was tramping the high hills with an unknown lady. That she was no countrywoman he was certain, for her slim body, her voice, her manner of speaking betokened breeding to one who had seen much of it while he lived in Lord Snowdoun's household. She was like—now of whom did she remind him? Incongruously enough it was Harry Belses. She had the same soft intonation, the same slight drawling lisp. The thought of Harry would ordinarily have set his mind off on the tack of his duty, but duty had for the moment been ousted by something more compelling.

Black as the night was, it was not difficult to find the way, for he had his countrymen's instinct for the points of the compass, and knew that he must keep due west to the head of the glen. Also he had the slope to guide him, since he was following the edge of a little tableland. But now and then he was uncertain of his course, and when he turned sharply he jostled his companion's shoulder. Once he caught her arm and its softness amazed him, for he had never before laid his hand on a woman.

Presently he was conscious that the steep slopes had bent to the right and that they were turning the uppermost cleugh of Yonder.

"Where do you want to go?" he asked her.

"Beyond the hills. There is a village in the next valley—they call it Grassmoor—I shall reach it in the morning."

"But what will you do there?"

"I will try—oh, I do not know . . . I need help, and there may be Christians there. I would have tried to reach Yondermouth, but I was too late—they were before me—I was driven up into the hills—"

"Then we should part here, for I am going north."

"Let me stay with you till it is daylight. I am blindish in the dark, and I might go astray, and return the road I came."

Nanty was conscious that she shivered as she spoke, and it could not be with cold, for the air was mild.

It was that darkest moment of the night which precedes the dawn. Suddenly Nanty had a revelation. Part Scotch! Hamilton of Mells! It could be none other. He knew his companion. It was that Delilah who had made a tool of poor Harry. That woman, half spy and half incendiary, who wove her foul plots in these wilds and found cover in a loutish husband. Jock's violent words came to his mind. He was tramping the hills with the high-priestess of all evil.

It was Nanty's turn to shiver. He did not stop to ask why so potent a conspirator should be a fugitive in the domain she ruled. He only knew that he was alone with a mystery of iniquity, and his flesh crept. There at his left hand went in the darkness something darker than Erebus. He had always been shy of women, and, having an acute sense of sin, he had been abashed by any flagrant wickedness. He shrank from this presence at his side as he would have shrunk from a loathly disease. He had the impulse to rush off on a road of his own, leaving the creature to the unclean spirits of the night. . . . Yet her voice was still in his ear, and it had been low and gentle.

On his right hand the black changed to grey, and a thin

wave of pale light ran up the sky. Very fast the grey thinned to a delicate web of blue, and the world beneath him sprang into shape. He saw the contours of the hills, though the valley bottom was still dim, and he realized that dawn would be upon him before he reached Tam Nickson's cottage.

"I must be off," he cried, and was just starting to cover the last mile at a run, when he saw that the morning had also revealed his companion. He stopped short, for what he looked at was not the Messalina of his fancies, but a pale girl with most tragic and beseeching eyes.

CHAPTER X

TELLS OF SUNSHINE AND THE HIGH BENT

THE waxing daylight cruelly revealed her weariness and dishevelment. The clothes were clearly not her own, but had been borrowed from some servant, yet they could not hide the grace of her figure. Her hair, black as a sloe, was in some disorder, but the head on the slim neck was exquisitely shaped. A delicate hand held the folds of her plaid about her breast. Her face was a broad oval, with a notable breadth between the eyes, and these eyes seemed almost colourless, like deep wells of water.

As Nanty looked at her, one thought came to him with the force of utter conviction. Jock Kinloch's tale was nonsense. This pale woman was not evil. He had pictured to himself meretricious graces, the allure of one skilled in all the arts of sex, and he saw instead an heroic, bewildered child. He forgot his urgent need of haste.

"You are tired," he said, and his voice was kind. "You must rest before you can go on. But not here, where we are in view of Yonderdale. We must get behind the ridge. Take my arm—it is only a step or two."

She obeyed, and it was plain by her dragging step that she was very weary. They climbed a few last yards of slope, and found themselves on a hummocky tableland which was the summit of the containing hills. There they were hidden from any one looking upward from the glen. Once he stooped and picked up something—two curlew's eggs from a scrape in the bent. "These will make our breakfast," he said.

They came to a hollow where the turf was green and fine around a tiny well. He pulled up some heather bushes and made her a couch. "Lie down," he told her. "Lie flat and let your body go limp. You are bone-weary, for I made you travel these hills like a deer. You must have food. I have some provender with me, and I will make a fire and roast these eggs. But first you will drink this." He mixed some brandy from a flask with water in a horn cup.

She drank, and did as she was told, stretching herself on the couch with a little sigh, while he gathered bent and roots for his fire. It kindled with difficulty, for the moisture of the previous day had not yet dried, and when he raised his head from the smoke he saw that she was sitting up.

"Will you tell me your name, please?" she said.

Her face had changed. The brandy had brought back some colour to it, and the eyes were no longer vacant, but anxious and questioning.

"My name is Anthony Lammas. I am a Scotsman, as you guessed."

She narrowed her eyes as if in some effort of recollection.

"But what are you?"

"I am a minister of the Kirk, but without a parish. My calling is to be a professor of philosophy in the most ancient of our colleges."

"A servant of God! And a philosopher! Oh, but . . . Lammas! Anthony Lammas! Where have I heard that name?" Some link coupled in her memory and brought her to her feet, her eyes suddenly ablaze with excitement.

"Were you not—a friend—of Lord Belses?"

"For some years I was his governor and tutor."

She clasped her hands, and then held them out to him with a gesture of infinite confidence.

"Oh, sir, I have been marvellously guided. It was for Harry's sake that I fled last night—to find help for him, for I could give him none—and by God's mercy I have stumbled upon his friend. He has always told me that you were his truest friend in the world. He is in deadly peril, sir."

"I know," said Nanty. "That is why I am here."

"You know! But you cannot know. No one can know except myself, and Winfortune, and—and my husband."

"I know that he has been challenged to fight by Sir Turnour Wyse, and that Sir Turnour does not commonly miss his man."

Her face was uncomprehending.

"I heard some silly tale of a duel," she said. "But that is a small thing. I have forbade Harry to fight."

"It is no small thing. Sir Turnour Wyse has come to Hungrygrain to force a meeting."

"It is not possible."

"Alas, it is only too possible. I saw him yesterday morning in Berwick. I saw him some hours ago marching through the wood above the Yonder. I came here to protect Harry, and it was while I followed Sir Turnour that I met others who would have disputed my road. I outdistanced them, but was driven far up the hillside, and there I met you. There you have my story. I think you are Mrs. Cranmer of Hungrygrain."

She dropped again on the heather. "What a wild tangle!" she cried. "Poor Harry has enemies on all sides, but Sir Turnour Wyse is not the deadliest." Nanty saw her face whiten, and dreaded a fainting fit.

"Not another word till you have eaten," he said with the firmness of his St. Andrews classroom. "When did you last break bread, I wonder? These eggs are ready, and a whaup's egg is fine fare."

He had with him bread and cheese and cold mutton, brought from the *Merry Mouth*. She drank two cupfuls of water, and ate half of one egg, while Nanty made a hearty meal. All the time her eyes were on him, appraising, questioning. She noted the firm set of his chin, his fresh colour, the fair hair growing a little scanty at the temples, the well-knit shoulders under the fisherman's jersey. It was a wholesome presence belonging to a wholesome world, and, having dwelt so long among sidelong glances, it gave her hope. Also the night had gone and its terrors, and above her a spring dawn was flaunting its banners. The sun was high enough in the eastern sky to flood over the lip of the hollow where they sat. It was no stormy sunrise of gold and crimson, but a steady upwelling of pure light, as tonic to the body and mind as a plunge into cool water. The thin, sour smell of the wet bent was changing to a thousand subtle odours. The earliest curlews were calling, and a lark's song came sweet and shrill from the heavens.

"I am trysted at Nickson the shepherd's house," he told her, "but my orders were to lie in the hills till nightfall if I could not reach it before dawn. You know the man?"

She nodded. "He's honest, I think, but I have seen little of him. He does his own work, and keeps apart from the rest of the glen. But what takes you to him?"

"My orders. I am not here alone. Since we are both on Harry's side, let us be frank with each other. The danger I fear is Sir Turnour Wyse. You come from Hungrygrain, knowing nothing of Sir Turnour, and you also are afraid. What is this other fear?"

"My husband," she said. "He is . . . but I cannot tell you. You must believe me when I say that Lord Belses has put himself in my husband's power at a moment when—when he may be tempted to use that power cruelly. He has come to Hungrygrain in secret, and he may never leave it. Do not press me further. You are my friend, and I beg you to take my word for it. Harry is in the utmost peril, and he must be delivered. That is why I ran away from the house last night—to find a deliverer, somewhere—anywhere outside this glen where all are slaves to evil. Thank God I have found you, and you say there are others at hand. We must make a plan at once—the urgency is desperate, for it will not be many hours till Hungrygrain is empty."

"Empty?"

"Empty." Her voice trickled away into languor. The single word as spoken by her had an ominous sound in Nanty's ear, but he saw that it was not the time for further questions.

"You are dropping with sleep," he said. "Lie down here where the sun will not reach you, and doze a little. You must, if we have a heavy task before us. I will go for a walk and try to get my head clear. When I come back and find you rested we will make a plan."

She obeyed, put the plaid under her head, and turned on her side like a tired child. Nanty walked north along the tableland, which was so full of hollows that there was no prospect beyond twenty yards. He could not be seen from any point in Yonderdale, and his route was not commanded by any higher ridge; only some one actually traversing the little plateau could find him. There were no sheep, for the land was all peat-haggs and coarse bent, and the ewes with the young lambs would be on the juicy lower pastures. He felt himself for a moment secure, and could think his own thoughts.

These thoughts were a fine confusion, but one conviction was crystal-clear. This woman, with whom he had been breakfasting on curlew's eggs on the hill tops, was not the beldame of Jock's tale. She had spoken of Harry as a sister might speak of a brother, or a mother of a lost child. Goodness and innocence looked out of her sad eyes. She had risked much in running away, and she had been pursued; that blew sky-high the picture of an arch-plotter with a wild folk to do her bidding. She was powerless, and her husband, the drunken boor of Jock's story, was the master. Harry was at his mercy, but why should he want to do Harry a hurt? Did he believe him to be his wife's lover? That seemed the likeliest explanation, and Nanty sighed for that was just the kind of situation he had dreaded. To defend the boy against a bravo like Sir Turnour was one thing, but to shelter him from a rightfully jealous husband was quite another, and he had a strong distaste for the job. Rightfully jealous? No, he could not credit that. Harry might have been a fool, but he had got no encouragement from the lady. He reflected ruefully that in a few hours his mind had swung to a new course, and that he had become her hot partisan.

He sat down in the shade of an outcrop of rock and tried to think. But his eyelids drooped, for the heat of the sun and the strong upland air had made him drowsy, and, except for fitful slumbers on the Edinburgh Mail, he had had no sleep for forty-eight hours. Gently he slid into unconsciousness.

Something damp and warm was on his face, and he awoke to find himself being licked by a young collie. An older and wiser dog stood a little way off, watching with some suspicion the antics of the younger, and behind it was a human figure.

Nanty scrambled to his feet in alarm, but was reassured by a voice.

"Ye'll be the Professor?" it said. He who spoke was a tall old man, a little bent, with shaven cheeks and a ragged white beard under his chin. He leaned on a great hazel crook, and had removed his broad bonnet to cool his forehead.

"Are you Nickson?" Nanty asked, now actively awake.

"Just so," the answer came in the soft slow drawl of Annandale. "I'm Tam Nickson, and ye'll be the professor they telled me o'. It's no often a learned man comes to Yonderdale. Since ye didna come to my house wi' the rest this mornin', I took a cast up the hill to look for ye. I gie the tops a look every second day, for, though the lambin' is bye, there's maybe twa-three late yowes among the haggs. But dinna fash yoursel', sir, for there's nae foot but Tam Nickson's comes this road at this time o' year. The rest o' Yonderdale has ither things to think o'."

"The other two, are they safe in your house?"

"There's three o' them. There's Bob Muschat, an auld friend whae has bode wi' me afore. There's a blackavised lad that they tell me is the son of a great judge in Embro. And there's a peely-wersh young man in braw clothes a wee thing the waur for wear. The threesome draibbled in at the back o' fower o'clock."

"The third?" Nanty cried excitedly. "Did you learn his name? Was it Lord Belses?"

"I speir nae questions, but I heard Bob ca' him my lord. He had gotten a clour on the heid, and lookit a wee thing gash. The three o' them made a gude meal o' milk and bannocks, and are now sleepin' as if they had been streikit. But dinna you stir a foot till the darkenin', for Hungrygrain the day is like a byke o' swarmin' bees. Purdey frae the inn gae'd off wi' horses at skreigh o' day, and Winfortune has a beast saddled, and is for the road. There's just Hartshorn and Meek and Sloan left at the house, forbye the Squire and his leddy."

Nanty forbore to correct him on the last point.

"Tell me of the lady," he said. "Is she like the rest?"

"When she first cam' here I thocht her a innocent bit bairn, but no doubt the pitch has defiled her."

"You know nothing of her?"

"Naething beyond a gude-day on the road. Ye maun ken, sir, I likena the broo o' Hungrygrain. There's nought for a believin' man to do in this glen but draw in his skirts if he wadna be spotted. I ken little o' what gangs on, for I hae nae pairt in it, but this I can tell you—there's much gangs on at a' hours, and there's nane o' it gude by God's law or by man's law. But I meddle not wi't, though I'm aye ready, like Rahab the harlot, to gie bield to the Israelitish spies that come up against Jericho. . . . Gude-day to ye, sir. It's a fine caller morn for the hills, but see that ye dinna leave the tops afore the darkenin'."

The old man raised his crook in a salute, and departed, with his dogs frisking among the heather.

Nanty went back to his breakfast hollow, where he found the girl asleep. But she slept light, for, though he stepped softly, the noise of his coming awoke her, and she sat up with startled eyes. She looked like one accustomed to painful awakings.

"I bring good news," he said. "I fell in with old Nickson on the hill. My two friends have got safely to his cottage, and they have brought with them—whom do you think? Harry Belses."

"He has escaped? He is safe?"

"For the moment. But how they found him I do not know,

nor did Nickson know. He said that Harry had got a blow on the head and looked pale, but that he had eaten well and was now sound asleep."

"O God be thanked! It is an answer to my prayers." She sat up and put a hand to her untidy hair. "Now I must leave you, sir. It was only Harry's danger that tore me from Hungrygrain. I must go back, for it is there my duty lies."

"But you cannot go like this. I will not permit it. I must have some assurance of your safety."

She smiled sadly.

"No man or woman can give you that. I am walking a desperate road, and I must walk it alone."

"Listen to me, Mrs. Cranmer. Something is happening, or is about to happen, at Hungrygrain, which bodes no good to you. Nickson is aware of it, and says it bodes no good to God's law or man's law. What that is you must tell me."

"It is no concern of yours, sir." He saw that she forced herself to a brusqueness foreign to her nature.

"It may be no concern of mine, except that misdoings are the concern of all good citizens. I came here for Harry's sake, and for his sake only. But it is most intimately the concern of those who came with me. You have not heard my full story. I would not tell it you if I were not convinced that you are on the side of decency, and that what is done wrong is done against your will. For I am putting my friends in your hands."

He told her what Jock had told him—that the doings in Yonderdale were known to the Government, that Hopcraw was being watched, that the net was closing. Her cheek flushed, and at first he thought it was anger.

"Three fishermen," she cried. "What can three fishermen do against Hungrygrain?"

"They have much behind them," he answered.

"Yet they are but rabbits against weasels. Oh, I cannot explain to you the bottomless futility of such ways. There is evil contemplated, horrible evil, and it is the work of desperate and subtle men. I am in the heart of it, and all that is left to me in life is the chance of thwarting it. I have little hope, but I can try. But you! And your fishermen!"

"Still we are on your side, and we can bring up potent allies. But we must know what the design is. If it is treason, there are the forces of the law to enlist. I have my duty, as you have yours."

"I cannot tell you," she said stubbornly. "I have reasoned out my duty and I see it clear. But it is my own duty, and I ask for no helpers."

"Then we must go our own ways. You are for Hungrygrain, and I am for Nickson's cottage."

"But you cannot," she cried. "You told me yourself that your orders were to wait till the darkening. Nickson, you say, was insistent too. You will be seen. All Hungrygrain is on the alert, like troops before a battle, and Nickson's dwelling is as bare as a table-top. You will ruin yourself and your friends, and you will ruin Harry."

"Nevertheless, a risk must be run. My duty to Harry is not the overmastering one, as the dear boy would be the first to grant. I must meet my friends at once, tell them what little I know, and prepare a plan."

Nanty's temper had stiffened. He felt like some bully who threatens a child, but he saw no other way. The girl dropped her head on her hands, but when she raised it her eyes were dry. Nanty was glad of that, for he was in dread of her tears.

"You would force me to unlock melancholy cupboards . . . and you would not understand."

But as she looked at him something in his appearance broke down her resolution. The long upper lip, the slightly prim mouth, the grave forehead disappeared, and she saw only youth like her own. Kindly wistful youth, eager to hold out a hand to distress. Competence, too, something audacious and masterful if the task were plain.

"Sit down," she said, in a changed voice. "Beside me, so that I need not look at you. I am going to do what I have prayed that I should never be forced to do—share my miseries with another. But I think this meeting of ours was predestined by God's purpose. You are a philosopher and may see deeper than other men. And you are a servant of the Lord and will be merciful."

She rested her chin on her hand, and kept her eyes fixed steadily on the green bank in front of her.

"I want you to see a picture," she began. "It is of a girl both of whose parents are dead, brought up by servants and an ancient aunt in a vast echoing house between the woods and the sea. That girl died long ago, but you must try to see her. She has few friends and none of her own age, and the world is a closed book to her. But she has other books, and roams wide in a good library. She is a great student, and her head is full of happy dreams. She is devout after her fashion, and had she been a Catholic might have found a vocation as a nun, for she shrinks a little from the bustle of life. . . . And then, as she grows older, vistas open for her, bookish vistas, for she is very ignorant. She is a romantic child, and has visions of wonderful enterprises in which she is to share. Her heroes are all paladins and saints and poets. She dreams of a lover, too, a fairy-tale prince who will some day ride under her windows."

She stopped. "Do you see the picture, sir? That girl died long ago, but she died slowly. She had a fortune, and her guardians were jealous that she should not be the prize of a fortune-hunter, so when she had grown up she was given but a sparing sight of men. Mostly they were heavy young squires, eldest sons, who thought only of horses and fat cattle, and who were shepherded unwillingly by their mothers to her presence. They were a little afraid of her, and she cared nothing for them, but all the time in her innermost heart she cherished her dream. And then one day it came true, and the fairy prince rode up. He was sad and dark and beautiful, and the world was against him. He was a poet, and a student, and a rebel against all dullness and cruelty. He had a cause to fight for, the cause of the poor and the downtrodden, and his beauty and his ardour melted her heart. They made a runaway match of it, and she became Justin Cranmer's wife."

"I can see your first picture," said Nanty. "Show me the next."

"The next is a blurred one, for it is the change of a girl into a woman, and of dreams into brutish reality. At first she was happy and they lived in Arcady—here in Yonderdale beneath us, among streams and flowers and country faces. Her lover had been a soldier, but he had resigned his commission out of honest scruples. He professed to be a friend of all humanity, and to be sworn to the cause of peace and loving kindness among men. He liked simple hearts, and the glittering world had no charms for him. Presently they went abroad and dwelt in beautiful places to which war had not come. He was always busy, and had many friends, some of them strange for one of his breeding, but she was too innocent of the ways of men to be surprised. . . . By and by she came to share in his business. She became his amanuensis, for she had a ready pen and was quick at foreign tongues. . . . In time she began to see the purpose of his work. It was to cripple the hands of those who made war and to force peace upon them. The end was so humane and she was so blind, that it was long before she understood that what she did was treason to England. And when she understood it she had gone too far, and her name was compromised. For he, her husband, did the work, but stood back and kept her in the foreground. There lay the strength of his position. In the eyes of the world he was a rustic squire who thought only of the hunt and the bottle, and that reputation he most jealously conserved. Who would suspect such a booby? And he had a second screen. If the name of Cranmer came into politics at all it should be his wife's name. She was his second stalking-horse.

"I was slow to see it, for love made me blind. What first opened my eyes was the knowledge that I had lost his love, if indeed I had ever had it. I detected him in flagrant infidelities. At first I bore it in silence and hoped against hope, until the truth was too harsh to ignore. . . . My suffering made my mind more acute. I saw what complexion his doings and mine must wear to honest folk. There was one night when I summoned up courage to demand an answer, and that answer I got—as plain as a blow in the face. He flung off the mask he had worn to me. He spoke frankly. His labour among the poor and oppressed in this land was not for charity and justice, but to kindle the flames of revolution. His dealings with other countries were designed to cripple his own. His purpose was not love of humanity but hatred of England. He defied me to betray him, for he pointed out that any revelation of his intrigues would be visited upon me, since I would appear as the chief conspirator. I was the spider that in the world's eye would be found to sit at the heart of his monstrous web, and who would believe that I was only a luckless fly. . . . Do you follow me, sir? I tell my story badly, for it is like opening graves to me."

Nanty bowed. He was getting Jock's tale, but from a strange new angle.

"I come to my third picture," she went on. "It is of a woman, girl no longer, who knew the blackness of despair. I do not think I feared for myself. I could have gone to the Government and told all, and suffered with a light heart the consequences of my folly. But if his love for me was dead, mine still burned for him. I could not forget the fairy prince of my dreams. My hope, I think, was that I might find a way of changing his purpose and undoing the ill, so I worked at his bidding, and waited for my chance with a sick heart. It never came. . . . And with one disillusionment came many. I learned more about his past. He had not honourably resigned his commission in the Army as I had believed—he had been broken, and for some scandal which made him an outcast to the few who knew of it. Slowly I came to understand him. He was consumed by a passion of hate. He hated the class in which he was born and the land that bore him. He hated all men except a few who were his slaves; but it was a cold, relentless passion with no honest fury in it, and it could brood and plan and bide its time. The more I saw of it the more I was smitten with a kind of palsy, as if I had looked on a snake. I had lost all power to act; I, too, was a slave, and he knew it. He was ostensibly kind to me, and had always an affectionate word and a caress, but I was as little to him as the pen with which he wrote his name. A tool, his principal tool, no more.

"But had you no friends, no one to counsel you?"

She shook her head.

"I could seek no counsel, unless I told everything, and that I dared not do, for I was a bird in a falcon's clutches. I had indeed a friend, one who had been my guardian, and whom my marriage had bitterly grieved. He was a good man, who had long ago found God and served Him dutifully, but his goodness and his high position made me shun my cousin Spencer and repel all his offers of kindness."

"Spencer? Who is he?"

"Mr. Spencer Perceval, the son of my father's brother. He who is now Prime Minister."

"Does he know anything? Does he guess?"

"He must know something, for the Government suspects me. I have evidence of it."

"So have I," said Nanty, remembering Jock's tale.

The April forenoon was bright around them, and a fresh, light wind was blowing from the north-west through the passes of Cheviot. But to Nanty, looking at the girl's tortured face, the world seemed a prison-house full of clanking chains.

"I had one other friend," she went on, and her voice quavered. "You can guess who he was. We met abroad and quickly became friends. My husband was gracious to him, for he made a third stalking-horse—the son of my Lord Snowdoun, His Majesty's Secretary of State. For a little Harry's friendship comforted me, for he saw in me only the woman I had once been. Many times I was tempted to tell him all, but I forbore for his sake, for I dreaded lest I should involve him in my miserable fortunes. Harry, as you know, is no temperate friend, and would have tried to cut the knot with violence. And soon I began to fear for him, lest my husband should treat him as he had treated me and lead him in his innocence into treason, for Harry has all the generous impulses which I once believed to be in Justin, and heeds nothing of worldly wisdom. So for his own sake I laboured to keep him at a distance. I forbade him to follow me, but he has disobeyed my bidding. Alas! I am born to be a grief and a peril to my true friends."

"At any rate Harry is safe for the present," said Nanty, but she interrupted him by springing to her feet.

"No, he is not safe. No one is safe. . . . I have delayed too long—I must go back to Hungrygrain. I have not told you all. In the last month I have learned something new . . . something terrible. Out of hate has come madness. My husband is mad, mad as any poor creature in Bedlam."

"I had guessed as much."

"I do not guess. I know. A thousand proofs have convinced me. He sleeps little now, and talks much to himself, and his face has changed. There are times when a distraught devil looks out of his eyes. . . . I think I have lost the power of fearing or I should go always in terror. He hates more than his kind and his country now—he has come to hate me. I have been his tool, and he would break me lest I should cut his hand. He used to treat me with a casual kindness. Now he is not brutal, for his voice to me is always soft, but he is planning subtle cruelties. He speaks to me with his lids half-closed, but sometimes they open and the devil looks out. I think I am about to pay the price of my weakness."

"Good God," Nanty cried. "You must never go back to him. Your life hangs by a thread."

"I do not think I mind that," she said, but there was no apathy in her voice. "My life is a small thing, and it would be cheaply spent if I could atone for all my folly. . . . But listen, sir. We may never meet again, but it would comfort me to leave with you my testament. . . . Something has brought my husband's plans to a culmination. He is no longer concerned to stir up revolution in England and to work treason abroad. It may be that too much is known and that the Government has now the power to unmask and checkmate him. But I think the reason is different. I think that his madness is come to a climax, and that he is meditating a more gigantic wickedness. . . . I do not think—I know. He is bringing his old work to an end and blocking his old channels. Hungrygrain is to be no more his *poste de commandement.* He is gathering all his powers and for all his madness his powers are great—for some desperate stroke. His purpose is murder."

"Yourself?"

"Me, but not by a direct blow. I shall be charged with it—there will be documents—ample evidence. He himself will escape, and from some refuge abroad will laugh a madman's laugh at the folly of mankind. But first some great one will die."

"The King? The Prince?"

"No, they are too well guarded, and in his eyes matter less than certain others. I think that if he had his will it would be Lord Castlereagh, whom he virulently hates, but my lord is ill to come at, for he is not in office. No, it is one whom he hates as a stalwart bulwark of England, and who may be accessible to him because of me. It is my cousin Spencer Perceval."

"But how? And when?"

"That I cannot tell. But it will be soon. Any hour my husband may leave Hungrygrain, and his errand is an errand of death. He will somehow find his chance, for he has an underground network to help him, and he is very subtle and bold. That is why I must hurry back."

"It is a good reason why you should put all England between him and you."

"No, for it is my only chance to redeem my wasted life. He trusts me as a creature wholly in his power, and soon I shall find out his plan. He has his accomplices, men like Winfortune and Meek from Yonderdale—and others, creeping things from the London kennels. But I am deeper in his secrets than they, and God may help me to defeat his purpose, though I have to receive his bullet in my own body."

It was Nanty's turn to rise. He caught her by the arm.

"Your husband is not the only mad one," he cried. "You are going to certain death. You are only one against a thousand. Let the Government know what you know, and crush this infamy in the bud. I will myself ride day and night to take the news."

"It is too late." She smiled gently at his vehemence. "The powder train is laid, and I only can hinder the spark that will fire it. Justin Cranmer is a match for any Government, for if one plot were exposed he would go to earth like a fox, and next day or the day after hatch another. You cannot conceive with what triple steel he is guarded. No, I am resolved to bring this evil at any cost to an end, and I believe that God will help me. I am strong now, since I know that Harry is safe. For a little I wavered when I learned that he was a prisoner in Hungrygrain, for I feared that Justin in his madness would not scruple to do away with an unwanted witness of his doings. But God has heard my prayer for Harry, and I am free again."

"It is monstrous." Nanty strode up and down the hollow in his agitation. "It cannot be permitted. You are undertaking more than flesh and blood can bear."

"I must dree my weird, as you say in Scotland," she replied. "I will not go back the way we came in the night, so that this corner shall be unsuspected. You will wait till the twilight before you move. You promise me."

"When do you leave Hungrygrain, and where are you going?" he cried in an agony of indecision, for it was suddenly borne in on him that he was being cast for a part in a drama more fateful than the affair of Harry Belses.

"We leave at any hour, but not, I think, before tomorrow morning. Where we go I do not know and can only guess. I think that first we shall visit my house of Overy, for there are papers there, some to be destroyed, some perhaps to be kept as evidence against me. After that I am in the dark. I think that the danger lies in London. . . . But stay, you shall have my full testament. I have gleaned one little fragment of knowledge. There is an inn called the Merry Mouth, which plays the chief part in Justin's plans. I do not know where it is, but my belief is that it is not a hundred miles from Norfolk. It is a place of assignation, and I think it may be for my cousin—that my husband has summoned him in my name. I tell you that, for you may some day have the chance of bearing witness that my heart was honest."

She gave him her hand, which he grasped in silence, for he could not speak. Her eyes were still tragic, but her voice was composed, and the weariness had gone out of her air. He crept to the edge of the hill, and saw her figure reappear on the far side of the cleugh and descend into the glen of the Yonder. For a long time she was visible among the links of the burn, till Yonder dropped into its green ravine, and she was lost in a sudden dip of the valley. . . . As he lay with the noonday sun warming his body he prayed fervently, and, having thereby lulled his emotions, he set himself to think. He had given his word or there and then he would have risked it and made his best speed to Nickson's house, for he saw ahead of him an urgent duty, which with bitter unwillingness he must undertake, or never again know self-respect.

In the early dusk he crawled out of the boulders of a little ravine, circumvented the sheep-fold and the dipping-troughs, and reached the back of the cottage. Two nights before, he reflected, he had at that hour been dining with Lord Mannour a hundred miles away, amid silver and candlelight and fine linen, and now he was pitchforked into a world where even lords of session were powerless. He gave the agreed knock on the lower part of the door, and, when it was unbarred and he entered the kitchen, the first figure he saw was Eben Garnock.

CHAPTER XI

TELLS OF ARRIVALS AND DEPARTURES

BUT it was not the unexpected sight of the Chief Fisher that held Nanty's eyes. In Nickson's elbow-chair, an ancient thing of oak padded with sheepskin, sat a pale young man with a bandaged forehead. In a second he was on his knees beside him.

"Harry, my dear Harry," he cried. "God be praised that I have found you. You are ill? You are wounded?"

The young man patted the hand that had been laid on his knee.

"If I were ill," he said, "the sight of you, old friend, would cure me. But I am well enough though somewhat stiff in the joints. My wound is a mere scratch. I have been dozing all day here, and feel ready for any exertion. . . . But tell me, Nanty, what Heaven-sent chance brought you here?"

"I came in search of you—to save you. I was told of your danger. I saw Sir Turnour Wyse last night. Have you met him?"

"My brave Nanty, did you propose to act as my second? Or, like my family, to spirit me away? Be comforted, for Sir Turnour and I have spoken together, and our feud is for the time pretermitted. Indeed, I think Sir Turnour may be in the same boat as the rest of us. Ask Nickson."

The little kitchen had an earthen floor, except for the stone flags round the hearth. There were the remains of food on the table—a braxy ham and a plate of oaten farles, an earthenware jug of ale, and a tun-bellied whisky bottle of the kind called a "mason's mell." The peat fire burned briskly, and everything in the place was clean and bright as a new pin. Jock Kinloch had curled himself on a sheepskin by the hearth like a great cat, and Bob Muschat balanced himself on a corner of the table. Nickson, the host, sat on the edge of the press-bed, and Eben Garnock, square as a Dutch lugger, stood in the centre of the floor, ruminating like a cow at pasture.

Nickson spoke. "If ye mean the gentleman that's bidin' at the inn, he got up this mornin' late and cried on Purdey. But Purdey was awa' south afore day wi' horses, and there was naebody about the place but servant lassies. So the gentleman sets off on his feet for Hungrygrain, tellin' his body servant that he wad be back or lang. But he's no back yet, and his man is rangin' Yonderdale looking for him. He was seen to enter the house, but no to leave it."

"He's likely to be in my own case," said Belses. "If you drop in at Hungrygrain you stay there. God! what a place! A man would be safer among the Moors in Africa."

"Tell me your story," Nanty demanded. "There's a puzzle here which I must piece together."

Belses repeated briefly what he had told to Sir Turnour the night before.

"Did Cranmer mean to do you a mischief?" Nanty asked.

"He meant to keep me shut up till after something happened—I do not know what. When I escaped, he and his folk meant black mischief. Muschat will tell you what befell after Wyse left me.

Bob, from the edge of the table, took up the tale.

"Ye mind when we parted company, sir, and I was to look in at the manse and get the news, and you were for followin' Sir Turnour. Well, I wasna long ower the brig when I met in wi' a wee body—Dott was his name, and he said he was the town-clerk o' Waucht. It seemed he was bidin' at the manse, and he had been settin' Sir Turnour on his road back. I saw that he was the man that we saw drivin' off frae the King's Arms yesterday mornin' and I minded ye had said ye kenned him, so I spoke your name and he was ready to talk. The body was a' cockered up wi' excitement. He telled me about Lord Belses and Sir Turnour and the wild ongaein's at Hungrygrain afore we got to the manse door. Now ye maun ken that the manse is on the bank o' Yonder, and when we won to it we were just about fornent whaur you and Mr. Kinloch were on the ither side. I heard the scrapin' o' your feet, and then I heard something mair—the sound of folk comin' the ither way that were no friends o' yours—I heard them cry out, and the noise o' rendin' busses and rowin' stanes. I jaloused what had happened, and I thocht to mysel' that if you and Mr. Kinloch could jink them—which I considered maist likely—they would come on to the manse, since they maun be seekin' Lord Belses. So when the auld wife opened the door, I cried on her that there was nae time to loss, and that we must get my lord out o' bed and awa' to Tam Nickson's afore the Hungrygrain folk got there. She's a wise auld wife, and it wasna lang or she had my lord into his breeks and we were ready for the road. The man Dott wadna come, though I pled sair wi' him. He said he had some law business wi' the mistress of Hungrygrain and wadna stir a foot till he had settled it. I hope he didna tak ony harm when the ithers got to the manse. He was fou' o' argyment, and Hungrygrain is no fond o' argyin'."

"He's maybe sorry now that he didna heed ye," said Nickson. "He took no harm last night. But this mornin' naething wad serve him but he must gang up to Hungrygrain to see the leddy. Gibbie Winfortune wasna there to shoo him awa', so he got inside the house, and gude kens how he's farin' there. He maun be a dour wee body."

"Stieve as a stane," said Bob, "but a stane can be broke wi' a smith's hammer."

"One thing more," said Nanty. "What brings Eben here? That was not in our plans."

The Chief Fisher had lit his deep-bowled pipe, and stood staring into the glow of the peats, a model of philosophic detachment.

"That's easy telled," he said. "I found things changed at Hopcraw. It's a kittle place to enter if there's ony wind, and there are marks to tell the channel to them that ken whaur to look for them. The marks are gone. The place is nae mair used and the shop is shut. I argued the thing out wi' mysel', and my judgment was that that side o' Hungrygrain's trade was done wi' and that the place for me was Hungrygrain itsel'. So I took the road up the burn, and I got here no mony minutes afore you, Professor. Na, na, I wasna seen. For a' my bulk there's few can see Eben Garnock by day or night if he doesna choose."

"We've been maist michty lucky," said Bob, "for we have a' forgathered here at the richt time. I can tell you I was blithe to see Mr. Jock when he stauchered in just afore daybreak. He had had a sore warstle ower half the Cheviots. And I was blither to hear frae Tam that you were safe on the high tops, Mr. Lammas. And we've gotten my lord here snatched frae the jaws o' his pursuers."

"You are wrong," said Nanty. "The men you saw last night were not seeking Lord Belses. Now you will hear my story. They were seeking Mrs. Cranmer, who had fled from the house."

Belses got out of his chair. "Great God! What new horror drove her to that? Where is she? Quick, Nanty," and he plucked the other by the shoulder.

"Sit down, Harry. It's a long tale. She ran away because she discovered that you were a prisoner and feared for your life. She hoped to get help from somewhere outside the glen."

"How do you know?"

"Because I found her—found her far up on the hill when I had outdistanced the pursuit. In the dark she accompanied me to the head of Yonderdale, for she wished to cross the watershed. We breakfasted together on the hilltop. Then, while she slept, I walked farther and met Nickson and heard that you were in his cottage. I returned and told her, and she became a new woman. . . . Jock, you are a ram-headed fool. The story you told me yesterday morning was wildly wrong.

If a saint of God walks the earth this day it is that lady."

"God bless you for these words," Belses cried. "She has found another champion. But where is she? Man, man, don't you see that I am in torment?"

"She has gone back to Hungrygrain. Back to her duty. She is as brave as Joan of Arc. Listen. Except for what you said of her character, Jock, all your tale was true, but it was not half the truth. For many a day there has been a factory of black treason in Hungrygrain and elsewhere. You thought that the cover was a drunken boor of a Northumberland squire, but you were wrong—the cover was the poor lady. Cranmer is the devil of the piece. She has been drawn innocently into treason, and it is her name, not his, that appears in the Government's books. You know him, Harry. You must have read his character."

"I think that he is altogether evil," said Belses.

"He is more—he is mad. That is his wife's verdict which I have heard from her own lips. The man lives and moves and has his being by naked hate. He hates the army from which he was rejected in disgrace. He hates the country which owns that army. This hate has driven him distraught, so he has come to loathe all humanity save the few whom he tolerates as his tools. Above all, he hates his wife, who is his victim. But this madman is no blind blundering thing, for his brain is cool and subtle and he has full power over all his faculties. He is the most dangerous man now alive on earth, and every hour makes him more dangerous. He has finished one campaign—he is leaving Hungrygrain, and Eben has told us that Hopcraw is done with. But it is only to begin another and a more desperate. Formerly it was treason—now it is murder. And he has laid his plot so cunningly that he himself will escape and from somewhere abroad will laugh at us fools in England. His wife will be left to bear the shame, and there will be so damning a weight of evidence against her that she cannot escape the gallows."

Belses had gone as white as the scoured flagstones by the hearth. "How do you know?" he croaked.

"She told me herself—unwillingly at first, and then frankly as to one whom she would never see again. It was a kind of testament before death. She has gone back to her husband in the hope that somehow she will be permitted to frustrate his purpose at the last moment. She has no care for herself, for she is beyond fear, as she is beyond hope. This day on the hills I have seen such courage as I did not know God had given to His creatures."

Nanty's solemn voice left a hush in the kitchen. The Chief Fisher broke it by shaking out the dottle of his pipe. In his broad comfortable speech he asked, "Wha's to be murdered?"

"The King's chief servant—Mrs. Cranmer's cousin and guardian—the Prime Minister."

"Keep us a'! That canna be allowed ony gait."

The matter-of-fact words seemed to dissipate the awe in Nanty's face and harden it into purpose. Suddenly he found himself taking command and giving orders.

"There is no time to waste," he said. "She has gone back to her husband because she believes that at any moment he may take the road. Hopcraw is done with, Hungrygrain is done with. The innkeeper, you tell me, has gone off early this morning with horses, and, Nickson says, so has the man Winfortune. Everything is in trim for the journey, and Cranmer any moment may follow with his unhappy wife. They will move fast, for relays of horses have been sent ahead. At all costs we must prevent them." He turned to Nickson. "Who are left in Hungrygrain? I mean, the desperate ones."

"They're a' desperate yins," was the answer. "There's vermin down in the village and along the waterside that are ripe for ony ill. But o' Cranmer's rank-riders, now that Purdey and Winfortune are gone, there's just the three left. There's Jerry Hartshorn, that's his first whip, as they ca' it, in the hunt. There's Sloan that was chief o' the Hopcraw pack. And there's Meek—him that they ca' Luck-in-the-Bag—the thrawnest deevil in a' Cheviot."

"Three desperadoes—four, counting Cranmer himself. There's five of us here if Harry has got back his strength."

"I have the strength of three men," said Belses. "If Cranmer is mad, I shall presently be raving."

"Have we any arms?"

Eben shook his head. "The Free Fishers dae their fechtin' wi' their nieves, or maybe a muckle stick. We've our whittles, but we're aye sweir to use them."

"We might borrow Tam's gun," said Bob, pointing to an ancient weapon above the chimney.

"It's bustit," said its owner. "Bustit thae ten years."

Jock rose from his sheepskin.

"What is this talk about weapons? We have our hands and our feet and our teeth, and that's enough. Nanty Lammas, you have harrowed my soul. I have been maligning a dove and shielding a kite, and now, by God! I'm going to have a hand in wringing the kite's neck. *En avant*, lads. We'll put a stopper on this ploy if we have to hough the horses and geld the men. The credit of the Free Fishers is at stake."

"Who knows the house and its environs?" Nanty asked, and his tone was that of a regimental commander.

"I've snowkit round it," said Bob, "and ken the lie o' the land."

"And I," said Belses, "have some sort of notion of it."

"You must keep in the background, Harry, for you are the only one of us that they have seen before. . . . Here is the plan we will follow. We will keep together till we are under the house wall—there are shrubberies of evergreens there which, according to Harry, make good cover. Then I detail Eben and Bob to go to the stables—Bob knows the road—and do what they can to spoil Cranmer's hopes of travel. It may have to be a brutal business, but that cannot be helped. Harry will remain in cover, as our reserves, and also to form a link between the stable party and the rest of us. Jock and I will get into the house by force or by guile and deal with Cranmer."

"How will you deal with him?" Belses asked.

Jock lifted a brawny fist and regarded it lovingly. "Knock him out—truss him up—whatever the Almighty permits us."

"Supposing he is not alone?"

"Oh, then, if his trusties are with him, there'll be a bonny rumpus."

Eben took from his pocket a silver boat-call which he presented to Nanty.

"Blaw that if ye want Bob and me, but no till we're needit, for there's like to be a heap o' wark in the stable."

Nanty pocketed the whistle. "The one thing to make sure of," he said, "is that we get to the house. Some of the vermin Nickson speaks of may be on the watch, and we cannot afford to be delayed. Thank God, there's no moon for hours. If we are forced to separate, the rendezvous is this cottage. . . . Now give me a bite of meat, for I haven't eaten since breakfast. In five minutes we take the road."

Jock regarded him with quizzical admiration.

"Man, Nanty, this is like old times. The professor's at the desk and we bejants sit doucely at his feet."

There was a cart-track which crossed Yonder water within a hundred yards of the house, the very road by which the peats had been brought that had been Harry Belses' means of escape. The five men had wormed their way to the bank of the stream without mishap. They had traversed the lower hill pastures, creeping by the dyke edges so as not to stir the sheep, and had crawled through a mile of thickets black as a tunnel, where there was no sound except that of sleepy birds. But when they drew together at the ford something struck on their ears above the rumble of Yonder. It was the sound of a horse's hooves.

A rider was crossing the water. There was an open glade there and sufficient light to see his figure. As he emerged on their side Eben—who considered anything to do with horses as his business—rose silently like a gnome from the bracken, and with his great arm plucked him from the saddle. Bob took the bridle and quieted the frightened beast, but its plunging made little noise, for the grass was deep.

"It's Meek," he whispered. "It's Luck-in-the-Bag. Canny, Eben, for he'll bite like a weasel."

The man in Eben's arms was small and skinny, bare-headed, and in his shirt-sleeves. Eben's great hand was over his mouth.

"One cheep, my mannie," he said, "and your neck's thrawn."

The captive did not struggle, but remained passive, till Eben laid him on the ground. He looked up to see five faces bent on him, for Bob had by this time soothed the horse, and it was grazing peaceably.

It was Nanty who spoke.

"You're the man Meek? Where are you taking that beast?"

"Ye would like to know, would ye? Well, it's bound for hell to mount the devil's grandma."

"Tie him up," said Nanty, and Eben, whose pockets always contained tarry twine, made a workmanlike job of it. The prisoner showed no alarm, and suffered himself to be bound without a struggle, whistling softly through his broken teeth.

"Gag him," said Nanty, and Eben was about to obey, using a bit of a cork float from the same capacious pocket. But suddenly from far off came a sound like a magnified curlew's call, or a huntsman's view-halloa borne from a great distance. The man on the ground cocked his ears and grinned.

"Ye may gag me if ye please," he said, "but ye won't make nothing by it. Tod Meek's goin' to do ye no harm, seein' he's left all lonesome in this valley. That call ye heard was Jerry's signal that him and me agreed on. It means that Squire and party are over Red Syke Edge. I'm afeard ye're come late for the fair, gentles, whosomever ye be."

"Gag him, Eben," said Nanty, "and roll him under the bushes. We can attend to him later. And tie up the horse to yon tree. The ruffian is right, and I fear the birds are flown. On to the house, and no more manoeuvring. You, Eben and Bob, have a look at the stables first—I doubt you'll find them empty."

He led the way through the shallow ford, raced up the bank, and came out on the shelf of ground which had been made into a shaggy lawn. Before them the house rose massive and dark, without one pinprick of light.

"Bide here, Harry," Nanty ordered when they were under the wall. "When you hear my whistle fetch Eben and Bob, if they haven't joined you. It would take a day to force the door, but we can break in a window. There—that's the one for us." The shutters were up on most, but this one was left unshuttered, though the sash had been bolted.

"That is the room where I last saw Mrs. Cranmer," said Belses.

Jock put his shoulder to the framework, and the whole thing crumbled inward with a crash of glass. "Rotten as touchwood," he said. "This place would never stand a siege. Wait on till I light Nickson's lantern."

Nanty and he squirmed through the aperture. There was still a spark among the ashes of the fire and the room smelt of recent use. The table, which, when Belses saw it, had been laden with papers, was bare, and the chairs stood about in disorder as if a conclave had just risen from them. Nanty cast an eye round.

"This was their last lair," he whispered. "Now for exploration. Caution is the word, for there may be an ambush at any corner."

They stole into a narrow passage, casting the lantern beam before them, and then into the shabby hall. No one of the doors on the ground floor was locked, and room after room was revealed empty. Some had clearly not been lived in for many days. In the huge kitchen, part of the old tower, there were hot ashes on the hearth, and, on a table, dishes with the remains of food. They crept up the staircase and found themselves in a maze of corridors, whose different levels marked successive stages in the house's architecture. Often they stopped to listen, but the night was calm, there was no sound to break the stillness, not a creak of woodwork or a drip of mortar, only the echo of their own steps. The place had suddenly lost its mystery. Man had used it and had finished with it, and it had been flung aside like an old glove, to crumble unregarded in the winter frosts and the summer suns. The race of Cranmer had done with Hungrygrain.

"Hist!" said Jock. "I hear a step."

They listened, and then moved softly in the direction of the sound. It came from the end of a corridor. As they halted it was repeated—footsteps hasty and careless, and then what seemed like dimly heard human speech.

"There are folk beyond that door," Jock whispered. "More than one. I have ears like a gled, and I can hear two different voices."

They waited, listening intently, and they heard the steps again. Then a crash as if a heavy foot had been driven against wood.

"We'll get the others," said Nanty. "Back with you, quick."

They raced down the stair to the room by which they had entered, and blew the whistle. In a second Belses was at the window, and behind him Eben and Bob. When the three were inside Eben reported. "The stables are empty. Not a bit or a bridle or a beast to need them."

"This house is not empty," said Nanty. "In a room upstairs there are men—two at least. Follow me, and be ready for anything."

In the room at the end of the corridor the steps had ceased. But there were voices, which came faintly through the thick door. Nanty tried the handle, but it would not turn. The key might be in the inside. "Open," he cried.

The voices ceased.

"Open," he cried again.

"How the devil can I open?" came from within, and the oak did not muffle the fury of the words. "You have locked the damned thing and got the key."

"I've heard that voice before," said Nanty. "It's none of the Hungrygrain folk. Put your shoulder to it, lads."

Eben did the work himself. His broad back took the door like a battering-ram, and lifted it clean off its rotting hinges.

It fell inward and the lantern revealed a big wainscoted room wholly bare of furniture. There were cobwebs in the cornices and in the cracks of the shuttered windows, and the floor was as deep in dust as an August highway. In its centre stood a large man with a very red face. He seemed to expect an attack, for his fists were in a posture of defence. But, as he glared at the newcomers, bewilderment took the place of wrath in his eyes.

"Now who in God's name are you?" he stammered. "I have seen you before." He looked at Nanty, but especially at Jock.

Jock bowed. "I was presented to you yesterday morning, Sir Turnour, in the Red Lion at Berwick by Miss Christian Evandale."

"The devil you were!" Jock's words seemed to restore to the baronet some of his composure, as if they reminded him of a saner world than that in which he now found himself. "And you," he turned to Nanty. "You also were there. . . . And, God bless my soul, there is my lord." The sight of Belses was the final straw. He put his hand to his brow and ruffled his crisp hair. "Gentlemen," he cried, "have the goodness to enlighten me. What are you doing here?"

Belses spoke.

"We came here to hinder the going of the people of this house, and to prevent a great evil. Me you know already, Sir Turnour—too well for your pleasure, I fear. This is my former governor, Mr. Anthony Lammas, now professor in the college of St. Andrews. This is Mr. John Kinloch, son to my Lord Mannour, of whom you have heard. The others are of the famous brotherhood of the Free Fishers. We are here on an errand which has the sanction of the Government, but we are here too late. The corbies have flown and left in their place a most reputable gentleman. Now how did that gentleman get into this dubious nest?"

The grave and slightly mocking courtesy of Belses' tone was a spark to the tinder of Sir Turnour's grievances. His precise speech broke into a splutter of fury.

"Nest!" he cried. "A nest of carrion! . . . I came here this morning to settle a private matter. The man Cranmer had lied to me; lied to me insolently, and I could not pass it by. I asked for an interview, and was admitted to a den of a room where the door was locked behind me. I was not armed, or I would have shot away the lock. Then came Cranmer with three ugly sprouts of rascaldom at his back. He demanded the purpose of my visit and when I told him he laughed in my face. Before I knew it the three ruffians had me pinioned, though I loosened the teeth in the head of one of them. Then, when I was at his mercy, this Cranmer poured out his venom. He said that he took little count of Brummels like me who should never leave St. James's Street. He invited me to return to my dressing-glasses and powder-puffs and the bullying of children, and not to meddle with the affairs of men. He said much more, but I shut my ears to it. They carried me to this place, cut my bonds, flung me in, and locked the door. I could hear Cranmer's giggling laugh in the corridor. . . . That is my simple tale, my lord, and by God! for every letter of it I will make that man sweat blood."

Belses bowed. "We are now allied in a common enmity," he said. "The help which I begged last night from you for charity will now be given for hate. The purpose. . . . What on earth is that?"

From beyond the other door in the room came a wailful voice. . . .

"Let me out, sirs," it moaned. "If it's you, Professor, let me out for the love of God. I'm half smothered with the stour."

"That," said Sir Turnour, "is my fellow-prisoner. I think it is the little man who was with us at the parson's house."

Where the baronet's boot had failed, Eben's shoulder succeeded. The door of what had once been a powdering-closet fell in, and from it staggered a melancholy figure. Its face was grimed with soot, and its clothing was in sad disorder. What had once been a spruce dark coat was now riven down the back, and its pantaloons were grey with dust.

"Losh, it's the wee town-clerk," said Bob. "I warned ye, Mr. Dott, that ye were set on a daft-like plan."

"You did that," said the scarecrow, "and you were right, but I had my duty to perform, and this is where it has landed me. I came here this morning seeking Mrs. Cranmer on a small matter of business. I inquired for her at the door and they let me in, but that was all the civility they showed me. A blackavised man with the glower of the devil appeared—he wouldn't listen to me—he just swore like a heathen—and the next I knew I was shut up in this press and the key turned. I was left my lone for hours, and then the door opened and a woman looked in. No, it wasn't Mrs. Cranmer—I couldn't see her right, but I think it was a servant lass. She flung a bit paper at me and ran for it, but first she locked the door. After that I heard an awful stramash, which must have been the arrival of this gentleman. I heard him swearing—such profanity I never dreamed of in all my days—so I knew that he must be in the same creel as myself. We entered into conversation, and he did his best to kick the door open, but the donnered thing would not yield. . . . I'm as empty as a whistle, friends, for I haven't broken bread since the morning. Is there no meat about the place?"

"Have you the paper?" Nanty asked.

He was given a torn and dirty slip which he held to the lantern. On it was written the words "Merry Mouth" in a fine pointed hand.

"It's the name o' our boat," said Eben.

"It's the name of something else," said Nanty. "This house is an empty shell, and it's no place for us longer. We must back to Nickson's, for there's much to be settled ere morning."

CHAPTER XII

TELLS HOW A CHASE BEGAN

"HARRY," said Nanty. "Will you do me a kindness? Lend me your coat and waistcoat and a spare cravat, for I assume you have baggage with you, and take in exchange this woollen shift that Eben provided me with."

"You may have my last shirt. But why?"

"Because I propose to set off instantly in pursuit, and my present garb is not very decent for a journey on the high-roads."

At his words the assembly in Nickson's kitchen woke to a sharp attention. For a moment no on spoke; then Mr. Dott, who had been engaged earnestly with a plate of brose, dropped his spoon and said:

"With your permission, Professor, I'll accompany you. I have still my bit of business to see to."

"Well done the town-clerk!" said Bob. "Man, ye're the game one."

"Why do you take this upon yourself, sir?" Sir Turnour asked Nanty haughtily. "Your concern in this affair is the smallest."

"Not so. It is the chief, for I alone have heard from Mrs. Cranmer's lips the true meaning of the journey. These others know it. Have patience with me, sir, and I will tell it you."

Nanty repeated the tale of his morning on the hilltops and his talk with the fugitive lady. He told it with a deeper emotion than he had shown at the first telling to the others, for the sight of that husk of a house had convinced him of the dark purpose of those who had left it, and he found himself keyed up to a great resolution. His mind hovered between fright and exaltation, and his quivering nerves put fire and colour into his words.

Mr. Dott was profoundly impressed. He had a dog-like fidelity to his client, and was also prepared to think any ill of those who had hindered a decent Scots writer in his lawful avocations. Not so Sir Turnour.

"You believe this rigmarole?" he asked coldly. "Cranmer I grant you. He is capable of any villainy, and you may be right that he is mad. His treatment of myself is warrant for it. But I cannot swallow this romantic lady. In my judgment she is a stool-pigeon for her blackguard of a husband. I have seen her, and I mistrusted her foreign looks and her tragedy eyes. I have heard too much of her to credit her innocence. In my judgment she is the most expert coney-catcher alive, and today in these hills she has added another to her bag."

"You forget, sir," said Belses fiercely, "that we agreed that for the present we should be neutral in this matter."

Sir Turnour bowed. "I stand corrected. I will say no more of the lady except that I am not her champion. My business is with her precious husband. Him I follow instantly, and, please God, shall soon call him to account."

The baronet's high colour had deepened, and his eyes had the fixed stare of one whose mind is unalterably determined on a purpose about which it is not wholly clear.

"Where do you propose to seek him?" Nanty asked.

"At his wife's house of Overy in the first instance. I understood from you that they will go there—must go there. If I miss him, be assured I will pick up the scent."

"I beg you, Sir Turnour, to listen to me," said Nanty. "This is a desperate affair, and those engaged in it are cunning men who have been weaving their plots for years. You have a just quarrel with Cranmer, and the Government has one not less just. Put aside for a moment the innocence or guilt of the lady. We are face to face with a matter of deep national concern, and would bring the conspirators under the weighty arm of the law. If you make your private vengeance your only thought and openly follow him he will escape you. Our only hope is to match secrecy with secrecy. That is why I claim that the chief task falls to me. You are known to Cranmer. Lord Belses is known to him. In vain will you spread the snare in the sight of the bird. But of me he knows nothing—he never saw me—he is ignorant of my name. I can follow him unobserved. But I am known to Mrs. Cranmer, and I may be able to give her that help which will permit her to circumvent him. We have an ally in the enemy's camp, but that ally cannot be used except by one who is unknown to the enemy."

"What do you propose, sir? I know nothing of you. I saw you for the first time an hour ago. Who are you?"

"You have heard that I am a professor of logic in Scotland. But I am also a young man, and I am privileged to be a member of that brotherhood of the Free Fishers to which these three others belong. I am as determined as you, sir, and my power lies in my obscurity."

"But what is your plan? Where would you follow them? To Norfolk?"

Nanty shook his head.

"Not to Norfolk. They will go there, but the danger-point is not there. It is at some place called the Merry Mouth."

"Merry Mouth! Merry Mouth!" Sir Turnour repeated. "An inn? I never heard of it, and I know most of the roads of England. There may be a score of Merry Mouths."

"I will find this one, and, having found it, I will trust the Almighty for the rest."

"Gad, you're a well-plucked one, Nanty!" said Jock Kinloch. "Are you for engaging the whole of that black crew single-handed?"

"Not single-handed. I will have Mrs. Cranmer with me."

"Stuff and nonsense!" Sir Turnour cried. "You come back to that woman's honesty, in which I most utterly disbelieve. I will go to Norfolk and pluck Cranmer out of his gang, and drub him as a man was never drubbed before. If he has flown I will come up with him. Norfolk is my own county, and my house of Wood Rising is within twenty miles of Overy. I am known to every man-jack in the shire, and can set a hundred scouts to work. I tell you I do not credit a word of the woman's story. I swear on my soul that whatever mischief is afoot she is deep in it—"

Mr. Dott interrupted. He had finished his meal, and rose to his feet, his solemn puckered face contrasting strangely with his ruinous clothes. The prominent eyes were ablaze.

"Swear if you like, sir," he cried, "by your broad acres and your braw house and your chariot and your blood horses, but do not swear by what you value so little as your soul."

The unexpected passion of the words, the unexpected defiance as if a chicken had turned to outface a hawk, made a sudden silence. Sir Turnour flushed deeper, and seemed to be drawing himself up for a violent rejoinder, when Eben's slow voice broke in. He had been puffing his pipe, and staring into the fire.

"Wait on, sirs," he said. "There's maybe gude sense in what the gentleman says. If them we seek gang first to Norfolk, what hinders us to try the same road? The wind is set in the nor'-west, and by my judgment it'll bide there for the next twa-three days."

"What the devil has the wind to do with it?" the baronet demanded.

"Mair than ye might think. Them we seek will travel by land, and, post as they please, they'll do brawly if they cover a hundred miles in the day. Let them take the speediest coach and they'll be little better off, for the road they seek is no the straight highroad. I've heard forbye o' coaches that break down and beasts that founder. As I judge, it's every yaird o' twa hundred miles—liker twa hundred and fifty—frae here to the Norfolk sands. If there's a quicker road it's common sense for us to take it, and birse in afore them."

"What quicker road can there be?" Sir Turnour cried scornfully. "I trust Cranmer to know all the short cuts."

"There's the sea," said Eben simply.

The baronet stared. "By God, I never thought of that. You're right. It's the long elbow you must make to get round the Wash that stretches out the distance. There's a straight course from the coast here to Overy Bar. But what are we talking about? Where is the ship? Have you a frigate lying offshore at your command?"

"We've a boat at Yondermouth that will dae as weel as ony king's ship. Better, for there's better folk to handle it."

"Man, Eben, that's an inspiration," Nanty cried. "Will the wind hold?"

"Under Providence I think it will." The Chief Fisher, who had seemed hitherto to be a silent spectator of the whole business, spoke now with the assurance of one used to plan and command.

"Do you know the Norfolk shore?"

Eben smiled slowly.

"No just as weel, maybe, as I ken the Fife coast and the Buchan nesses. But there's no a fleet or a deep frae Spurn Head to Brancaster Roads that I kenna the way o', and mony a time or this I've waded the glaur o' the Wells sea-flats."

"Can you take us to Overy?"

"Ay. I've been there on lawfu' errands and on some not so lawfu'. I wad maybe be a wee thing fickled if an easterly haar came down on us, but still I think I micht smell my way in there in ony weather."

Sir Turnour unbent. "You seem an honest man and a capable seaman. I like your plan, so the sooner we start the better. My servant will take my chaise back to Berwick. How far off is the harbour where your boat lies?"

"Fifteen mile, maybe less. I left the *Merry Mouth* wi' Davie Dimmock for some sma' repairs. They'll be done by this time, and she can sail when it's our will."

"The *Merry Mouth*?" Sir Turnour puzzled, then turned to Nanty. "I thought that was the inn of your fantastic tale."

"It is also the name of Eben's cutter. A queer omen, and I think a good one. If we have luck with one *Merry Mouth* at sea, we'll maybe have luck with another on land. . . . I have a favour to ask, Sir Turnour. I want the loan of your chaise and your galloways."

"Are you mad, sir?"

"I am desperately sane. I have the land journey to make, and while you try to intercept the fugitives in Norfolk, my business is to await them at their rendezvous, which I can assure you is the real point of danger. Otherwise Mrs. Cranmer would not have been so urgent. My request is that you let me have your chaise to York, where I can get a coach that will take me to the Midlands. I am convinced that the Merry Mouth, be it inn or hovel or mansion, is at some place where a road from Norfolk joins the main London highway. I will find it, and I will wait there till I get some enlightenment."

"Then you will wait the deuce of a time, sir. Why should I entrust my chaise to you, when I utterly discredit the tale to which you have pinned your faith? Besides, you have not the look of a whip. Can you handle cattle?"

Nanty shook his head.

"I never in my life tried. But I will have one with me who can," and he looked at Jock. "Mr. Kinloch is not in your class as a charioteer, Sir Turnour, but he has driven the Perth coach, and I have seen him make a fair show with a blood beast in a curricle."

Sir Turnour brooded with a sullen face.

"Can you handle a pair?" he turned to Jock.

"I have driven a pair of Barnton's roans," was the answer. "I can promise you that neither the galloways nor your chaise will take any hurt from me."

The young man spoke haughtily, for he had not forgotten his grievance against the baronet, but the latter was too preoccupied to observe it.

"You are a man of sense," he turned to Eben. "I heartily approve your plan of the sea journey, but what do you say of this wildcat search for a place that may exist only in a madwoman's fancy?"

Eben lit his pipe before he replied.

"I think it wise, sir, and I counsel you to do what the professor asks. I am an auld hand at this trade, and I never like to put a' my weight on one foot. We fisher folk like what we ca' cross-bearin's. And this word 'Merry Mouth,' comin' as it did, is ane we daurna neglect. . . . But the chaise hauds three, for there'll be little baggage. The professor and Mr. Kinloch maunna gang their lane. Bob maun be wi' them."

"Can you sail the boat alone?"

"Fine. Besides, I'll hae able-bodied passengers to gie me a hand if I need it. Bob maun gang wi' you, Professor, for otherwise the twa pairties will hae no way o' gettin' word to the ither. Mr. Kinloch is ane o' oursels, but he's a new member, and he's no yet perfectly acquainted wi' our ways. Ye maun understand that the Free Fishers gang far afield and into queer bits, and there's few corners o' this land where they canna pick up a friend. We've our ain canny ways and our ain private lines set, and Bob has been lang enough wi' us to hae learned the set o' them. I can get word frae Norfolk to Bob wherever he is, and he can get word to me, and wi'out Bob the twasome o' ye wad be like coos in a strange loanin'. Forbye, there'll maybe be trouble at the Merry Mouth or whatever they ca' it—waur trouble than may be waitin' in Norfolk—and three stout fellows are better than twa."

A change suddenly came over Sir Turnour. The hard lines in which his face had fallen mellowed into good humour. He stood up to his full height, stretched his arms, looked round the company, and burst into a great jolly laugh.

"Cranmer is mad," he cried. "So, I think, is his lady, though that is denied. But we are all mad—mad as hares in March, mad as a Meath filly! I come raging up into this accursed north country to read a lesson to a foolish youth who had forgotten his manners. When I find this youth he is so humble that the schoolmaster is at a loss, and so bold that he reads the schoolmaster himself a lesson. I find a boor whom I heartily detest and from whom I am compelled to seek satisfaction for gross insults. And then, to tangle further this already tangled business, I stumble on a gang following the same boor's trail for another purpose, and hear dark tales which lift my private quarrel to the height of a patriotic duty. I am an orderly man, and you have made my life as disordered as a mob fair. So I am setting out, I who detest salt water, in a boat I have never seen and in charge of a sailorman of whom I know nothing except that he has an honest face. And I am asked to lend my chaise and the cattle I have hired to a bedlamite Scotch professor to go seeking a fantastic name through the length of England! *Vive la bagatelle!* Motley is the only wear! I surrender, gentlemen. I fall in with your crazy plans, and may the best man win!"

He turned to Belses.

"You, my lord, will, I take it, return to your distracted family?"

"With your leave, Sir Turnour, I will accompany you to Norfolk. I have the deepest interest of any in your errand."

"I guessed as much. You have certainly my permission, if you can get that of our chief mariner."

"And me, too, by your leave, sir," spoke up Mr. Dott. "I have still my bit of business to dispatch, and I cannot go home till it is finished."

"Just listen to the town-clerk," said Bob, who had attached himself specially to Mr. Dott. "There's staunch folk about Waucht."

"So be it," said the baronet. "I make no complaint. The more the merrier when it comes to seasickness. I stipulate only that you do exactly as I bid you when we reach Norfolk, if we are ever so fortunate.

"And now," he buttoned his coat and smoothed his beaver, "now, by God, for food. I have eaten nothing all day, and am as empty as a bad filbert. I am in command, and my order to all is that we make for the inn. The worst villains have gone out of Yonderdale, including the innkeeper. If any one tries to stay us on the road there are six of us and we will wring his neck. Food I must have, and if there is none in the inn we will get a sheep from the hills. I summon you to dine with me forthwith on whatever fare we can find. Anyhow, there is good liquor, and my servant is a pretty hand at compounding punch. *En avant.*"

"We maun gang cannily out of this place," said Eben, "and cannily till we're a mile or mair off. Meek is still here, and the Hungrygrain folk will return, and it would never dae to bring trouble on Tam Nickson."

The moon lit them down the stream and up the hill to the inn. To Nanty it seemed that the glen had a new atmosphere. It had lost that oppression which had weighed on his spirits from his first entrance into it. Except on the high tops it had seemed a tainted land. But now it was a hill valley in all the sweetness of the spring night, a place of running waters and sleeping birds and springing flowers. Mr. Dott, whose perceptions were less acute, seemed also to be conscious of the change, for his spirits rose, and he was no longer the anxious and frustrated lawyer. He cheered the road with songs of his native land. He it was who at the inn managed to summon the pale wife, and, promising that all would be handsomely paid for, demanded beds for the party and an immediate supper. He even, pursued by the gibes of Bob Muschat, made his way to the kitchen and cajoled a maid to make him a dish of toasted cheese after a recipe of his own.

Nanty shut down his thoughts, which waited like a great army in the background, tumbled into bed, and slept for eight hours a dreamless sleep. He awoke to a world of blue skies and light airs and the fresh scents of morning. He awoke also to a heavy preoccupation, which did not seem to be shared by the rest. A gig had been found to carry the party to Yondermouth. Jock Kinloch would accompany it, and bring back some clothes more suited to a lowland journey than fishermen's togs. The others seemed to take everything as a matter of course. Sir Turnour gave his orders as if he had been in his training stable at Newmarket, and was notably civil to Jock, who had awakened in a high mood for adventure. Harry Belses was silent, but there was hope and purpose in his eyes. Eben Garnock smoked his first pipe as if he were on the quay at Pittenweem. As for Mr. Dott, he had again visited the kitchen, and was accused by Bob of a purpose of love and not of greed. Bob had a verse of a wicked song:

> "A bonny may went out one day
> Some fresh fish for to buy,
> An' there she spied a wee toun clerk,
> An' he followed her speedily—
> Ricky doo dum dae, doo dum dae,
> Ricky dicky doo dum dae."

The singer almost got his ears boxed, and Mr. Dott departed in the gig with a high air of wounded dignity.

"That's a fine wee body," said Bob, as he looked after him. "I wouldna say but he's the teuchest o' the lot. Love and anger will carry a man a lang gait, but when a Scots writer is out in the way o' business, he'd walk barefoot ower the plainstanes o' hell."

CHAPTER XIII

OF SUNDRY DOINGS ON THE SOUTH ROAD

JOCK and the gig did not return till close on midday. He brought Nanty's baggage, who was now able, without borrowing from Harry Belses, to present again that appearance of sober dignity with which he had left St. Andrews. Jock wore his green coat and corduroy breeches, a sufficiently workmanlike attire for the road, though at the Red Lion in Berwick it had shown up poorly in contrast to Sir Turnour's elegance. Bob had somehow managed to procure a black coat of an ancient cut, and a shirt and neckcloth in harmony with it. "Eben Garnock's," he explained. "Eben aye carries his Sabbath coat in the *Merry Mouth*, for he's an elder o' the Kirk, and winna miss a diet o' worship if he's in port at a weekend. He lent them readily, for he says there's nae means o' grace about Norfolk."

"What do we look like?" Jock cried, as he tested the buckles of the galloways' harness. "You're the professor again, Nanty, or maybe a stickit minister—no, your skin's too brown and your eye too bright for a stickit minister. I'm the country bumpkin off to see the world—it's the devil's ill-luck that I haven't my new suit from McKimmie's. And Bob—God knows what Bob is—a cross between a Cameronian preacher and a fish-couper! Anyway, there's nothing randy about the look of us—just three quiet lads travelling on their lawful occasions. It's the chaise that troubles me. There's a Corinthian dash about it that doesn't set well with its occupants, and there will maybe be questions asked down the road."

Bob alone had some knowledge of the country, and he had consulted with Tam Nickson and Sir Turnour. The view-halloa of Cranmer's huntsman the night before showed that the party had taken the hill road to the south, and Sir Turnour had been clear about their purpose. Relays of horses had been sent on ahead, and they must mean to cross the Tyne at Corbridge, and make straight across the Durham moorlands to the great Carlisle-London road at Catterick Bridge. There they would no doubt take coach for their secret destination in the Midlands. Nanty, who felt himself in command, had no other purpose than to follow their track, a track which would soon be lost in the bustle of a great highway. He was looking for a single inn in a vast unknown land, and all he knew was that it must be somewhere adjacent to the shire of Norfolk. He must go south—ever south—and trust to Providence.

Jock proved that he could handle the ribbons, and, more important, that he could nurse his cattle. The galloways were fresh after their two days' rest, and, easing them on the hills, and giving them their heads on the flat, he took them at a rattling pace over a switchback country in the bright afternoon. They crossed the bridge of Tyne long before sunset, and when the twilight fell were high up on the Weardale moors. The road was of hill gravel, often half overgrown with grass, but in the dry spring weather it was as good as the broadest highway. The air was fresh and tonic, the countryside full of the sound of young lambs and curlews, and weather and scene would have ordinarily sent Nanty's spirits soaring. Yet he was profoundly depressed, and while Jock babbled cheerfully and Bob on his seat behind was a fount of rustic music, he wrapped himself gloomily in his thoughts.

For he was convinced that somehow the main responsibility of success or failure would rest on him and he felt himself inadequate to the burden. What had become of the competent young man who had hitherto prided himself on meeting each task with an easy mastery? Not even the donning of his proper clothes had given him back his former self. The professor of logic, the St. Andrews Questor, the legate of the Senatus and of Lord Mannour, had been lost by the wayside. Also the boy who had been queerly mixed up in these personages and had longed hungrily for adventure. He felt himself to be crude, ignorant, callow, a blundering hobbledehoy who sought to match himself against the cunning of grown and desperate men.

Cranmer especially had become a figure that hag-rode his fancy. He had never seen him, but Bob had, and Bob had drawn his picture—a dead-white face—black, finely pencilled eyebrows—cold, wise, cruel eyes. He was afraid of Cranmer, he confessed to himself, afraid not so much of any bodily hurt Cranmer could do to him as of the malevolent power of his spirit. There lay evil incarnate, and he had never met evil, and shuddered virginally at the thought of it. Yet every mile was taking him nearer to Cranmer. He had no doubt about their meeting. He would find the Merry Mouth inn, and terrible things would befall there. There his courage would be tested and might fail him.

Yet he must not crack. His trouble was of the heart as well as of the head, for, if he failed, the pale woman he had met on the hills would be the victim. He remembered all her sad graces, the sudden childlike innocence of the eyes when they were freed from their tragic preoccupation, the lines about the mouth of an almost forgotten mirth, the soft voice, the exquisite modelling of the small face. He had never seen, never dreamed of anything like that girl in her rough clothes, so fragile and yet so resolute, so fine and yet so massive in her hopeless fidelities. Was he in love with her? He knew one thing only, that this was what he had dreamed of all his day, and had cherished too deep in his heart ever to profane with his reason.

He shut down the thought of her, for it only increased his nervousness, and tried to think coolly ahead, as became the leader of a forlorn hope. Sir Turnour had given him advice. In his inner pocket he carried several of Sir Turnour's modish *cartes de visite* with a line scribbled on the back asking courtesy for the bearer, in case his journey took him into company where the baronet's was an honoured name. There was also a letter on Sir Turnour's personal notepaper to Richard Monckton, Esquire, of Flocksby Hall, a seat adjoining the Carlisle highroad, where the chaise was to be left when the travellers took the London coach. . . . That night they had better avoid a town, for he could not disguise from himself that their company was an odd one and might invite questions. Some wayside hostelry of the humbler kind was their mark. No need to change horses, for the galloways would carry them next day to Catterick Bridge. . . . Nanty got some consolation from recapitulating his meagre plans, and a little beyond Wilton-le-Wear he saw an inn which offered the sort of lodging he desired.

It was a small place, but with good stabling, for it was a noted meet of the local foxhounds, and within a quarter of a mile of the local kennels. It proved to be empty of guests, the landlord was friendly, they were shown clean bedrooms, and, when Jock had seen the galloways stabled and fed, they sat down to a comfortable supper. The curtains were not drawn on the window looking out on the road, and, while they were busy on a dish of Wear trout, there came a clatter of hooves which stopped at the taproom door.

Bob, who was sitting on the window side, took one glance at them, and then rose and, with a finger at his lips, left the room. He did not return till the fish had been removed and a loin of mutton set in its place. The others had meantime heard the hooves again, and observed a rider, leading several horses, pass on to the north.

"We're on the right road," said Bob. "Who think ye it was? Hartshorn, the Hungrygrain huntsman, nae less. Awa' hame wi' the beasts they rode the first stage on. He's mighty dry, for he had two-three chopins o' yill afore his thirst was slockened. Na, he doesna ken me, but I ken him. Afore this I've lookit on the ill-faured face o' him frae the back o' a dyke. I had a word wi' the landlord, and he tells me a party gaed by about midday, a gentleman and a leddy and three serving-men. Hartshorn was ane o' them. Purdey the inn-keeper will hae the beasts for the next stage. We'll maybe hear him jinglin' by in the night."

Next day they topped the last ridge of intervening moorland and came down to the broad haughs of Swale. Now they were on a much-frequented highway, with on each side a wide ribbon of grass—no longer the smooth hill gravel, but a surface still scored by winter ruts, which a dry spring and much traffic were beginning to level out. At the inn at Catterick Bridge they had their midday meal, and were there overtaken by the coach from Carlisle to the south. The Rapid was crowded in every inch, outside and inside, and they were told that there would be no vacant seat before York.

The landlord, a friendly Yorkshireman, scratched his head and gave them his best counsel. Clearly he took Nanty for some great man's secretary, travelling in a hurry with two lesser servants. "Give your cattle two hours' rest," he said, "and they will carry you to Boroughbridge. There at one in the morning you can get the Umpire, which never to my knowledge has carried a full load. You're for the south, you say, and have no mind to call at York? Well, the Umpire's the thing for you. She'll carry you to Doncaster, where you can take your choice of coaches—for Nottingham, Leicester, Brummagem, anywhere you please—or if it's London you're making for, you can follow the Great North Road. You can sup as snug at the Green Willow in Boroughbridge as at any house in the dales."

The galloways took them all afternoon through a country which to Nanty's northern eyes seemed the very tropics for richness. Every hedge was white with may, every orchard a sea of blossom, the ploughlands were green with sprouting corn, and in the fat meadows there pastured cattle of an amplitude strange to one accustomed to the little lean kine of Fife. The landscape soothed and satisfied him; surely he had come into a land so warm and settled that law-breakers would find their task harder than on the bleak Northumbrian moors.

"A change from the East Neuk," he observed to Bob over his shoulder.

"A sore change," was the answer. "I dinna like it. We're ower far frae the sea. It wad choke me to bide here."

At a toll-bar the gatekeeper called their attention to the fact that one of the galloways had cast a shoe. There was an inn a mile ahead, he said, and a blacksmith's shop behind it. Boroughbridge was a matter of six miles farther.

The inn proved to be a roomy place, for it served a wide hunting country. The galloways were unyoked, the smith was found, and soon the music of his bellows was loud in the quiet evening. On the benches outside the door sat a row of countrymen with pots of beer, and from the inn parlour came the sound of men's talk. One galloway was tethered to a bridle-ring in the signpost, and the chaise with its pole erect stood in the space between the highroad and the inn door. Jock clamoured for ale, but Nanty and Rob declined refreshment. They stood a little shyly apart from the rustics on the bench, with that sense of mingled insecurity and distinction which attends all travellers.

To them there entered from the back parts a man with a string of horses, a tall fellow wearing a homespun coat with big pockets, corduroy breeches, and frieze leggings. At first he did not see the chaise. The landlord came out to speak to him.

Bob dug Nanty in the ribs.

"It's Purdey," he whispered. "The Hungrygrain innkeeper. I thought we wad hae passed him langsyne. He has come an unco way south. . . . Na, we're safe enough. He has never cast eyes on ony o' us, though I ken his thrawn face weel."

Purdey was talking to the landlord, as one professional to another. He had a loud voice, and Nanty could hear every word.

"Grand weather for the road," he was saying. "My gentlefolk have the luck o't. No, I'm in no great hurry home.

I'll bed the night at Catterick Brig and be on Cheviot side the morn before the darkening, if I start at skriegh o' day."

A maid brought him a mug of ale.

"Here's health," he said. "I'll no be travellin' the roads for a bittie, but if ye hear of any young beasts of the kind we spoke of, ye can get word to me by Catterick Brig, or by Johnny Trot when he comes north to look at our yearlings. . . . Did ye say that ye had a gude-brother a hostler down Huntingdon way?"

"Not in Huntingdon, but nearby. Fenny Horton, they call the place. Been there for two-and-twenty years. Jem used to buy cattle from the fenmen, and he had the fortune to marry a pretty wench that was the only child of Bill Ashe—him that had the change-house and likewise brewed his own beer. Ever heard of Bill? He was a great man in them parts. By and by he died, so Jem hung up his hat and ever since has been as snug as a flea in a blanket."

Purdey had finished his mug.

"That's what I told my master. Knowing yourself, he likes the breed, and might put a bit o' business in your brother's way, when he's down there. Well, I maun ride. Hold these beasts while I mount. . . . God in Heaven, how came that here?"

He had turned round and seen the chaise—a type of vehicle, with its exceptional breadth, by no means common. It was plain that he recognized it. Then he saw the galloway by the signpost and conjecture became a certainty.

There was lively suspicion in his eye—anxiety, too, for he was a faithful servant. Three days back he had seen the same chaise and the same horse in his own yard in Yonderdale. What had wafted them into Yorkshire? His eye ran over the toping countrymen, and then fell on Nanty and Bob. He was no longer the easy-going traveller, but a man fiercely inquisitive.

"Who brought that here?" he demanded of the landlord.

The latter nodded his head towards Nanty.

"There's the gents," he said. "The other nag is being shod in the smiddy."

Purdey marched up to Nanty, looked him over, and apparently did not like what he saw.

"Is that your chaise, sir?" he asked, and his tone was menacing.

"No. It has been lent to me by a friend," was the answer.

"Lent?" The stress on the word was insolent. "And where, may I ask, have ye brought it from?"

"I do not see how that concerns you."

"It concerns me very closely." Purdey's speech had lost the burr of the hills, and had become sharp and precise. He must, in his time, thought Nanty, have filled other callings than that of innkeeper, and dwelt in other places than Yonderdale. "Here's dirty work, friend Robbins," he called to the innkeeper. "This chaise put up at my place three days back. It is the property of a man of fashion, a baronet, who was a guest with me, and whom I left residing there. Now I find it a hundred miles off in the charge of God knows what. Who are these landloupers? I don't like the cut of them. Lent, says they. Stolen, says I. It's a case for a constable and the nearest justice."

Jock had come out of the inn and joined them, and Nanty was conscious that the trio might present an odd appearance—Bob in a coat that had not been made for him, Jock in his half-raffish provincial clothes, and he himself like a cockerel in the company of jackdaws. It was plain that the landlord regarded them unfavourably. The rustics on the bench had lifted their faces from their alepots and were looking at him with slow, suspicious eyes. And there was Purdey bent on mischief. He saw in Purdey's face something that was almost fear. The sight of this link with Yonderdale had roused the dread of pursuit. He would stop at nothing to wreck their plans.

"Ye've got to give some account of yourselves," said the landlord. He was a short, fat man with a superficial air of good-fellowship, but his eyes were shifty and his mouth was cunning. "This gentleman speaks sense. Ye're a queer crew to be driving a gentleman's chaise, and unless ye can satisfy me as it's right come by it's my dooty to arrest ye pending further inquiries. There's been overmuch thieving on this road of late, and us honest folk has got to be careful."

The rustics had risen from their bench and were drifting round the disputants, foreseeing a better evening's amusement than gossip. Nanty realized the delicacy of their position in a place where they were unknown and suspect, and where Purdey was at home.

"I assure you, sir, you have no cause for your suspicions," he said. "We are lawful travellers and honest men. The chaise and horses were lent us by a friend to expedite the first part of our journey. I will give you the friend's name. It was Sir Turnour Wyse."

The landlord laughed.

"Ye've chosen the wrong lie. Sir Turnour Wyse, by God! There's no man better known on the road. I knows Sir Turnour. We all knows Sir Turnour. He's as likely to lend his fine chaise to fellows like you as to come here seeking a job as stableboy."

"It's Sir Turnour's chaise," said Purdey. "He is the gentleman I spoke of. I last saw him in my own house with his body servant and his braw clothes and his shiny boots and his silver dressing-case, the very pattern of a Corinthian. And you have the impudence to tell me that he lent his chaise to three blackguards—one looking like a dominie, and one like a clerk in his Sunday best, and one like a ploughboy."

The last word touched Bob on the raw, and his jaw set.

"Canny, my man," he said, "or I'll lowse every tooth in your heid."

Purdey shrugged his shoulders. "He has a Scotch tongue. This is a new kind of Scotch packman. It's a case for the constable, friend Robbins,"

Nanty drew from his pocket one of Sir Turnour's cards.

"Will this convince you?" he asked the landlord. "Here is Sir Turnour's card with his name engraved on it, which he gave me as an introduction to any of his friends I might meet. There are some words in his own handwriting on the back of it. You know Sir Turnour, you say, so you know that he is an ill man to offend. Be careful, sir. If Sir Turnour comes to hear of this insolence he will flay the skin off you."

The landlord was plainly shaken, but not so Purdey. "It's maybe Sir Turnour's card," he cried, "but how was it gotten? Tell me that. Maybe the same way as the chaise—by violence or stoutrief. Sir Turnour is a braw fellow, but three to one is heavy odds, and these three are not weaklings. I tell you there has been murder done. As like as not, Sir Turnour is lying in a ditch with his throat cut."

At the mention of murder the interest of the rustics perceptibly quickened. They drew off a little, but they never took their eyes from the three strangers. Here was entertainment for a fine evening. "Shall I fetch constable, master?" one of them asked, and the landlord nodded.

Nanty saw the position growing ugly. He feared not only some maddening detention, but the making public of an errand in which secrecy was everything. For one moment he looked round the group with a wild idea of knocking down anybody who barred their way. He was not accustomed to this kind of scene, but it stirred some little ancient devil of his boyhood.

Then suddenly the grown man replaced the boy. He remembered Sir Turnour's letter, and took it from his pocket-book.

"Whereabouts is Flocksby Hall?" he demanded, forcing his voice to an assurance he did not feel. "I have this letter from Sir Turnour to Squire Richard Monckton of Flocksby."

Utter silence greeted his words. Purdey looked sharply behind him, embarrassment crept into the landlord's malevolence, the rustics began to edge away. A high ringing boyish laugh came through the open window from the inn parlour.

"That be Squire Dick," said some one.

"Then I shall present my letter," said Nanty, and marched indoors.

There was no doubt where his errand lay, for talk and laughter drifted from behind a door on the left side of the little hall. He knocked, and a voice bade him enter.

Five gentlemen sat round a table discussing a magnum of claret. One had the look of a sporting attorney, an oldish man with horn spectacles on his nose, and before him a sheaf of papers. Of the others, two were elderly and fat, and one was a long lath of a man in a bright bird's-eye neckerchief. The fifth, who seemed to be presiding, was scarcely more than a boy, with fair hair and blue eyes set wide apart in a freckled face. His cheeks were a little flushed, and his clothes, though cut in the extreme of fashion, were worn with an air of country undress. He lifted his head at Nanty's entrance, but there was no incivility in his stare. Here was one who looked charitably upon the world.

"Can I speak with Squire Monckton?" Nanty asked, and four solemn heads nodded towards the boy.

"I ask pardon for my interruption, gentlemen, but I bear a letter to Squire Monckton from a friend. Sir Turnour Wyse."

"Sir Turnour!" the boy cried. "How goes that imp of fame?" He tore open the envelope, read the page, and then held out a hand to Nanty.

"You've hit it off to a marvel, sir. I'm as ill to find these days at Flocksby as a mayfly in August, and here you get me at the first cast. These are my fellows of the committee of the Flocksby Hunt, met to review the season's sport." He named four names. "And this, gentlemen, is Mr. Anthony Lammas, just out of Scotland, commended to me as a cock of the right breed by a most sovereign judge of cocks. No, by God, not Mister, but Professor. You abash me, sir. I'm too fresh from Brasenose College not to have still some awe of the academic gown. Consider me as at your service. I'll see that Sir Turnour's chaise is returned to his Half Moon Street stable, and the cattle can go north to Berwick with my next convoy, and meantime find stalls at the Hall. . . . Our sederunt is finished, and I move we adjourn to Flocksby.

You'll sup with me, and I'll send you to Boroughbridge to join the Umpire. Tell you what, I'll post a man ahead to book you a seat."

"You are most kind, sir," said Nanty. "But I have two companions with me. One is a young man, the son of an eminent judge in Scotland, and the other a fisherman who is essential to our business."

"We'll have 'em all," cried Mr. Monckton. "Bless you, sir, at Flocksby we often sit down thirty to dinner and forty to supper. . . . Let us be going, for I am deucedly peckish! Your horse must be shod by now, and we five will attend you like a sheriff's mounted posse. The place is not three miles off."

"Thank God I found you here," said Nanty. "The landlord was inclined to suspect our honesty, since he held that our appearance did not match our equipage."

The boy drew down his brows in a way that showed that his temper lay handy. Then he laughed.

"Robbins is an oaf," he said. "God made him and doubtless he must pass for a man, but he's a cursed bad judge of a gentleman. I'd get rid of him tomorrow but for his wife, who was my father's kennel-maid. Hey, Robbins," he cried as he straightened his cravat and clapped a beaver on his unruly mop of hair. "Get the other horse in the gentleman's pair, and quick about it."

But there was no need of the command, for when Nanty emerged from the inn he found the galloways being put to the chaise by an obedient ostler. The landlord stood obsequiously by their heads, the rustics were back on their bench, and Purdey and his horses had disappeared.

The Squire of Flocksby accepted Jock and Bob with the same complacence with which he had received Nanty. "You're the whip, ain't you?" he asked the first. "Nice little tids, but too slow for my taste. I could fit you with a pair of spankers.". . . Bob he looked over with a connoisseur's eye, and consulted his friends. "Gad, what shoulders!" he cried. "He'd buff magnificently. If your fish stop taking, you try the ring. Come to us and we'll have you a champion in a twelvemonth."

At Flocksby they supped at a board at which dukes and drovers, peers and pugilists, were regaled indifferently. The fat member of the Flocksby Hunt became drunk and slumbered. The attorney had to leave halfway through the meal, and the lean man, who had ambitions to represent the county, talked politics when the decanters had been thrice round, till he was silenced by his host, after which he sang a song. They all sang, Jock in his bass, Bob in his fine tenor, and Nanty gave the company "Dunbarton's Drums." At midnight Squire Monckton, still warbling choruses, packed the three of them into his curricle and drove his "spankers" tandem to Boroughbridge, where the Green Willow received them with open arms. "If there's no room in the Umpire," was his parting injunction to the landlord, "fling out a brace of bagmen. I'll pay the shot."

Presently, in a night as balmy as a Fife June, Nanty on the box seat was watching in the glow of the headlights the ribbon of the great road unwind before him. The young Squire had given him an inspiration. Difficulties must be faced with a light heart and with a high hand. He was almost happy. But he wished he did not look like an unfrocked parson. The phrase rankled; he had heard it whispered by a member of the Flocksby Hunt.

Then he laughed and reminded himself of his true rôle. He was no swashbuckling youth roaming the land for sport and adventure, but a grave man to whom had fallen a heavy duty. His strength lay in his head, not in his hands or heels. He had won the first point in the game, for he knew from Purdey's remark that somewhere by Huntingdon was a place called Fenny Horton, and that somewhere near Fenny Horton was Cranmer.

CHAPTER XIV

TELLS OF A VEILED CHAMPION

AT nine o'clock on a very wet morning a chaise from Huntingdon deposited the three travellers in the market-place of Fenny Horton, where, at the sign of the Roman Urn, John Blanchflower invited company. Two nights and days they had been on the road, for the coach from Boroughbridge had missed the regular day mail on the Great North Road.

To Nanty's surprise the little square was full of people, and the landlord, two ostlers and three serving-maids awaited them at the inn door. Soon it became clear that this was no accident, but that they were really the object of popular interest. Every eye was turned on them, an ostler ran to the horses' heads, the landlord himself, smiling like a harvest-moon, assisted them to descend.

It was Bob apparently who caused the excitement. He wore his big seaman's coat, and had a blue woollen comforter knotted round his neck. "That's him," Nanty heard from the crowd. "That's the Scotty. Lord, he do look a tough 'un."

Mr. Blanchflower bobbed his head.

"Welcome, gentlemen. The Urn is honoured to entertain you. We got word to expect you, but heard nothing more, so I had given up hopes of you."

"Who sent you word?" Nanty finessed, for he was deep in bewilderment.

"It came down the road—I couldn't just say how—it's

been in everybody's mouth that Fisher Jemmy was on his way. A week ago some said he had passed Newcastle. Then, as the time went on and the big day came nearer, there was word that he had gone to a mill Darlington way. You've cut it fine, gentlemen, for the championship is only two days off—the first round to be fought at ten o'clock on Thursday morning. Five of the boys has arrived, two at the Dog and Unicorn, one at the Duke's Head, and two with Sir Miles Furmilow at Hay Hall. Now the Urn has got its man, too, for which I kindly thank you. Your rooms are ready, and I promise you they'll be as private as your own parlour, and the food of the Urn is reckoned the best in three shires. There's a nice barn for sparring practice, and a quiet little meadow for a run in the morning. Follow me, gentlemen. . . . May I be honoured by your name, sir?"

Jock took charge, since Nanty still blinked puzzled eyes. "Hold your tongue," he whispered fiercely to Bob, who was the embarrassed recipient of many appraising glances. "As dumb as a doorpost till I give you the word." Then to the landlord, speaking broadly like a jockey from Cupar Fair: "This is Mr. Anthony Lammas, the gentleman that backs the Fisher and pays his shot. I'm his trainer, and a damned pernickety one ye'll find me. We want three rooms—one for Mr. Lammas, one for me and the Fisher that'll bed thegither, and one for our meals, and for each door we want a key. Ye'll send our food to our room—the best ye've got for me and Mr. Lammas, and underdone steak and wheaten bread for the Fisher. We could manage fine with a second breakfast when we've washed our faces and dried our breeks."

Jock's tone had the mixture of authority and vulgar familiarity which the part required. The three in the landlord's wake withdrew from the gaze of the crowd, who raised a faint cheer in Bob's honour. Ten minutes later they sat before a sea-coal fire in a room full of flowered chintz and ancient mahogany, drinking tumblers of rum and milk. Another twenty minutes and they were busy with a platter of bacon and eggs as large as a milk-pan. There was also a dish at which Bob took one shuddering look and replaced the cover. "Eels," he cried. "Waur than frogs. They're a queer folk, the English."

"This is a merciful Providence," said Jock, when called upon to face the situation.

"It's a calamity," said Nanty. "Here are we full in the public eye, with every movement we make a matter of interest to some hundreds of idlers. We might as well have printed a handbill and sent it round with the bellman."

"Not so, Nanty my dear. Your logic is deserting you. We're a fighting party and therefore privileged folk in Old England. Bob can do what he likes within reason, and no one will question him—not till after Thursday's fight. He can lie all the time in his bed. He can sit in his chair before the fire. He can trot round the meadow and break the nose of any man that looks at him. His privacy will be respected as if it were a royal accouchement, and you as his backer and I as his trainer will have the same indulgence. We're sportsmen, hang it, and till we're beaten we're cocks of the walk. That's the grandeur of the English character. In Fife they'd jail us as suspicious characters."

"But we'll have people coming here—to talk about the fight—to look at Bob—"

"Not them. We're sacred characters, guarded like race-horses. Nobody will come near us. It would be a breach of the unwritten laws of the game. I had a word with the stable-lad who brought up our baggage, and it seems that the meeting on Thursday has been got up by one Sir Miles Furmilow, a local sporting baronet, and that fighting men are coming from all over the land, since the championship stake is a belt of five hundred guineas. They are to draw lots for their opponents, and to fight in bouts of ten rounds each till the best man wins. There'll be a lot of blood lost in Mill meadow come Thursday."

"But supposing the real Fisher Jemmy arrives?"

"Bob's the real man, for he is first comer. Any one else has to prove his title against Bob's fists. Are you prepared, Bob?"

“ ’Deed I am that,” was the answer. “But, mind ye, I ken naething about fightin’ inside a ring o’ ropes wi’ a clout round my middle. I’ve grand wind, and I’m light on my feet, and when I’m thrawn I could fell a stirk, but naebody ever learned me what they ca’ the science o’t. I’ll no stand up like a jumpin’-jaick and mak mysel’ a show for thae English.”

“You’ll not be asked,” said Jock. “What we’ve got is a hidy-hole for the present. Long before Thursday we must be up and off on our proper job. Man, Nanty, don’t look so glum. We must take what cards fortune gives us and play boldly. Up to now we’ve had the luck on our side.”

But Nanty was not glum; he was thinking hard. Thursday, the day after the morrow, was the big day, and the countryside for thirty miles round would flock to the spectacle. Cranmer would know of this, for a dispeopled land was what he wanted. Somewhere near must lie the Merry Mouth, a quiet place that day with Fenny Horton as the magnet. Thursday must be the day he had fixed on for his purpose—Thursday, or, more likely, Thursday night. He was now in Norfolk, for Gabriel (he thought of the girl only as Gabriel) had told him that their first goal was her house of Overy. Some time on Thursday he would return, and the crisis would begin.

He told the others his conclusion. His spirits had risen again, for the hand of Providence seemed to have thus far guided them. The time of waiting was nearly over, and in two days the worst—or the best—would happen.

“I must bestir myself,” he said. “You two stay here till I come back, for I’m the least conspicuous of the three. I can pass unnoticed in the streets, when every eye would be on the pair of you. I must find where the Merry Mouth is.”

“Ask the landlord,” said Jock.

“Not I. He looks a decent soul, but inns are the breeding-ground of tattle, and if we mentioned the Merry Mouth to him or to anybody about the place it would be over the town in an hour. I’ll take the air like a curious traveller, and maybe I’ll find some native to crack about the countryside so that I can edge in my question. Don't stir a foot till you see me again."

The rain had ceased, but the brimming gutters showed that there had been a heavy fall. With the collar of his greatcoat turned up and his hat low on his brows, Nanty passed unremarked out of the inn door and mingled with the throng on the kerb. The little town stood on a knuckle of high ground, and he followed the main street which straggled eastward. He gazed with interest at the brick houses, some of them with stuccoed porticoes and fanlights, and with admiration at the great sprawling grey church which looked as ancient as Largo Law. "But for John Knox," he reflected, "we should have had the like in Scotland and not be forced to put up with barns."

Clearly there were many incomers in the town, farmers in top-boots as thick as on a market-day, raffish young gentlemen in waxcloth coats, staring countrymen, dusky gipsy folk, and a motley of the lantern-jawed sporting breed which he had seen at Cupar races and which is the same over all the world. The street descended and widened, and he found himself looking over straggling cottages to a great expanse of flat country very clear under the rain-washed sky. It was of a curious grey-green tint, without any of the brighter colours of spring, except where patches of mere caught the sun. The road in front of him presently became a causeway embanked above a sluggish watercourse. The whole land seemed strangely foreign. The folk in the street, rosy or sallow, were of a different race from his own, and to an eye accustomed to sharp contours there was something infinitely dreary in the unfeatured vista and the smudged horizon.

But when the sense of forcignness was most strong upon him, he suddenly encountered a familiar face. It was long and white and melancholic, and it rose above the folds of a voluminous white muffler. He recognized Mr. Ebenezer Pitten, the Balbarnit butler.

He was recognized in turn. The doleful features became almost cheerful, and a not very clean hand was thrust forward.

"It's the Professor," cried Pitten. "I'm blithe to see a kenned face in this foreign land. What in the name o' a' that's wise has guidit ye here? I was just thinkin' I was the first Scotsman that ever set foot in this wersh countryside, which is a' glaur and flowe-moss."

"That is the question I would ask you," was Nanty's answer. "I thought that you and your ladies were bound for London."

"So we are—so we are—in the hinder end, but there was aye a notion of stoppin' on the road to visit a young lassie that was at the school langsyne wi' Miss Kirsty. Landbeach Manor they ca' the bit, but it's mair water than land. The lassie's name is the Leddy Jean Hilgay, and she bides wi' her auld grannie the Countess o' Horningsea. Grand names and grand folk, but a dowie habitation. We came here twa days syne in a post-shay, and yestereen it rained as if the Almighty had forgotten His promise and ettled a new Flood."

"Do you stay long?" Nanty decided that he would not mention to Jock that Miss Evandale was in the neighbourhood, fearing to revive black memories.

"They were speakin' about a week, and it'll be the sairest week I ever put in. Miss Georgie is content eneugh sittin' sewin' her piece and crackin' wi' the auld leddyship. But Miss Kirsty yawns her heid off, for she has been accustomed to exercise like a young cowt, and the Leddy Jean is no that weel, and spends the feck o' the day lyin' on a sofy. But it's me that's gotten the warst job, for there's no a hand's turn o' work for me to dae, and I'm feared o' yon muckle English serving men wi' their pouthered heids. It's a drouthy bit, too, for I dinna like their yill, and there's naething else allowed in the housekeeper's room. I cam' in here this mornin' to get a dram, for there's nought to be had at the Merry Mouth."

"The what?" Nanty cried.

"The Merry Mouth. A queer name and a queer house. It's the nearest public, about a mile frae the Manor yetts, but it's no the kind o' canty public we're used wi' in Scotland.

Merry Mouth, forsooth! I never saw onything less merry, and there's naething in't for a man's mouth. It stands down by the edge o' the flood water, a' by its lane among saugh trees, and there's a thrawn bitch o' a wife wha shoos ye awa' like a tinkler dog. . . . But ye haena telled me what brings you here, Professor. I last saw ye in the hottle at Berwick-on-Tweed wi' the Kinloch lad."

"A mere accident," said Nanty. "Like your mistress I had to visit a friend before going on to London, and followed him here. My stay will be short, but it may last a day or two. I have a distant acquaintance with Miss Evandale, and we come from the same shire, so while I am in the neighbourhood I may be privileged to pay my respects to her. How far off is this Landbeach Manor, and where does it lie?"

"About three Scots mile—five maybe, as the English reckon. Ye canna miss the road. Gang on as ye are gaun, tak the first turn to the north, and syne east again whaur ye see a muckle windmill that pumps the water frae the sheughs. Then head straight on by the Merry Mouth till ye come to the lodge yetts. I cam' here in an hour and a half, but a young lad like yoursel' wad hae come in less. Will I gie Miss Kirsty ony message?"

"Not a word. I'll take my chance of finding her at home. Here's something for you to quench your thirst with."

Pitten pocketed a shilling with loud expressions of goodwill, and Nanty continued his walk till he found a lane which enabled him to double back and reach the market-place. He entered the inn in a state of high excitement, to find Jock and Bob languidly playing cards with a dirty pack they had borrowed from the landlord. Nanty locked the door behind him.

"Wonders will never cease," he cried. "The kingdom of Fife has decanted itself into the Fens. What do you think I met in the street but Pitten, Miss Evandale's butler? Miss Evandale and her aunt are staying at a house only five miles off."

Nanty had expected, and feared, that Jock's face would

fall, and that he would resume the part of the wounded and desperate lover. Instead he received the news with extreme composure.

"There's nothing wonderful in that. Miss Georgie told us at Berwick, you remember, that they had a visit to pay before going to town."

"I have other news, tremendous news. I have found the Merry Mouth."

This brought Jock to his feet.

"It's not a mile from the gates of Landbeach, the house where Miss Evandale is staying. About five miles from here."

"The Lord be thanked!" Jock cried. "This makes me feel solemn. A word on the top of Cheviot—a name overheard from yon blackguard Purdey—and here without a false start we are hot on the scent. But the next step, Nanty Lammas? That's the puzzler. Tell me your notion of the logic of it, my wise professor."

"Here's the logic of it. On Thursday, when every man, woman, and child will be drawn to Fenny Horton and will be slow in returning, Cranmer has arranged his villainy. He has Winfortune and Sloan with him, and the man they call Aymer, and I do not know how many more of his London sewer-rats. Some of them are probably now hanging about the Merry Mouth, and Cranmer himself will arrive presently from Norfolk—Cranmer and his wife. It is a long road, and I do not think they will come before Thursday. That day, in the evening doubtless or the early night, Mr. Perceval will appear, summoned by his ward. The stage is prettily set for a quiet murder, of which the lady will be permitted to bear the guilt. No doubt in her house of Overy, and in the Government's pigeonholes, there is ample damnifying evidence. That is the first proposition in the syllogism. The second is that we are here to prevent it, to save the life of the Prime Minister and to rescue the lady from an intolerable servitude."

"So far the court is with you," said Jock. "But the third proposition, Nanty lad? That's the rub. How the deuce is it to be done?"

"Let us set out our assets. We are three against a multitude, so nothing is to be done by our frail strength. We are opposed to a subtle brain, so we are not likely to succeed by guile. There is no help to be got from the countryside, which that day will be an empty barrel. We cannot appeal to the authorities of the shire, even if we knew where to find them, for we have no credentials and would not be believed. . . . Ergo, we must add to our forces. In Norfolk, if God has been kind, there is now, or will presently be, the crew of the *Merry Mouth*—four men, two of whom are as resourceful as Ulysses. With their help we might do much, for Eben is a master of wiles, and Sir Turnour is as formidable as any man in England. But Overy is sixty miles distant by the shortest road, and we have sixty hours to spare—not more. Read me that riddle, Jock, and I'll take off my hat to your wits. We're confronted with the eternal categories of space and time that have always puzzled philosophers."

"It cannot be done," was the doleful answer. "We're like three pigeons purposing to attack a colony of eagles, and without a weapon among the lot of us."

Bob put his hand through his tow-like locks.

"Wait on, sirs. Sir Turnour is a great man for horses, and if he kent where the Merry Mouth was he'd drive like Jehu. Norfolk is his ain countryside, and his word there gangs far. Now the way I look at the thing is this. If he gets to Overy while Cranmer is still there, there'll be a bloody battle, and whatever comes o't Cranmer's ither plan will be knocked endways. If he finds at Overy that Cranmer has gone, he'll follow him like a hound-dog—make your book for that. I ken the teuch breed o' him. Keep in mind that Cranmer has nae suspicions o' our whereabouts—doesna ken that he's followed. Now my dread is that Cranmer will hae ower big a start, and may get here and work his will lang or Sir Turnour meets up wi' him. From what I mind o' this countryside there's queer jinkin' roads atween here and Norfolk. Our first job therefore is to get word to Sir Turnour about the Merry Mouth inn."

Bob took a pull at his mug of ale, for he was not accustomed to long speeches.

"It a' depends on Eben. There's one thing certain, that whatever road Cranmer rides and Sir Turnour follows, it will be through the burgh-town they ca' King's Lynn. Now we maun try and read Eben's mind. I had word wi' him afore we started and we made this plan. Sir Turnour will no delay at Overy, but tak the road as soon as he can get beasts. Eben will follow in the cutter, and if this wind holds—as there's every sign it will—he'll be at Lynn afore him. If we can get word to Eben there I'll no say but what we'll hae Cranmer beat."

"But it's forty miles to Lynn," said Jock. "I asked the landlord. Four hours by the fastest coach."

"We can spare four hours—maybe six—maybe ten," said Bob. "Onyway, I'm for tryin'."

"By water?"

"Water! "Bob cried. "Nae fears. If I were aside the sea it's water I would try, for it's the thing I ken. But here amang thae fen slodgers ye'd be a week working a wherry down the dykes, and there's no open water till ye get to Lynn and the lamentable sea they ca' the Wash. We o' the Free Fishers have aye been guid friends wi' the fenmen, and I've but to speak a certain word doun by ane o' their watersides to get a' the help I want. But there's nought the fen camels—that's the name we gie them, for they gang on stilts—there's nought they can dae to help. They're a douce folk, and a sure folk, but they're no a speedy folk. Na, na, there's just the one thing for us. We maun put our trust in horses, as the Bible says. We maun be off to Lynn afore the darkenin', and tak our chance o' findin' Sir Turnour and Eben there."

"I believe you're right," said Nanty. "We must get a chaise and the best beasts, and Jock must force the pace. No post-boys for us. . . . But wait a minute. We cannot all go. One of us must stay here to keep an eye on the Merry Mouth. We're like soldiers in a campaign, and while some bring up the reserves others must hold the front."

He sank his head in his hands and brooded.

"I have it," he said at last. "My meeting with Pitten was providential in more ways than one. Jock, what kind of a woman is Miss Christian Evandale? Is she one to ride the ford with?"

The boy's face clouded. "Confound you, Nanty, why do you ask me? I'm done with her—I'm done with all women. Mars for me, and Venus can go hang."

"But is this particular Venus a kind goddess? Will a sad tale move her? Has she bowels of compassion? Above all, has she a stout heart?"

"She is a cold-blooded hussy, but she has spunk enough. Ask the Fife Hunt."

"That's all I want to know. If she has courage she has likely enough got the softer virtues. Here is my plan. You two leave me behind, and tomorrow I pay a visit to Landbeach Manor and ask for Miss Kirsty. I'll see the dragon Miss Georgie, too. I'll tell them the truth—and maybe they'll believe me. If they do, I have got me an advanced base—how I am acquiring the military talk!—a secret base, too, within a mile of the enemy. Off the two of you go to Lynn. We'll have up that landlord that has a name like a minor poet."

Jock looked glum.

"I don't like it, Nanty. I see the sense of it, but it's leaving you to the post of danger. You'll go snowking round the Merry Mouth and get your throat cut."

"Not I. I'm too much of a coward. It's the game Bob and I played longsyne bird-nesting in the Dunnikier woods, and Bob will tell you that I'm as cautious as other folk. My joints are as supple as they were in those days, and I've learned more wisdom. The worse risk I run is to fall in love with Miss Kirsty."

It was the right word. "You're welcome to her as far as I'm concerned," said Jock, and made no more question.

To the landlord Nanty was high and mighty, a great man giving orders and not condescending to explanations. They had altered their plans, he said. The Fisher and his trainer would set out in the evening for a place where sparring practice had been arranged. A chaise and pair of the best must be provided, and he would pay a deposit of twenty pounds for its hire, since the time of its return would be uncertain. No coachman or post-boy was needed, for, as the landlord would understand, there must needs be some secrecy about their movements. He himself would spend the night at the Roman Urn, but the following night he might lodge with the Countess of Horningsea at Landbeach. Mr. Blanchflower bowed at the name, and promised exact compliance; he bowed again when Nanty counted him out twenty pounds from money destined by the University of St. Andrews for a very different purpose, and was given a laboriously written receipt.

After a meal which Bob ate heartily and at which Nanty only pecked, the two set out in the early twilight. Bob, wearing a big overcoat and a mighty comforter, was again an object of interest to the crowd, who would have been more inquisitive but for Nanty's severe face on the doorstep. For Nanty had suddenly swelled into a formidable dignity. All the consequence of professor and questor and university ambassador was now in his carriage, and something, too, of Lord Mannour's envoy, and the confidant and friend of great men. He gave his orders in a firm voice, and his eye was magisterial, so that the stablemen and maids and the landlord himself ran to serve him. . . . But within he felt hollow, and his magnificence was only bravado, designed to cover a fluttering heart.

He confessed to himself that he was black afraid. He had always been—ever since he had felt the oppression of Hungrygrain, and had seen Meek's evil squint, and had had Cranmer's picture drawn for him. A pale face, with the heavy dark brows bent and the thin lips parted in mockery, was ever before his eyes. It ousted another face, a woman's, on which he would have loved to muse. He had made his plan in a sudden moment of clear vision, and the making of it had given him a boyish exaltation. But now he realized that it had sent his two comrades from him and left him alone. His solitariness weighed on him like a mountain of lead. Horrid little tremors shot up his spine, and took the strength from his knees. He was alone in a very queer place, and on the morrow, still alone, he must make acquaintance with a queerer. His thoughts recoiled with a spasm of terror from the dark inn among the willows.

He sat in his room while the darkness crept in, striving to bring the powers of philosophy and religion to his aid. He thought himself into a kind of resolution, but his body still played him false, for his imagination had got the better of his logic. Then he forced himself to action. This would never do. He must stir his legs and drink the air of Heaven, for his trouble now was of the shrinking flesh, and lethargy would only heighten it.

The streets were more crowded than in the daytime, and it seemed that many of the citizens and incomers of Fenny Horton had looked too kindly upon the bowl. Quarrelsome little groups crowded the causeway. A company of strolling acrobats had arrived, and in a corner of the market-place were performing under flaring lanterns. Nanty sought the quieter streets, and presently found himself above a pool of water where one of the fen canals opened into a basin. In the clear spring dark he could see wherries and barges drawn up by the quayside, and farther out stumpy masts. There was no sign of life except a stray dog, but in the semicircle of low-roofed houses beside the quay a bright light and a hanging sign revealed an inn. He longed for the proximity of his fellows, something to swing his thoughts from their dismal orbit. The place, judging by the sounds that came from it, was crowded, and in the then condition of the town his presence would cause no remark. He entered the taproom, and found a seat on a bench near the door.

The room was lit by two smoking lamps and a bright fire. It was crowded, and, so far as Nanty could judge, most of the occupants were of the heavy-built, sallow, fenland breed.

One or two were clearly strangers—gamesters, and jockeys out of engagements, the riff-raff drawn hither by the coming fight. Beer in mugs and spirits in thick, footless glasses circulated freely by means of two slatternly maids with hair in elf-locks. It appeared that the company had drunk well, but were not drunken, for they were singing. A man would give a verse of a familiar song, and all would join in the chorus. Even the raggle-taggle sportsmen shaped their lips to some kind of noise.

Most of the songs were unfamiliar to Nanty, slow drawling ballads of the fens and the cornlands, which reminded him how far he was from home. Their words he did not understand, and the tunes had none of the brisk lilt of his own land. They were heavy, earthy, placid as the fen waters. As he sipped his ale his eye roved round the company, and he remarked one man, near the fire and very clear in its light, who was different from the rest. He was tall, with a horseman's stoop in the shoulders; he wore a frieze coat and corduroy breeches, but, plain as his clothes were, he seemed to be of a slightly higher social grade than the others; his face was lean and long, his jaw slightly underhung, and when his thin lips opened they revealed a gap in his upper teeth. Clearly he was regarded as a person of some consequence, for he had the best armchair. He sat with his head a little turned away from the company, sucking a churchwarden pipe, and staring at the fire.

Some one was mulling ale on the hearth, and the man held out his mug to be filled.

"A tune for your drink, friend," said the muller. "Give us a catch out of the north. We've got Fisher Jemmy down for the championship, and there's many as fancies him. I've a crown on him myself, for they tell me he has a drive like a smith's hammer. Pipe us a tune of the Fisher's country."

"I'll give you a tune of my own country," was the answer. "I'm no lousy Scot. Here's to the bonny hillsides and green howms o' Northumberland."

He raised his mug, and broke into a brisk song with the

quick-step of dancing feet in it. It was about a Lentron Fair to which all the dales gathered, a gross and merry ballad, given in a rich tenor and accompanied by the beating of time on the chair arms. The man scarcely opened his mouth as he sang, and the words must have been meaningless to the company, but the lilt of it caught their fancy and all joined lustily in the chorus.

"O the laughin' and the daffin' and the quaffin'," went the refrain, and Nanty, as he listened, and watched the lean weathered face, had a sudden conviction. This was one of Cranmer's men. It must be the chief of them, Winfortune himself, for had not Tam Nickson described him as "lang and blackavised and broken-chaftit"?

"Another," was the cry as he finished, for the quick-step had stirred the muddy company to a new vivacity. Even the slow fenmen hammered their applause.

"I'll give you another, and then I must take the road," said the dark man, and, looking into the fire, he hummed a little to himself, and then broke into a song which was very different from his first. It had a slow sad rhythm, which died away now and then into an infinite regret.

> "It's up and farewell unto you, Spanish ladies,
> It's up and farewell to you, ladies of Spain,
> For we are a-sailing beyond the bar of Cadiz,
> And never, no never, we'll come back to you again."

The man who sang had changed his character with the song. He was no longer the rustic gloating over coarse jollities, but an old man and a sorrowful man, who had seen the glories of the world and found them ashes. He was the eternal wanderer, outside all class and rank, free of all bonds of honour and duty, but with a shrunken heart within him. As Nanty watched his passionless face and listened to the tragic passion of the voice, he wondered in what strange doings, in what strange corners of the globe, this man had amassed that melancholy burden for his soul.

The song finished in silence. With a curt goodnight Winfortune pushed through the crowd and left the room. In passing his coat brushed Nanty's cheek, and from it came the unmistakable odour of peat-smoke. Nanty paid his modest lawing and followed a minute later, and it was with squared shoulders and a brisk step that he walked back to his inn. For the chanty, which to Winfortune was the confession of his heart's bitterness, was to him the trumpet-call of youth. The larger world called him; he was on the highroad now, far away from his dusty classroom; and if the highroad brought peril, it also brought shining rewards. He had stopped thinking about Cranmer. The face that now filled the eye of his mind was a woman's.

CHAPTER XV

HOW A PHILOSOPHER LAID ASIDE HIS PHILOSOPHY

NANTY wandered down a road which ran from the main highway to the little fenland boroughs of the north. He had read the names on the first milestone out of Fenny Horton—Ely, Downham, King's Lynn; that was the road Bob and Jock had travelled the night before, and now by the grace of God they should have reached their journey's end. He had the day before him with only one duty to fulfil, and he deliberately sauntered to quiet his nerves.

He remembered that it was the last day of April. Spring was almost past, and in this soft southern land summer had already begun. The reedy watercourses were ablaze with marsh marigolds, the wayside banks were white with marguerites, the fat pastures between the dykes were gay with daisies and buttercups—"enamelled" was the word that rose to his mind—he remembered it from Dunbar and the old Makars. At the turn of the road the sails of a huge old windmill were slowly turning, and he heard the chack-chack of the pump. Beyond, like a pale green cloud, lay what must be the woods of Landbeach, and somewhere on the left, where the tall trees declined to sallows and brushwood, must be the ominous inn. Larks were singing high up in the blue, and wailing lapwings skimmed the fallows. There were two hawks in the air, and the russet gleam as they turned told him that they were kites. Only once before had he seen a kite, and the sight brought back to him the bird-nesting of his childhood.

But these were not the friendly woods of Dunnikier. The richness of the flowers was strange, and strange, too, the sweet rotting smell of the marshlands. Only the spring wind was familiar, and he took off his hat and let it blow through his hair. That wind and he were old companions, and it had not failed him now, though his learning and philosophy had gone by the board. He had lost the painful sinking of the heart which had troubled him yesterday. He told himself that he was cool and wary, but he knew that he was strung as tense as a bow.

A mile from the windmill the side-road, still oozing water from recent floods, rose slightly to a ridge of hard land which made the park of Landbeach. To the north lay a great fleet, now glittering in the sun, and covered with a multitude of wildfowl. Then came a tangle of willows already in leaf, and a clump of ancient oaks, many of them with broken boughs, some of them laid prostrate by winter gales, all of them gnarled and stunted. In the midst of this decaying grove stood a decaying house.

The Merry Mouth had no sign, for above the door only the iron stump remained of the bar on which had once swung its nameboard. It looked like the shell of a very old house which a hundred years before had been encased in a square Palladian frame. It had the solid sashed windows of the early Georges, and a portico from which the stucco was peeling, so that the pillars had hollows in them, like trees from which branches had been lopped. Once it had been a gentleman's dwelling, for to left and right there were the ruins of a pleasance—crumbling terraces and shaggy bowers. It stood by the roadside, but it had none of the welcoming air of an inn. Pass by and leave me alone, it seemed to say, for I am sick and old, sick and weary.

There was a side entrance which appeared to lead to the taproom. Nanty pushed his way in and found himself in a dirty passage. He tried one door and found it locked; another, which gave under his pressure, and showed only a lumber room full of sheepskins and broken furniture. He hammered with his staff and shouted, and presently an old woman limped in from the back parts.

"A mug of ale, mother," he said. "I have had a long walk and I have a longer in prospect."

She blinked, as if she did not understand him, and he repeated his request. Her eyes were red with rheum, and she had a foul mutch atop of her dishevelled grey hair.

"We are not serving customers," she said at last, and he noted that, like Winfortune, she had not the speech of a peasant.

"You are bound to serve me. It is the law, for this is an inn."

"Not these seven years," she replied. "The sign is down, if you had eyes in your head to see."

"Then where can I get a drink?"

"Go six miles on and you'll come to Twyford, or five miles back to Fenny Horton. Good-day to you. I have no time to chatter with idle men." And before he knew he was jostled by the crone back to the open air, and the door shut behind him. The blotched white façade of the house seemed to grin at his discomfiture. It was utterly silent, and the banging door had made a startling echo. Two moorhens scuttled across the road towards the mere.

Nanty left the place, and turned to his right into the grove of oaks through a gap in a mossy brick wall. He wanted to prospect the house and get a view of its back parts. Not knowing who might be about, he went stealthily, keeping out of sight of the windows. But he found that in that flat place there was no chance of a view, so he climbed a tree and sat in a crutch of it.

There he could reconnoitre at ease. He was looking at the east side of the house, but he could also see the back quarters. At the rear some one had built on a low wing, beyond which lay what seemed to be stable-yard. There was a tower which had once held a clock—the empty hole gaped like an eye-socket. In the yard was a huge litter of straw, as if a stack had been pulled to pieces and flung about wantonly. The place seemed empty, but his sharp eyes noted fresh horse-dung. Most of the outbuildings were of brick, but one or two were of old lichened wood, and against them the straw was piled like rifts of dirty snow.

From his perch Nanty got a new impression of the loneliness of the place. There was that flapping windmill in the west, and to the east lay Landbeach. But the windmill had no dwellers, and Landbeach was the home of a very ancient lady and an invalid girl, and no doubt a host of fatted alien servants. There were no countrymen near with the countryman's curiosity, and whatever happened in the Merry Mouth there were none to know or to tell. To the north lay mere and fen, and to the south leagues of desolate pasture. It was a lonelier place than the most distant glens of Tweed, which had hitherto been to him the Ultima Thule of solitude.

He was just about to descend, when he saw a figure cross the stable-yard. There was no mistaking the long lean body and the horseman's stoop. He had had a lucky escape, for he had no desire as yet to come under Winfortune's eye.

Nanty crept out of the shadow of the oaks and regained the road, and he was not easy in his mind till he had put half a mile between him and the Merry Mouth. Presently a high brick wall began on his right, which must mean the park of Landbeach. He scrambled up at a part where the coping had been broken, and looked into a wide demesne of bracken and turf and young oaks. Then he came to a lodge with a thatched roof and absurd Ionic pilasters, and turned in at the gates.

The drive wound in meaningless curves through the pastures, and dipped to a reedy lake. It was a very untidy drive, and Nanty inferred that the domain in the hands of an aged lady was not over well managed. Fallen timber lay rotting, and the windfalls of the winter had not been removed—very different from the spruce little Fife estates where not a penny's worth was allowed to waste. But this great park had a noble spaciousness, and the fallow deer under the trees and the fantastic turreted boathouse on the lake were proofs of a past magnificence. The place, too, was riotous with light and colour, full of bird-song and flowers, and after the gloom of the inn seemed a haven of honesty and peace. He had a glimpse of a big house on his right at the end of an avenue of trees, and since the drive seemed determined on foolish circuits, he left it and struck across the turf. He was trying to think just what he should say to Miss Christian Evandale.

His thoughts would not marshal themselves, for they were distracted by the beauty of the carpet on which he trod. It was all of blue and gold, the blue of the tiny bugle and the gold of ranunculus and primrose, and in the adjacent shadow of the trees were great drifts of wild hyacinths. . . . He would begin with Fife. He had never met the lady there, but he knew many of her friends, and he could speak of Balbarnit, of Jock, too, though that might be a perilous subject. He had been seen by her at Berwick, and she might recall his face. He remembered that he had been struck by her beauty, though not her manners. Still, Jock had said that she had spirit. . . .

He raised his head to see, coming out from the trees, a girl with an armful of hyacinths.

She wore green, not yellow as on the former occasion, and even in that bright place she shone like a jewel. All pink and white, and golden, she was as dazzling to Nanty's eyes as sunshine. He swept off his hat, and his words came stammeringly.

"Miss Evandale?" he faltered. "Have I the honour—"

Her face was surprised, but not unkindly.

"I am Miss Evandale," she said. And then recognition woke in her eyes. "I have seen you, sir—only a few days back. At Berwick, was it not?"

"I was there with young Mr. Kinloch. I would present myself to you as a Fife neighbour. My name is Anthony Lammas, and I profess logic and rhetoric in the college of St. Andrews."

The lady laughed, a pleasant ringing laugh. She seemed

no more the modish miss, but a country girl. Nanty began to understand Jock's infatuation. This young Diana leading the Fife Hunt would turn any boy's head.

"And what does a St. Andrews professor in the Fens, Mr. Lammas?" she asked.

"That is a tale which I ask permission to tell you. Yesterday I met your man Pitten and heard that you were here. I have come to appeal to you—for your sympathy, and maybe your help. We are in a very desperate perplexity."

Nanty's solemn voice made her face grave.

"We?" she asked. "Who are we?"

"Besides myself, there is Mr. John Kinloch, whom you know. And two Fife fishermen. And Sir Turnour Wyse. And my lord Belses."

Again she laughed.

"La! What a company! Jock, my madcap comrade, and two kail-suppers. Sir Turnour Wyse? That was the splendid gentleman who befriended us at Berwick? And Harry Belses! You have swept the ends of the earth for your companions. What high business does this mission portend, and what does it in this outlandish spot?"

"It is a mission of life and death, and it concerns a place close by called the Merry Mouth. We are racing against time for the life of a great man and the soul of a greater woman."

The girl's face sobered. Something of the shrewdness entered it which had made the Ebbendaal fortunes. She looked steadily at Nanty.

"You look a man of sense, sir," she said. "You can have no purpose in coming to me with a fairy-tale. I will hear it. But first let me summon my aunt, who is somewhere hereabouts. You saw her at Berwick, I think—Miss Georgina Kinethmont, my mother's sister. She has somewhat the air of a dragon who would have accounted for twenty St. Georges. But she is a kindly dragon, and very, very wise."

She gave a high, shrill view-halloa. There was an answer in the voice of a peahen, and presently from a side-walk emerged a striking figure. Though the day was mild, Miss

Georgie was heavily cloaked, and her hat was tied to her head by a Paisley shawl which ended in a great bow beneath her chin. She carried a staff like a weaver's beam, which she must have borne as a weapon of offence, for she did not walk like one in need of artificial aid.

"Aunt Georgie, I present to you Professor Anthony Lammas of St. Andrews, of whom you had but a glimpse at Berwick. He has come to beguile us with a tale—come from Sir Turnour Wyse and my beau Harry Belses."

Miss Georgie rested her gloved hands on the handle of her staff, and made a silent and searching inquisition of Nanty's face and person. It appeared that the result was not unfavourable, for when she spoke her voice was civil.

"Lammas! Lammas! I have heard of you, lad. The auld Principal speaks well of you, and our neighbour Lord Mannour says the feck o' the brains of the college is under your hat. This is a sing'lar bit to forgather. You say you come from Sir Turnour Wyse? How the deil did you fall acquaint with him?"

"Mr. Lammas has a story to tell us," said the girl. "He promises that it is exciting. Let us get inside one of Jane's arbours and hear it."

She led the way to a little summer-house, with a rustic table and benches. Miss Georgie disposed herself comfortably in a corner, with Nanty beside her, while Miss Evandale sat on the table. "On with the good work, sir," said the old woman, "as Burley said when he stuck the Archbishop on Magus Muir."

Nanty found a difficulty in beginning, the story had so many facets. Then he resolved to make his narration a diurnal of his own doings. He told of his St. Andrews mission, his dinner with Lord Mannour, and the lamentable quarrel between Sir Turnour Wyse and Lord Belses. He spoke of Mr. Cranmer, and at the mention of the lady and the young man's infatuation Miss Kirsty laughed. Clearly Harry had made no conquest of her affections.

Miss Georgie's thoughts were on a different tack.

"Cranmer!" she cried. "The wife owns half this countryside. All from the Merry Mouth public for five miles west and ten miles north. I had it yestreen from the auld Countess. Like me she's fond of redding up folk's pedigrees and knowing who owns what lands, and she's like a gazetteer for these parts. Perceval was the wife's maiden name—a fine house in the auld days, she said, but sore declined."

Nanty told of his visit to Yonderdale, of the chase in the night, and the vigil with the lady on the hilltops. He told his story well, for as he recapitulated the events he revived the emotions that had accompanied them. He pictured Hungrygrain as a Dark Tower from which a web of intrigue had been spun over all England. He told of the colloquies in Nickson's cottage, of the visit to the empty house, of the plan of campaign, and of the coming to Fenny Horton. With the point of his stick on the earthen floor of the summer-house he drew a map. "See," he said. "Here am I. There is the Merry Mouth inn. There, if the fates are kind, is now, or will soon be, the *Merry Mouth* boat. Somewhere between us is Cranmer. Soon, too, there will be another on the road, and that is the Prime Minister of England. Tomorrow the two last will draw together on the Merry Mouth, and unless Sir Turnour and his men arrive in time there will be murder done. Cranmer will not suffer, for he has made his plans cunningly for escape, but it will be the death of his lady."

The two women listened intently to his story, and it seemed to him that Miss Kirsty's cheeks lost something of their roses. But Miss Georgie snorted.

"Havers, Professor! Heard you ever such a daft-like tale? This is a law-abiding country, and none of your Muscovies. What hinders you the morn to raise the countryside and make a tolbooth of the inn? That is, if you're right in your conjecture, which I take leave to doubt."

"Cranmer has chosen tomorrow well!" said Nanty. "It is the fight for the championship in Fenny Horton, and every male thing that can stagger will be there. That's the English way of it, if you strip two men to the buff and set them up to pound one another."

"Mr. Lammas is right," said the girl. "I had it from Jean's maid, and from Pitten. All the outdoor servants will be off tonight, and will camp in the open so as to be in time. Tomorrow we will feast upon cold mutton, for there won't be a man in the house."

"We'll see about that," said Miss Georgie fiercely. "We'll compel the bodies. A servant's a servant."

"Not in England when the word sport is breathed," said her niece. "Besides, what good would they be? The Landbeach keepers and stablemen are mostly ancient and doddering, and have been used to the slack sway of an old woman. The Landbeach footmen are trencher-fed hounds. Our Pitten is the best of them—he might at least fire a blunderbuss before he ran away."

The old woman had knit her brows and was thumping her great stick on the ground. "Maybe you're right. At Balbarnit we could have raised a dozen stout fellows, but this is not Balbarnit. A bonny kettle of fish, Professor! Murder—and the King's chief Minister! An unholy blackguard that maunna be allowed to have his way! And a madman, too, says you. And the lady! To be honest, it's just the lady that sticks in my throat. I've heard of her, and of Harry Belses' infatuation. A daft Methody, I was told, and a wild Jacobin. And here you come with a story of a suffering saint. I've nothing to say against Harry, except that he's a young man and what they call romantic, which means a head stuffed with maggots. And you—well, you've ower long and serious a face to be lightly regarded, but you're a philosopher and a minister of the Kirk, and therefore maybe not very well acquaint with the things of this world. As for John Kinloch, he's no more than a will-o'-the-wisp. But Sir Turnour now—there you have a muckle, massy man of sense. Do you tell me that Sir Turnour takes your view of Cranmer's wife?"

"I will be frank," said Nanty. "He does not. But I would

remind you that Lord Belses and I are the only ones of our company who have seen the lady. Sir Turnour is still sceptical of her virtue. It was on that point that he quarrelled with my Harry, and he is not a man to give up readily a prejudice. But Sir Turnour is wholly convinced of Cranmer's villainy, and assured that some time tomorrow it will come to a head in the Merry Mouth. Therefore he is now hurrying here as fast as wind or horses can carry him."

Again the stick thumped. It thumped rhythmically as if it was an aid to Miss Georgie's thoughts.

"You come seeking help?" she cried. "What help can you get here? There's me and Kirsty, two weak women. Inbye there's another pair that's a hantle weaker, an auld Countess and an ailing lassie. As Kirsty has told you, there's not a man about the place to depend on. What is it you seek?"

"I do not know." Nanty shook a weary head. "I hoped for counsel from kind and honest folk. I wanted a refuge at hand for Mrs. Cranmer if she should need it. I think that I also hoped for lodging, for it is imperative that I should be near the Merry Mouth."

"I can promise you the latter two. But counsel—faith, it's hard to see what counsel you can get. Have you riddled the thing out? Have you a plan in your head?"

"I have set out the case to myself a hundred times, but I can reach no finality. There are too many unknown things that must be left to fortune."

"Fortune is a hussy that's likely to be in a better temper if you meet her halfway. Hearken to me, and I'll give you an auld wife's reading. I'll set out the facts, as I've many a time had to do on Kirsty's business to glaikit Edinburgh writers."

Miss Georgie settled herself on the bench, and laid her staff across her knees so that it looked like the mace in a court of justice.

"First, for Sir Turnour and Harry Belses. They must have won to Norfolk today, or the whole plan flies up the lum and Cranmer gets his will. If they reach Overy—is that the name of the place?—before the Cranmers go, what next?"

"I do not think that Cranmer will ever go."

"Well, that's the best that could happen, though it might leave something to be redd up at the Merry Mouth. Now, say that they find Cranmer gone. They will follow?"

"Like the wind. Sir Turnour is a master whip, and in Norfolk he can command what horseflesh he wants."

"So be it. Sir Turnour must make up on Cranmer on the road, or reach the Merry Mouth before the mischief begins. Otherwise he might as well have stayed at home. You are right, Professor. There's a feck o' things we must leave to fortune. There's got to be a fight at Overy, or on the road, or at the Merry Mouth, or the kail-pot's coupit. . . . Now turn your mind another gait. Mr. Spencer Perceval is hasting here to his niece's summons, and will arrive some time the morn. If the mountain is coming to Mahomet, is it not possible to set Mahomet off on another road? There's nothing we can do to stop Cranmer or hasten Sir Turnour, but can nothing be done to shoo away the Prime Minister?"

"I have thought of that. But we do not know where he is coming from. It may be from a neighbouring country-seat. If it is from London he has a choice of roads. He may come from Huntingdon, or he may come by way of Cambridge."

"It's the last day of April, and Parliament is sitting. He'll come from London, and so there's but the two roads to watch. He'll be coming post, and he'll have his body servant, and he's a notable wee body with his white face and his perjink clothes. There's maybe nobody about Landbeach that's much good in a fight, but somebody might be found to watch the roads and carry a letter. That wants thinking on. . . . Meantime, what are your own plans? You can get a bed at the Manor, but what will you do with yourself for the next four-and-twenty hours?"

"I must keep watch on the Merry Mouth. Tomorrow, if no help arrives, I must see what I can do alone."

"Alone! But you're a man of the long gown and not of the sword. Bethink you, Professor, you'll have desperate folk to face if the one-half of what you tell me is true."

Nanty shivered.

"I am a broken reed, I know well. . . . But I cannot fail Mrs. Cranmer. . . . I should never know another moment's peace."

Miss Georgie did not look at him. She was addressing her staff, and her tone was unwontedly gentle. "Maybe he'll not know many more moments either of peace or dispeace. . . . It's a queer thing, but they've at last gotten a man in the Senatus of St. Andrews. I must see the Cranmer wife—she must be fair by-ordinar."

In the early twilight Nanty slipped through the bracken of the park to the western corner of it, which was within a stone's throw of the Merry Mouth. He had been duly presented to the ladies of Landbeach, the old Countess who sat all day stiff in a chair with a head nodding like a china mandarin's, and the young Lady Jane, who each spring suffered from a feverish languor. A groom had been sent to bring his baggage from the Fenny Horton inn, and he had made his toilet in a bedchamber which would have held, with room to spare, the whole of Mrs. McKelvie's dwelling. He had donned the breeches and buckled shoes of ceremony, and before dinner had strolled with Miss Kirsty down the great avenue to the lodge gates, and then along the road to within sight of the Merry Mouth. In the mild bright afternoon it had seemed an innocent place, silent, tenantless, gently decadent. No chimney smoked, and there was no sign of human life—only a mallard in the adjacent sedge, and the first swallows skimming the mere.

"You are certain?" the girl asked. "You are clear that you are not on a wild-goose chase? That place looks as harmless and as empty as the old doocot at Balbarnit."

"I am certain," Nanty answered, "that very soon it will wake up into a hellish life."

But he had not been certain, and that was his worst trouble. He could have keyed himself up for some desperate trial of fortitude, but this doubt was fraying his nerves. At any moment his manhood might be tested; yet again it might not; a thick curtain was over the future, and he could only wait miserably by its fringe. He had scarcely listened to Miss Kirsty's chatter. She was curious about many things—Jock's behaviour, Sir Turnour, Harry Belses, notably Mrs. Cranmer; but when she saw his distraction she turned the talk to Fife and the friendly tattle of its burgh-towns. He saw her purpose and was grateful. She understood that he had his own private battle to fight, in which she could give him no aid but goodwill.

Dinner was a business of stiff ceremonial, and Nanty, when the ladies rose, was left to a ripe port and his own thoughts. This waiting was maddening him, and he felt the need, at any cost, for action. So he changed again into his second-best pantaloons and frieze leggings. The moon was in its last quarter, and night when it fell would be very dark. Now was the time to reconnoitre the Merry Mouth and see if life was yet stirring in it. He had a sense like a cat's for movement in the dark, and it might be well to get the topography of the place into his head, for he did not know what might await him on the morrow.

Kirsty, with a silk scarf over her golden hair, found him on the terrace about to drop from its balustrade into the park. She knew his purpose without asking it.

"You will not be late?" she said. "I will give orders to the servants to sit up for you. And you will be careful—promise me."

"I will be careful. There is no danger, and this night-hawking is a game I played often as a boy. I am very quick and light on my feet, though I have sat so much at a desk. I cannot bide still tonight, for my thoughts trouble me."

"I understand," she said. "Aunt Georgie is preparing for action. She has got herself a road-book and a map, and is studying them with two pairs of spectacles. She means business tomorrow. God be kind to you, Mr. Lammas."

Nanty waited till the oak grove was in deep dusk before he entered it. Before him were the ragged back-parts of the inn, and the only sound was the cry of a hunting owl. He reached the containing wall, scrambled up on it, and looked down into the stable-yard.

Here there was sound. It came from a building apart from the rest, which seemed of newer build. The yard was empty and the house was silent. He dropped from the wall and crept in the direction of the sound.

There were horses there—he could hear their impatient movement, and the champing of their jaws. They had just been fed; therefore Winfortune or some other was in the neighbourhood. The barred windows were too high for him, and the door was locked, so he could not inspect them, but he knew their purpose. No doubt they were blood beasts, and tomorrow would be fresh for the road. They would be the means of escape for Cranmer and his gang.

Nanty was happier now, for he had business on hand. He had found one thing of moment, and he might find out others. But he must be very wary, for Winfortune was near.

He crept round the yard, finding himself much impeded by the immense litter of straw which he had seen that morning from his crutch in the oak-tree. Straw was everywhere, except in the vicinity of the stabled horses. It was pitched in great drifts against the wooden shed which abutted on the house. . . . Now he guessed the explanation. Some time soon the place would be fired.

Again he was comforted. This mission of his was not fruitless. The telling of his story had made it seem almost too fantastic, and there were moments when he had been inclined to Miss Georgie's scepticism. But now he had confirmation—the horses and the straw. The stage was being duly set for a black drama.

His assurance of this fact gave him confidence. The house was still silent and utterly dark, with not a glimmer of light in any window. Somewhere on the west side the old woman must have her lair, and she might well be asleep. But Winfortune would be about, for he had fed the horses within the last half-hour. He must be very careful of Winfortune, who was no doubt indoors eating his supper. But he must find out the lie of the land in these back parts, for it might be fateful knowledge in a crisis.

He skirted a kind of pent-house, and came to a line of low barred windows, with many broken panes. Feeling his way he found the hollow of a door, and to his surprise it yielded to his pressure. He stopped for a moment to collect his thoughts, and see if he had the plan of the building in his mind. This was the back entrance, leading into a wing, a storey lower than the rest, which had been added to the main block. Why should he not enter? He was quick on his feet and could move as softly as a cat. Also, he had the gift of half-vision in the dark which the Greeks said that Artemis gave to her votaries. If Winfortune was there he might spy on him, but he was pretty certain that he could not be spied upon by Winfortune.

He found himself in a passage as dark as the inside of a nut. The floor was flagged and uneven, and he had to pick his steps. Presently it bent to the left, and he was aware of a thin line of light below a door.

There was no sound in the room beyond, but the light flickered, as if it came not from a lamp but from a fire. Gently he felt the door, and found that it was ajar. Gently he pressed it open, and looked in. The room was empty. A small fire burned on the hearth, and there was a table which held the remains of supper—a loaf of bread, the knuckle of a ham, and an empty beer jug. It held something more—a quantity of papers arranged in little piles as if some one had just been sorting them.

It was borne in upon Nanty that here was matter of extreme importance. At all costs he must see these papers. He moved forward to the table, and had his hands on one packet. . . .

Suddenly he realized that the door had closed. More, there was the sound of a key turning. Some one had entered the room. He heard flint strike upon steel, and a candle flared up.

It was Winfortune. And Winfortune had not come there by accident. He had been following him, for his dark face showed that he had found what he expected, and his gap-toothed mouth was stretched in a grin.

"Ay," he drawled. "And who may you be, mannie?"

Nanty, whose heart had missed a beat at the sight of him, forced himself to a forlorn boldness.

"Are you the landlord?" he demanded. "I am a traveller who could find no way into your accursed inn by the front door, so I was forced to try the back. Are your people all dead or asleep?"

"Just so. Dead or asleep. But I am uncommon alive and wakeful."

Winfortune raised the candle and let it fall upon Nanty as he stood by the telltale papers.

"You tried at the front door, did you, and got no answer? And being hungry and drouthy you would not be denied, so you came round by the back seeking the kitchen? You'll be for a bed and a bite o' supper."

Nanty nodded. He did not like the bantering drawl or the bright, malevolent eyes.

"You're a traveller?" Winfortune continued. "Where from, may I be so bold as to ask?"

"From Scotland."

"Ay, you'll be for the great fight the morn in Fenny Horton. But if you come from Scotland you've come in on the wrong side of the town. What's your trade? You've the look of a schoolmaster, or a preacher, or maybe an attorney's jackal."

He drew the candle back.

"I'll tell you your trade. You're a liar. I watched you snowking in the yard and I set a trap for you, and you're caught. You're some damned kind of spy. Well, your travelling is done for a bit, my bonny lad. The Merry Mouth has no liking for you and your kind."

"You're an uncivil fellow. Open the door and I will go my way."

"Nay, nay. Here you are and here you bide. You'll get a night's lodging, though I'll not speak for the comfort of the bed, and maybe a long, long sleep."

The figure in the flickering candlelight was so uncanny that Nanty had to put a strong compulsion upon himself to choke down fear. But anger came to his aid. It would be ruin to all his plans if he were trussed up in the Merry Mouth, and prisoner before the battle was joined. Now he knew a different kind of fear, not of the man before him, but of his own failure.

"I require you to open that door," he said, and his voice was firm.

"I'm listening. Any more commands from your worship?"

Nanty measured his opponent with his eye. He was a big man, lean and bony, but he must be a score of years his elder. So far as he could see he was unarmed. There was nothing for it but the ancient appeal. He swept up a packet of papers and dashed it in his face, and at the same moment struck hard with his left hand at the gap-toothed mouth.

He found himself caught in a hug like a bear's. He was lifted from his feet, but crooked his legs in the table, while he belaboured the man's face with his fists. He might have been battering a smith's anvil. A great wrench dragged him from his anchorage, he felt himself swung in the air, and the next second his head crashed on the stone flags of the floor.

CHAPTER XVI

TELLS OF A SCEPTIC'S CONVERSION

ABOUT the time when Nanty was dropping from the wall into the stable-yard of the Merry Mouth, the cutter of that name was moving with the tide up a dark channel among mud-flats over which the waters were steadily rising.

The *Merry Mouth* had crossed the bar with the flood, its only piece of good fortune on the voyage. For, though the wind had not moved from the north-west, it had threatened to die away altogether. Off Flamborough Head the boat had lain becalmed for the better part of a day, and no seamanship of Eben Garnock's had been able to conjure up a breeze. The result had been black depression on the part of Harry Belses, and explosive irritation on the part of Sir Turnour. Eben, accustomed to the fickleness of the sea, had sucked his pipe in silence, and Mr. Dott, who had never before embarked on salt water, and had dreaded nausea, had been sunk in deep bodily content.

But that afternoon the wind had been brisk, and they had made landfall well before the darkening. Eben, who seemed to have a special sense and had been there before, nosed his way into the mouth of a narrow channel between the sand dunes, and the last light revealed wide samphire-covered flats gleaming pale under the steady lipping of the tide. Then darkness had fallen, and presently the *Merry Mouth* was at a rude landing-place, above which rose a black mass which must be trees.

"God's curse on all winds," Sir Turnour cried, stretching

his stiff limbs and shaking himself like a big dog. "Cranmer will have been gone for hours. Overy House is a mile off, and Overy's our mark. I'd give a thousand guineas to catch the hound before he leaves his kennel. Make haste, Eben, and tie up that damned boat of yours. If the fellow has left we must pick up his scent before it is cold."

Beyond the trees lay pasturelands, which to east and west became saltings where the tide crept among the little creeks. At first the four of them ran, Mr. Dott labouring heavily, but soon they dropped into a jog, and then into a walk, for the voyage had cramped their legs. They crossed rushy meadows, full of nesting snipe, and came to a mossy brick wall which fringed the park. After that they were on cropped turf, and made better going. They took no precautions, for under Sir Turnour's leadership they were not secret spies but brazen pirates new landed from the sea.

The house rose before them, a huge Palladian structure, with in one window far up a solitary spark of light.

Sir Turnour unbuckled one of his pistols and handed it to Belses.

"You're something of a marksman, my lord? Take that, but use it discreetly. Remember that Cranmer is my portion. No eavesdropping. Straight for the door."

There was a big old-fashioned bell which woke a babel of echoes. Sir Turnour rang it a second time, and a third, and then with his fists he beat a heavy tattoo on the door. "The place is a shell," he said. "I greatly fear that the birds have flown. Another minute and we break in by a window."

But, though there was no sound of feet inside, the door was suddenly opened, and in the crack was the light of a candle and a woman's white face. Harry Belses recognized it.

"It is her maid," he cried. "Mollison, where is your mistress?"

The voice was familiar to the woman, and she advanced the candle so that it shone on the wrathful visage of Sir Turnour, the gravity of Eben, the solemnity of Mr. Dott, and on Harry's face, which she knew well. The fear went out of her eyes, and her cry was of relief.

"Oh, my lord," she cried, "she is gone. Not an hour ago. She and the master and the others. I thought it was my lady returning, for she said that—"

"Let us have the story indoors," said Sir Turnour, "for this doorstep is a trifle conspicuous. Go first, Belses. The woman knows you and may think the better of us on your account. Phew! The place is dank. It has not been lived in for a twelvemonth."

The maid led the way into a big square hall, and the thin ray of the candle showed only a line of forbidding Roman busts and the rims of great dusky pictures. She lit a bunch of candles in what had once been a Spanish altar lamp, and the light made the place less ghostly. She was a thin, elderly woman, in felt slippers and a night wrapper.

"Mollison, my dear," said Harry, "you must forgive our haste. We come on your mistress's behalf, and you know me for a friend. Who is in this house?"

"I am alone," she said, and shivered.

Harry slipped off his greatcoat and put it over her shoulders.

"There! You will be warmer now. You say your mistress left an hour ago. Where has she gone? Quick, for it is a matter of life and death to her."

"I do not know. She did not tell me. I was to wait here till word came for me."

"It was you who at Hungrygrain gave this man a paper with words written on it," and he pointed to Mr. Dott.

She nodded. "It was by her order, and a difficult job I had of it."

"The words on it? The Merry Mouth. Where is that place?"

"I do not know." Her face had again become stupid with fear. "My lady—I do not think she knew either. I once heard her ask the master, and he laughed at her."

"When did you come here?" Sir Turnour demanded, and his peremptory tone frightened her into stammering.

"Last night—I cannot remember when—but it was dark. I was blind-weary with travel—and my lady, too. Blind-weary." Her voice tailed away into a moan.

"What scares you, woman?" Sir Turnour demanded. "We are your friends."

There was more spirit in her reply.

"It is my lady. I love her and she has gone from me. I am terrified for her sake. All this day she had a face like death, and when she left us she was weeping—and she does not often weep. She is threatened by some terrible thing—and I do not know—I cannot help her."

"Then by God we're all on the same side. No need for more talk. Action's the word, for Cranmer's on the road with an hour's start. We must get horses and follow. There'll be no beasts in the Overy stable—Cranmer would see to that. Wood Rising, curse it, is twenty miles off, so I cannot get my own. . . . Wait a minute. There's the Cup and Cross not a mile off. John Cherrybook has the inn, an honest fellow that can breed a good greyhound. John will find us horses. Is there any man about the place to take a message?"

"I do not know," the maid faltered. "I know no one on the estate. When I have been here before I have never left the house."

"Then, Eben, you must go. You know the inn?"

Eben nodded. "Ay, the auld house aside the mill dam?"

Sir Turnour scribbled something on one of his famous *cartes de visite*.

"Any conveyance he has got—curricle, gig, chaise, drag—any blessed thing so it be not a farm cart. Four horses if he can find them—if not, a pair—but they must have pace. John can put his hand on good blood. I've seen him win a race at the hunt meeting on a tit of his own breeding. There's ten guineas in John's pocket if he can fill the bill, beside a handsome price for the hire. Quick, man, not a moment's delay; and if John makes difficulties, fetch him up here for me to handle. . . . What are you after, my lord?"

Harry Belses had been talking apart with Mollison and

was now lighting two tall pewter candlesticks which she had fetched.

"I am about to make an inquisition of these chambers. Cranmer did not come here merely to give his wife a chance of bidding farewell to her old home. He had some damnable purpose which I intend to unravel."

Sir Turnour grunted. "I'm for forty winks, for God knows when I may get sleep again." He made a bed out of a great leather divan and a couple of rugs, and flung himself down on it. Mr. Dott did the same, and since the salt air had made him drowsy, was soon asleep. Unfortunately he snored, and did not desist till Sir Turnour stretched a long leg and kicked him in the ribs. After that for the better part of an hour there was peace.

It was broken by Eben's return and the inrush of wind from the hall door. Sir Turnour, a seasoned campaigner, was in an instant on his feet.

"The landlord will dae his best," Eben reported. "He sent his humble respects to your honour, and he'll get the beasts and a curricle for them to run in, but ane o' them is five mile off at a farm-toun, so it'll be the back o' midnight afore they're ready. His word was that he'll have breakfast at the Cup and Cross whenever we like to come, and that we can start if we're willing on the chap o' one. He kenned that Cranmer had been here, but nae mair, for it seems the body gangs and comes like a warlock, and though he's the mistress's tenant, he has little wark wi' the maister."

Sir Turnour consulted a massive watch. "Then I've time for another snooze," he said. But at that moment candlelight wavered on the staircase, and Belses and the maid appeared.

Harry's face was white in spite of the weathering of the sea winds. He had made some sort of toilet, and his fair hair was brushed neatly back from his brows. Again Sir Turnour was struck by his unpleasing resemblance to that young Lord Byron whom he did not love.

"Will you come with me, sir?" Harry said. "I have found something of moment, something which explains much."

Sir Turnour rose grumblingly to follow, and so did Mr. Dott, rubbing sleep from his eyes. Eben, after a word with the maid, joined them.

On the first floor was a pilastered upper hall, out of which opened a drawing-room and a library, and what seemed once to have been a boudoir. Much of the furniture was under dustsheets, and the great chandeliers were in linen bags, but in the library certain articles had been cleared. In particular the dust had been partly rubbed from a low bookcase intended for folios, which had also a long drawer. There was a big writing-table where the same thing had happened, and in the boudoir a little escritoire showed signs of recent use.

"Mollison has the keys," said Harry, "for these pieces of furniture are for her mistress's special use. Look at the contents, Sir Turnour."

In the drawer of the bookcase were plans and maps, which at first sight seemed innocent enough. But a second glance dispelled the impression. There was a chart of a patch of Suffolk shore with soundings marked, and certain routes traced and annotated. These annotations were in the French tongue, and seemed to be for the guidance of a hostile landing, for there were notes on the strength of the coast defences. The thing may have been a clever invention, but, to any one scrutinizing it, it had the look of the work of an enemy intelligence department, prepared with the assistance of an ally. There were other papers of the same kind, including an elaborate list of east coast garrisons, with details of proposed troop movements.

"You see the purpose, sir?" said Harry. "This house is searched, and the first thing to be discovered is this damning evidence. But that is only the beginning. Look at this," and he opened two drawers in the library table. In these lay piles of neatly docketed correspondence, some of it in a cypher, some in French in a variety of hands, but also various copies in English of letters to gentlemen of strange names mainly derived from Latin literature.

"I have skimmed some of these, and find them mostly

unintelligible. But that is because I have not the knowledge which would give the key. Others, the agents of His Majesty's Government, will possess that knowledge. I have no doubt about their meaning. They are the papers of a secret organization which has now served its purpose and has been disbanded. Mark you, many of them are in Mrs. Cranmer's hand, which I know well. To any searcher she will seem to have been the arch-intriguer. There is no line written by Cranmer, and I'll be sworn that there is no mention of him.

"But there is worse to come," said Harry, as he led the way into the boudoir. The paint on the panels was dim with age and dirt, the curtains were shabby, and the silk of the embroidered sofa was tarnished, but the gilt mouldings on the escritoire were bright, as if this were the only cared-for object in an uncared-for house.

"There is little in the drawers," he said, "but there is, of course, a secret receptacle which was not hard to find, and which any searcher would look for. Mollison had no key to it, so I broke it open." He plunged his hand into an inner crevice.

"Look at these. Not docketed and tied with silk, but hurriedly stuffed away as if in haste. They are a queer motley. Here are ill-written and foully ill-spelt scrawls from some of Cranmer's London vermin. No names, of course, but the Secretary of State could doubtless throw light on the correspondents. . . . And here is a letter from Mr. Perceval dated a week ago, making an assignation for tomorrow night."

"Tomorrow night!" Sir Turnour exclaimed. "Gad, we have run it fine. In a few minutes it will be *this* night. Where in the devil's name is John with his horses? Let us have done with this trifling and get us down to the inn."

"It is no trifling," said Harry. "I show these things to you to convince you of the reality of the lady's danger—and of her innocence. That last letter of the Prime Minister is enough to hang her. . . . And mark this other bundle. They are Cranmer's letters, the bungling schoolboy epistles of an oafish Northumbrian squire from whose mind treason is as remote as philosophy. Written to his wife, and treasured by her loving hands! They are sufficient to acquit Cranmer—and to destroy his lady. I take off my hat to his cunning. Are you a convert, Sir Turnour?"

"I am convinced of the man Cranmer's devilry."

"And of the lady's innocence? Would any human being with a guilty heart thus build up a damning accusation?"

"I am convinced of her peril. About her innocence I do not know. She may be a rotten-hearted baggage, albeit a fool."

"Yet she told the truth to Nanty Lammas on the hill. This is precisely what she feared. Had she been in any plot would she have thus exposed it?"

Sir Turnour's patience was exhausted. "A plague on her and all her works," he cried. "This folly is delaying us. It is Cranmer we seek, and whether his wife be guilty or guiltless is no concern of mine. Let's to the Cross and Cup, a speedy breakfast, and the road!"

He strode from the room, but at the top of the staircase came to a sudden halt. There was an alcove there which may once have held a statue. In that alcove there was a wicker basket, and in that basket there was a dog.

He was a small black cocker spaniel, and his wet nozzle and flapping ears were raised just over the rim of the basket. Sir Turnour stood over him.

"Now I wonder where you come from?" he said, and stooped down to scratch his head. The spaniel heaved his shoulders and made as if to rise, thought better of it, and reclined over the rim, lifting his melting eyes to Sir Turnour. He knew with the certainty of all wise dogs that here was a friend.

Mollison hastened to explain.

"It's Benjamin, sir—I beg pardon—my lord. Benjamin is my mistress's dog. She thinks the world of him, but he ain't allowed to go north in case he should be killed by them wild hounds at Hungrygrain. He has hurt his leg, poor little dear, and my lady was nursing him and fussing over him. She tied the leg up all nice and comfortable, and she gave me instructions about doctoring him, and money to pay for his bits of meat. Last word she says was, 'Mollison!' she says, 'be kind to Benjamin, and see that whatever happens he has a home.' " At the recollection the woman's voice trailed off into tears.

Sir Turnour continued to gaze at the dog, and as he gazed his mind suffered a violent dislocation. He was slightly ashamed, though he did not realize it, of his speech in the boudoir. His dislike of Cranmer seemed to make it imperative to include the lady in his disfavour. Also his pride forbade him to renounce an opinion which had been the cause of his still unredressed grievance against Harry Belses. But he was an honest man, and he was beginning to feel that his harshness could not be wholly justified by facts. Also he was a lover of all dogs, and the spectacle of this little beast, the last thought of his mistress as she went out into darkness and danger, suddenly melted his heart. He stooped again and patted the black head, and then turned to the others with a very red face.

"Belses," he cried, "I'm an oaf, a lout, a cur, a curmudgeon. Don't contradict me. I make you a present of these confessions to use as you please. I've been talking like a common blackguard. Damme, she must be a good woman, and I defy any man to deny it. A woman with her own neck in peril who would think about her dog is a fine woman, a great woman. Damme, she's a saint."

He stooped, poked in the basket, and felt the bandaged leg. The spaniel got to his feet and lifted the wounded paw.

"A deuced workmanlike job, too! Feeling pretty bobbish, little dog? Not much the matter, says you. Good job, for by God you're coming with us. You'll see your mistress in twenty-four hours, or my name's not Turnour Wyse. I'll wring Cranmer's neck for my own sake, but first of all I'll wring his nose for the sake of his lady. March," he cried, picking up the dog in his arms.

Then a thought struck him.

"Woman, have the goodness to kindle a fire," he told Mollison. "Belses, get that stuff out of those cursed drawers. We have five minutes to make a bonfire of it."

Harry protested. "Let us take the papers with us. There is evidence which may be useful"—but he was cut short.

"Burn every dangerous paper—that was my father's rule, and I mean to follow it. They are safer in charcoal than in the hands of meddlesome lawyers. Won't Cranmer be mad when he hears of it!"

Like a tornado Sir Turnour swept them downstairs, and on the hall hearth superintended the burning of an armful of documents. Like a tornado he swept them out of the house. "You stay here with a quiet mind," he told Mollison. "You'll have your mistress back to you within the week, and I'll be shot if you ever again clap eyes on your master. Benjamin is my particular charge, and I'm a good hand with dogs." Like a tornado he stormed across the park at the head of his little party, saying no word to them, but speaking much to himself. The part of champion of distressed beauty was new to Sir Turnour, but he would not fail in it for lack of zeal. The fury of his purpose was like an equinoctial gale.

John Cherrybook was a little man of forty, with the sallow skin of the marsh-men, and that indescribable rakishness of gait, that wise cock of the head, and that parsimony of speech which marks all those whose work is with horses. He knew Sir Turnour as a famous figure in the shire, and he had laboured to do his bidding. Horses he had got, a pair not over well matched, one a bay four-year-old with obvious good blood in him, the other a big rangy chestnut which looked more like a 'chaser than a roadster. They were waiting in an ostler's charge, and at the inn door stood an odd conveyance, a kind of rustic curricle seated for two, with immense red wheels and a pole which might have belonged to a stage-wagon. Indeed, the whole concern looked like a coach which had somehow lost three-quarters of its body on the road.

"Best I could do, your honour," said John. "The quads is

all right, barrin' that the bay is blind o' the left eye, and the chestnut a bit weak in the off fore. Bad firing's done that. You'll find they run nicely together, and if it's pace you wants you won't get a faster rig in Norfolk."

Sir Turnour examined the horses with a critical eye.

"A devilish bad match," he said. "It looks to me as if their paces would be like a peal of bells. And where in God's name did you find that Noah's Ark?"

" 'Twas Mr. Walcot had her built—him we called Mad Jack Walcot, wot broke his neck a year come Martinmas. I reckon 'twas the fastest turn-out in Jack's hands between here and Norwich."

"About as much balance as a hay-wain," Sir Turnour said sourly.

"Maybe so, your honour," John replied cheerfully. "But if you're for the south your honour knows that the roads is easy going, and on good roads them 'osses will make as light work of that curricle as if they was yoked to a baby-cart. Speed, you'll mind, was your honour's word."

"So be it. Now for breakfast."

The landlord ushered them indoors. "I've lit a fire in the blue room, and there's a tasty bit of mutton from the saltings. Follow me, gentlemen, and mind the step down!"

Sir Turnour was a stern commander. In a quarter of an hour he had bustled them through the meal, to the disgust of Mr. Dott. "Damn it, sir," he told him, "if you are still hungry, take a hunch of bread in your pouch." Then he gave his orders. "My lord and I will take the curricle. And the spaniel—I won't be separated from the dog. You two must follow as you can. I'm for King's Lynn. If Cranmer is bound for the Midlands he must pass through it."

Eben looked out of the window and appeared to be making a calculation. "In anither half-hour we'll get the ebb. Me and Mr. Dott, if a' gangs right, will be at Lynn as soon as yoursel'. The wind's better than weel. If ye're there afore us, wait on us; and if we're first, we'll wait on you."

"What's the sense of that?" Sir Turnour demanded.

"We're chasing Cranmer and dare not lose a moment."

"But how will ye chase him, sir? By speirin' along the road if such or such a party has passed that way? That'll dae fine as far as Lynn, for up to Lynn there's but the one road for him to take. But ayont Lynn he has the wind o' ye, and has the choice o' a dozen ways. We dinna ken where the Merry Mouth inn may be, but he kens, and he'll gang straight to it like a solan goose fleein' hame to the Bass. It's a slow job speirin' for a man that kens his ain purpose."

"And that's God's truth. But how will it help matters to forgather with you at Lynn? You're as much in the dark about the Merry Mouth as I am."

"I'm in the dark, but maybe Bob Muschat's no. Bob and the Professor has come by anither road, and it's possible—I'll no say mair—that they've found the whereabouts o' the Merry Mouth. If they havena', weel, the Almighty's no kind to us. If they have, Bob will try to get word to us. He kens we're at Overy, and he'll say to himsel', 'Eben will be lookin' for me, and there's but the one place for a tryst, and that's Lynn. Eben will come by sea, the wind and tide bein' what they are'—ye'll no fickle Bob wi' wind and tide. 'Eben,' he'll say, 'will mak a plan wi' Sir Turnour, for it wad be daft-like to part company, and someway or ither I'll find the hale clanjamphry at Lynn. So, kennin' what I ken, Lynn's the port to steer for.' Ye maunna pass Lynn, sir, till ye've seen huz and Bob."

"Ye seem mighty sure o' your friend's habits of thought."

"Aye. We o' the Free Fishers ken each ither's minds, or we wad be as feeble a folk as the coneys."

Sir Turnour burst into a laugh, which made the spaniel by his side shiver delicately.

"You're talking horse sense, and I'll do as you say. But by God I believe you've another reason. You and that pirate Dott are determined to be in at the finish."

A slow smile flickered over Eben's iron face. "I wadna say," he admitted, "but that my thoughts were workin' that road."

So while Sir Turnour and Harry Belses, with a little black dog at their feet, were bestowing themselves in the curricle, Eben and Mr. Dott were stumbling over a dark mile of saltings to the channel, where the *Merry Mouth* was beginning to strain at her moorings with the turn of the tide.

CHAPTER XVII

TELLS OF A GREEN LAMP AND A COBWEBBED ROOM

NANTY came to himself in a darkness which smelled foul and oppressive. It was a long time before he had any clear consciousness, for his head throbbed maddeningly, there was a band of hot fire above his brows, and he had fit upon fit of retching nausea. And when the physical misery subsided a little, he could not get his brain to work. His one active sense was smell, and he puzzled hopelessly over the rank odour. It seemed to him like a tan-pit, and he knew only one tan-pit—that beside the harbour at Dysart. He struggled to think how he had got there, and the effort brought back his sickness, so that he could only lie still and moan. Slowly he dropped again into uneasy sleep.

That second sleep wrought a cure. He woke from it with the wheel in his head almost stopped, and only a flicker of pain left above his brows. He was fully conscious now, and could search for his injury. This, apart from an aching shoulder and sundry bruises on his thighs, proved to be a deep cut on the left of his forehead, the blood from which had congealed into a big spongy clot. Cautiously he moved his head, and found that the action did not greatly pain him. He felt his arms and legs and they seemed to be unbroken. . . . Then, bit by bit, the recent past returned to him. He remembered nothing of the fight with Winfortune, but he remembered Winfortune's fierce eyes, and he assumed that there had been a fight. His head was a witness.

He had got thus far—that Winfortune had struck him down. The next thing was to find out where he was. The purlieus of the Merry Mouth were his last memory from his former consciousness, and he concluded that he was somewhere in its back premises. The smell of the place assailed his nostrils again. It was not a tan-pit—or a lumber-room of old harness—or a charnel-house—though there was rottenness in the air. It was black dark, so sight gave him no aid. . . . Then, as he sat up, his hands touched something soft on the floor, and the impact seemed to send up stinking wafts. He had it—there were fleeces and hides all round him. This was a country of sheep and cattle, and at one time the tenant of the Merry Mouth may have done some farming. . . . His mind was now clear; he was in a loft or attic, at the back of the inn, a prisoner, but an unshackled prisoner.

He had no means of striking a light, and his watch had stopped. It must be long after midnight, for he believed that many hours had been passed in unconsciousness or sleep, but he could not tell whether it was now early morning or broad daylight. It might be far on towards noon, or even later, for, though he felt no hunger, that might be due to the nausea following his wound. The thought maddened him, for here was the day of the crisis, and he was a helpless log. It got him painfully to his feet, and set him groping round the place. If his eyes were useless he could at least use his hands.

Stumbling over bales of rotting sheepskins he found his way to a wall. The skins were heaped far up on it, and in his effort to reach it he was half suffocated by the stench. Feeling his way along he came to a blank space, and his finger touched the jambs of a door. The door was a heavy thing, and it was securely locked. He ran his hand over it and reached one conclusion. He was not in any outhouse or attic, but in a principal room of the inn, for the edges of the panels were ornamented—he could feel the cup-and-ball pattern.

Beyond the door he found a wall at right angles where

there were no skins. He groped along it and judged the length to be more than twenty feet, so the room must be an important one. In that wall there were two windows, each at some considerable height above the floor, and each shuttered heavily and bolted with huge transverse bars, which fitted into sockets and were firmly locked. He tried to remember the look of the inn as he had seen it from the road. So far as his memory served him the windows on the ground floor had extended to within three feet of the ground, and on the first floor they had also been tall. This room was therefore not on the main front. It must be at the east or west end, and the windows must look down the road from Fenny Horton or over the oak grove.

These speculations were useless enough, but they served to keep his mind from raging at his complete futility. He had no weapon, not even a pocket-knife, with which he could assault door or window. He turned to the last wall and found it a blank space, though the floor was cumbered with old barrels and boxes. He had now explored all four walls, and a question suddenly occurred to him. There must be another door somewhere. If, as he believed, the door he had already found opened upon the garden or possibly upon a staircase, there must be another entrance, for a chamber so grandiose could not be a mere cul-de-sac. If there was a second door, it must be in the wall against which the skins were piled. It would probably be bolted like the others, but he must do something or go mad.

The first plunge into the skins brought back his nausea, and he had to sit on the floor and gasp till the fit passed. Never had he encountered so fiendish a stink, for at every movement of the pile an effluvia arose which took the breath from him. He persevered, and very slowly got sufficiently behind the skins to enable him to touch the panelling. . . . Suddenly his hands found a cornice, and he realized that here was a door, a narrower and shallower thing than the one he had just examined. He pressed it and found it unyielding. . . . Yes, but it might open inwards. Retching and half blinded, he set himself to remove the hides in front of it.

That task must have occupied him the better part of an hour, for the foul air and his wound seemed to have taken the pith from his arms. But he wrought steadily, for he had an odd illogical feeling that some hope might lie this way, that the fates which had thus far been kind to him would not leave him in the lurch. Especially he had the mystical belief that he was destined to meet Cranmer, and he could not meet Cranmer if he were caught like a rat in a stopped hole. His expectation grew so high that, when he had cleared the skins and made a passage to the door, he had to stop and take a grip on his nerves. His heart was behaving like a gate in a high wind, and he tried to steady himself with a prayer before he touched the handle.

The door was not locked—that was plain. The pile of hides had been considered sufficient to block it. But while the handle turned it would not open, though it gave ever so little, for the grime of ages had clogged its hinges. Nanty wrestled and strove till the sweat ran into his eyes. Three times he stopped to rest, and three times returned to the struggle. Then a sliver of wood seemed to crack at the top, and the thing swung back on him.

He listened with anxious ears, for the opening had been noisy; but he might have been in a cavern for all the sound there was. Before him there was the same black darkness, but by stretching his arms he found that he was in a corridor. . . . Suddenly a tiny spear of light shot out—a slender line close to the ground, and a star twinkled at the level of his waist. Some one had lit a light in a room in the corridor.

From that moment dated the resurgence of Nanty's courage. Hitherto he had been battling like a cornered animal, but now he was human again. A sponge seemed to wipe the film from his mind, and the energy of youth flowed back to his limbs. He was wary now, and resolute to face anything, for was not the way made miraculously plain before him? In that room was some one whom God purposed that he should meet. He tiptoed stealthily along the bare boards towards the door.

There was no sound from within. He turned the handle gently and peered inside. The light was ghostly, and he saw that it came from a big lamp with a green shade which stood on a dressing-table. That lamp must have been lit only a minute before, but the lighter had disappeared—gone out by the other door. The room was a bedroom, for there was an old-fashioned four-poster with dark damask curtains, and the table on which the lamp stood was a dressing-table. The windows were uncurtained and heavily shuttered. There were other articles of furniture—a big Dutch armoire, a chair or two, a couch, and in a corner a tall needlework screen. Once this had been a principal guest-chamber, for the plaster ceiling was delicately wrought, and inlaid with painted medallions now black with dirt.

The silent room with its eerie green light had the effect of checking Nanty's new ardour. He stood perplexed, listening for some clue, but no sound from the outer world came through the thick shutters. Outside it might be any hour—high noon, afternoon, evening—but here it was a timeless dusk, like some country under the sea. Nanty shivered, for it seemed a stage set and lit for any evil.

Suddenly there was sound—some one was approaching the other door, some one with heavy feet. Nanty slipped behind the needlework screen, and put his eye to a hole in it. He was less frightened now, for soon there must be a call to action.

A man entered, carrying a saddlebag which he flung on the bed, a big rough fellow with the air of the hills rather than of the fens—perhaps the man Sloan from Hungrygrain. He stood sideways in the doorway to let some one pass him. That some one was a woman.

She wore a short riding-habit and ill-cleaned boots, a bodice of some white stuff, and a loose green coat. On her head was a little tricorne hat, which might have been coquettish, had it not been pathetic. For the woman's air when she found herself alone was one of utter weariness and dejection, as if solitude at last gave her the chance of doffing a cruel mask. She pulled off her hat and flung it beside the saddlebag, but she did not go to the mirror on the dressing-table to arrange her hair. Instead she dropped on the couch, and lay back with her head resting on one of the arms and her eyes closed. Nanty from behind the screen saw her face in profile against the damask bed-curtains, and it was the face of a child tired beyond endurance, too tired to rest, almost too tired to breathe. Her cheeks had no longer the clear healthy pallor that he had seen on the hills, but were pale as a death-mask. Her limbs sprawled in an extreme listlessness. She might have been dead but for the slow rise and fall of her bodice.

Nanty slipped from behind the screen. Not for one moment could he eavesdrop on this tragic figure. For a second he stood looking down at the heavy, closed eyelids. Then, "Mrs. Cranmer," he whispered. "Mrs. Cranmer! Gabriel!"

Her eyes opened as if she were hearing voices in a dream. He spoke again, for he had got a glimpse of his own appearance in the mirror, and knew that he was no pretty sight, his forehead foul with congealed blood, his coat torn, face and hands black as a collier's, and his hair in wild disorder. She would think him a maniac unless reassured by his voice.

"Gabriel," he said gently. "Don't be afraid. . . . I'm here to help you. You remember . . . the hills above Yonderdale."

Her eyes were not startled—they were beyond the surprise of fear, and that in itself was the most tragic proof of her suffering. But for a moment they were mystified. Then it seemed as if a light flickered in their darkness. She sat up, and her hand flew to her hair.

"You are the Scotch professor? Mr. Lammas? Oh, what cruel fate has brought you here?"

"I have followed you. You spoke the words 'Merry Mouth' to me, and you wrote them on a paper for another. I sought for the place, as I was bound to do, and by the mercy of God I have found it."

She put her hands over her eyes.

"I am to blame," she moaned. "I am born to bring ill to my friends. Oh, why did you follow me? Why did I speak those foolish words?"

Her dejection was a goad to Nanty's spirit. For this little lonely figure he felt such an uprush of tenderness that it wrought on his head like wine. No more the leaden compulsion of duty for him, but the swift spur of youth and love.

"There's one friend of yours who wouldn't for worlds be elsewhere. I've had a weary time getting to you," and he told briefly of his journey. Life came into her face, but at the mention of Winfortune it clouded again.

"He thinks you are his prisoner in the room of the sheepskins? Any moment he may look for you there, and if he finds you gone he will . . . But no, he is away for the present—I saw him when we arrived—my husband sent him on an errand to see that the roads were guarded. . . . We have a short breathing-space in which to plan your escape."

"Not mine," said Nanty. "Yours, Mrs. Cranmer. If we can get you out of here there is a house nearby with friends in it, good women who will take care of you—"

"You do not understand," she said wearily. "I cannot go out of this place. I fear that you cannot, but for me it is beyond hope. I am the centrepiece in their game. This day, as you know, is a holiday in all the countryside. Tonight, and I think for most of tomorrow, it will be as empty of life as a grave. We have come from Overy, where my husband has done what he wished. He is here, and Winfortune and Sloan, and Vallance has brought his Londoners, and the roads are watched, and the place is a fortified castle. Tonight, as I told you, my cousin will arrive at my summons, and unless God works a miracle he will not go away. What can you do to help me, except share in my danger? You are weaker than the mouse with the caged lion."

"You have forgotten the fable," said Nanty briskly, "for the mouse released the lion. I have not come all this long road to fail you. There are others besides me, for there are three stout fellows at Overy, and there are two more that I sent off forty hours ago to guide them here. Any moment they may arrive, and your fortified castle will have its resolute besieger. One of those at Overy is Harry Belses."

"Harry," she cried—and her eyes had the same troubled maternal look that he had noted in them when he had first mentioned Belses' name on the hill. "Oh, I thought that Harry was safe out of my troubles. Who is with him?"

"Sir Turnour Wyse—the man who challenged him, and who has now transferred his wrath to your husband. I had rather not be the one who offended Sir Turnour Wyse."

She scarcely listened. "Harry at Overy!" she repeated. "He will see Mollison . . . and Benjamin. . . . We often talked of Overy. . . . Oh, Heaven send that he be not in time."

"Heaven send that he be. I think, madam, that you underrate the devotion of your friends. Harry has but the one thought, and that is to be at your side, for your own salvation and to frustrate your husband. When he and the others arrive they will blow this infamous plot into fine dust. They have still ample time. I do not know the hour of the day, for I have been living in the dark, but it cannot yet be the afternoon."

"You are mistaken," she said. "When I came here it was after four o'clock. Soon it will be twilight. We have but an hour or two's grace."

"God bless my soul! Then we must be up and doing. There is no way out by the road I came, for the outer door is locked and would resist a battering-ram. What lies that way?" And he pointed to the door by which she had entered.

"My husband," she cried. "Any moment he may come for me. Hist! There he is. Quick, behind the screen."

It was not Cranmer, but Winfortune, and he entered softly as if he had come on a private errand. He seemed embarrassed, too, and he took his hat from his head with an effort at courtesy. He stood with his back against the door, his long dark face like green bronze in the light of the lamp.

"The master will not be here for a bittie," he said. "I want a word with you, my lady, before he comes. There'll be rough work tonight, and rougher to follow. I've no ill will to you, for you've always treated me honest, so I make bold to say something in your ear."

He hushed his voice to a whisper.

"Master is sending you north—with Sloan. Things will be done tonight, as you maybe guess, which won't make the country healthy for some of us. Lucky we've got our bolt-holes waiting. But you, my lady, will be in the worst pickle, for you're the decoy to draw the chase."

He lowered his voice still further, and, leaning forward, spoke in her ear.

"You can't get away, for you aren't meant to get away. Sloan will ride cunning and save his own bacon, but you will be ta'en. It's not for me to question the master's plans, but here is one I cannot like. You're young, and there's some would call you bonny, and you've always been kind to Gibbie Winfortune, which is not as common a thing as it should be. So I've come here with a word for you. You'll ride through Huntingdon and bait at the Dun Cow. There you must give Sloan the slip and get to the house of Goody Twynham in Church Row. It'll be the dark o' the morning, but hers is a door that never shuts. Give her this writing from me, and she'll take you in and hide you so that all the King's army would never find you. It'll be coarse fare and coarser lodging, but you can bide safe with her till you get word to your friends."

He handed her a letter folded and sealed with a blob of green wax.

"That's the best I can do for you, my lady," he said, "and the master must never hear of it. I'm off, with a God bless you."

There were tears in Gabriel's eyes when the door had closed on him. She looked at the letter which had no superscription, and, as Nanty came out from behind the screen, she put it in her bosom. "I did not know," she said, "that

Winfortune had a kindness for me, and now I know it too late. Had I known sooner he might have helped me, for I did not dare to turn to any at Hungrygrain.

"There are elements of decency in the man," said Nanty, "which may stand him in good stead in the next world, but will scarcely save his neck in this. Have no fear—you are not going to Huntingdon, and will not need Goody Twynham's ministrations. Here, in this place, an end will be set to your tribulations."

Nanty's voice matched his words. He had got a sudden uplift of spirit which made it needless to counterfeit cheerfulness. This pale woman woke in him an utter certainty and a desperate valour.

She shook her head. "Your friends will not arrive in time. Overy is a long journey, and they may not be at Overy. What if wind and tide have delayed them? We travelled with relays of horses and we did not linger, and yet we have but new come, though we started yesterday evening and rode through the night."

"Then I must do the business myself," said Nanty.

She looked at him with wonder in her eyes, but no hope, and that nettled him.

"What can you do, my brave friend?" she asked. "You are a scholar and a man of God, and you have not been bred to struggle with ruffians."

"Nevertheless, I am young, and strong, and God will show me a way."

"You are unarmed among armed men."

"I have my right hand, and an exercised body."

Suddenly her face flushed, and her eyes, which had been open and fearful, clouded and looked down.

"I am armed," she said. "That is my one hope."

From a leather handbag she took a pistol.

"I have schemed and lied for this. It is loaded and primed and ready, and I too am ready. There is only one way. Innocent blood can only be saved by the shedding of guilty."

"Can you shoot?" Nanty asked.

"I have never tried, but no one will suspect that I have this . . . and I will be very near . . . and I do not think I can miss."

"Give it me," he said, and reluctantly she laid it in his hand.

It was a heavy two-chambered cavalry pistol. Nanty, who knew little about such weapons, fingered it, balanced it in his palm, and regarded it with a kind of awe. It was David's sling against the two-handed sword of Goliath. This frail woman clung to it as her solitary hope, and the pathos of her lonely valour smote on his heart till his eyes blurred.

"This is for me," he said slowly. "If your husband is to find an executioner I must be the man. It cannot be you, for it would break your heart. Once you loved him—and you have lain in his arms. His death at your hands would be a righteous judgment, but the memory of it would haunt you all your days."

"Give it me back," she cried piteously. "I have no length of days to look for. I shall soon be dead. Oh, you cannot be so cruel! It is my child, my only hope."

"I will use it, have no fear. You are right, Cranmer must die, but I will fire the shot. That is no work for a woman's hand, still less for a wife's. But it is work for me, since I have been divinely guided into this business, and must see it through to the end."

"But you cannot," she cried, her eyes wild and imploring. "I shall be alone with him. He is here and soon he will call me. You cannot follow. You will be taken—"

His uplift of spirit was now mated with a pleasant coolness.

"You forget that I have the master hand in this game. No one knows I am here, except Winfortune, and he thinks that I am lying helpless among the sheepskins. They mean to fire this place, and he doubtless imagines that I will burn with the rest of it. Wherever you are taken I will follow, and the chance of surprise is with me. I will cherish this pistol as I cherish my hope of salvation, and I swear when the time comes the bullet will go true, though I have to press the muzzle against his heart."

Suddenly she drooped before him, all the power gone out of her limbs. He caught her in his arms, he whose arms had never before held a woman, and the scent of her hair was like spring flowers. He pressed his lips to it.

"Courage," he whispered. "God will not desert us. In a little while—a very little—"

There was a voice from beyond the door.

"Gaby," it cried. "Come to meat." And when there was no answer, it sank into a mutter, "What ails the bitch?" and a step sounded on the floor without.

Nanty, behind the screen, saw the woman with a great effort compose herself and move to the door. He could not see the man beyond it. The door was left ajar, so he heard the footsteps in the short corridor. There was the creak of another door opening, a door very near at hand, and then silence.

He waited for a few minutes, while he thought out his course. Cranmer had talked of meat, so nothing was likely to happen for a little. He must not be premature, but must put off the decisive act to the last moment, to give his friends the chance of arriving. Oh, where in Heaven's name were all the others? If they did not come, he himself would be torn in pieces. Not the woman—Winfortune would protect her. And Mr. Perceval would escape—if Cranmer were dead, it was likely that his satellites would not have the nerve to consummate the plot, if indeed they knew of the proposed consummation. Cranmer must die, but at the right moment.

To his surprise he felt no fear. Coming events seemed to fall into a scheme as exact as a set of propositions in logic, and fully as abstract. He calculated his own chance of living much longer at about one in a hundred—if his friends did not come. The latter contingency he could not assess, for he had no data. He was not greatly perturbed. He had heard of drowning men living over again in their extremity their past lives, but his thoughts had no inclination to travel back. His one anxiety was that at the due moment he should not miss, and he lifted the pistol and pointed it at the green lamp. It was a heavy thing—if he missed he thought he could brain a man with the butt. He had a notably powerful right arm.

He must have waited a quarter of an hour before he decided to move. It would be well to find out what Cranmer was doing, for he must not miss his market. He pushed wider the door, and very stealthily tiptoed into the passage. The light of the green lamp followed him, and revealed a closed door at the end of it. He stood and listened outside it, but no sound came. The Cranmers were making a silent meal.

Suddenly he heard an oath, and then a cry followed, a small stifled cry like some small thing in pain. It was the smallness and feebleness of it that stabbed his heart and woke a primeval passion. He opened the door.

The light was dim, but it was not of lamps but of daylight. He saw nothing of the place save two figures, a man's and a woman's—the woman crouching as if she had been struck. They were preoccupied, and would not have noticed his entrance had not his boots slipped upon a grease stain on the floor. He recovered himself with a scrawl of nails on wood, and the man swung round to face him.

Nanty, having no confidence in his marksmanship, came at a bound within a yard of the man, held the pistol to his breast and pulled the trigger. The priming must have been faulty, for the hammer only clicked on the nipple, and before he could use the butt the man had leaped aside, and swung a heavy chair before him. The next second Nanty was looking into the barrel of another pistol.

He hurled his own weapon at his adversary, and at the same instant ducked his head. Something bright flashed in his eyes, and something hot and sharp furrowed his scalp. Now he was berserk mad, and sought only to grapple with his foe, though he carried a whole armoury. But the foe did not shoot again—instead he blew a whistle. He slipped like an eel from the clutch of Nanty's arms, and in a trice had put the table between them. In doing this he flung from him the third occupant of the room, who had tried to impede him.

Then things began to happen to Nanty with a furious speed. Other figures appeared on the scene, and a hundred hands seemed to be reaching for his throat. He struggled desperately, but a giddiness came over him, and something of the nausea he had suffered that morning. The next he knew was that his legs were being trussed up with ropes and his arms bound to his sides. He resisted no more, for the strength had gone out of him.

"Bring a lamp," he heard Cranmer's voice. "I must have a look at him."

The green lamp was fetched and set on the table, Nanty was placed in a chair beside it and Cranmer stood opposite him. "Get out till I call you," Cranmer told the others. "I want to be alone with this madman." Nanty had a confused vision of men with evil faces passing him. Winfortune was not among them.

The film of passion had gone from his eyes, and he was at last fully conscious of the scene. He was in a long room with three windows which let in the hazy purple twilight. Once it had been a noble apartment, but now cobwebs hung in the cornices and festooned the window shutters, and the panes were leaden with grime. The floor was of bare boards, and there was no furniture except the table and several chairs, and an ancient oaken cupboard of which the door swung half open on broken hinges. The remains of food were on the table, and a case bottle of brandy. Every detail Nanty saw with an acid clearness.

He could not see Mrs. Cranmer, for she was behind her husband, who stood opposite him beyond the table. Cranmer was plain in the green circle of lamplight. Unlike his wife, he had made his toilet since his journey from Norfolk, and was now a resplendent figure in a blue coat, a double-breasted satin waistcoat cut high, dark pantaloons and strapped boots. He was busy reloading a pistol and meticulously measuring the charges. His slim white hands moved in what was almost a caress, and as he wrought he spoke—not to Nanty, but to the figure behind him in the shadows.

"One of your many lovers, my dear? Nay, do not deny it, for he is the kind that would follow your *beaux yeux*. A most determined fellow. He would have made you a widow, but for an unlucky misfire. His foul hands were very near my throat. Your taste was always for the kennel, my sweet, but I had thought you might have chosen something cleanlier."

He laid down the pistol and looked at his watch.

"Seven by the clock. You are nearest the window, Sister Anne. Do you see anybody coming? I must finish with this carrion before eight. Eight, I think, was the hour our friend fixed, and, as befits the head of the State, he is a punctual gentleman."

He was looking at Nanty now. "You have only a matter of minutes to live, sir," he said. "You may care to satisfy my curiosity as to who in hell you may be. On the other hand, you may not. I do not press you."

Confidence and enterprise now utterly fled from Nanty's soul, and every spark of hope. He was confronting Cranmer, the man who had haunted his dreams, and the reality was more dreadful than his fear. The figure before him had a demoniac air of mastery. The oval of dead white face, exquisitely modelled, the horseshoe eyebrows, the mocking mouth, had a corrupt Satanic beauty. The eyes, large, luminous, and impenetrable, had lost all human quality; they were only windows from which looked out cruelty and unutterable hate. Here was no madman in the common sense, but an immense perverted genius. Strangely enough the picture of Sir Turnour Wyse flashed across his vision. Once he had detested that bluff figure, but now it seemed to embody all in the world that was sane and wholesome and human. Oh, why had his pistol missed fire, and not sent this spirit of the Pit to its begetter?

Mingled with his repulsion was the acutest fear. His early boldness had been only the valour of ignorance. His bonds supported him or he would have crumpled in a heap. It was terror that made him answer Cranmer's question.

"I came here last night," he said in a voice which trickled

from a parched throat and between dry lips. "I thought it an inn, and I looked for hospitality. I was attacked by a servant and struck down and locked up in a lumber-room. I found means of escape and groped my way in the dark to this room. Here I saw you in the act of maltreating a lady, and I—I—endeavoured to shield her."

Cranmer grinned, but with an unsmiling face.

"A very pretty tale," he said. "Some of it may well be true, but some of it is manifestly false. What kind of *preux chevalier* are you that draws on a man merely on the supposition that he has spoken harsh words to a woman? Will you swear, you that have so short a time to live, that you have never seen my wife before?"

Nanty remained silent, for it seemed hardly worth burdening his conscience with a lie. Cranmer spoke to the darkness behind him. "As I thought, Gaby dear. It is another of your lovers." Again he looked at his watch. "The quarter-past—nearly the twenty minutes. I will finish with him at the half-hour. Sister Anne, Sister Anne, do you see anybody coming?"

He stopped to listen. "I thought it was horses. It is only the swallows chackering."

Then he turned to Nanty.

"I am not interested in you, so I will let your past alone. Soon it will be all past, for at the half-hour I propose to kill you. You have a few minutes to make your peace with whatever gods you worship."

The words restored Nanty to his manhood. His life was over, with all its pleasant ambitions and quiet dreams. No more for him the blown sands of Forth, and the broomy uplands, and his snug little study in whose drawers lay the unpublished masterpieces of youth. He renounced these things with scarcely a regret, for his soul was consumed with a passion of pity for the woman whom he had so tragically failed. His brave words had been folly, and now she must tread her bitter road alone. To where? The answer to Cranmer's question came back to him out of the memory of his childhood's fairy-tales. "Only the wind blowing and the grass growing." For the youth of both of them wind and grass would soon be but the appurtenances of a grave.

Cranmer seemed to read his thoughts, for he spoke again. "You will have a pyre like an ancient Roman. In an hour or two this place will be crackling, and tomorrow it will be ashes."

He took his watch from his fob, and what he saw there made him stretch his hand to the pistol on the table. But as he moved the figure behind him rose and plucked his arm. "Justin," she cried. "Some one is coming. Listen. There are horses on the road."

He listened, and then shook her from him.

"You lie. The time is up, and I am a man of my word." Again he put out his hand.

Suddenly upon Nanty's strained ears fell the sound of a horn.

CHAPTER XVIII

HOW SUNDRY GENTLEMEN PUT THEIR TRUST IN HORSES

THE curricle with its oddly matched pair swung out of the inn-yard as the moon rose above the poplars. Sir Turnour sat in the best Four-in-hand Club style, head erect, shoulders squared, hands well down, elbows close to his side; but though immobile as a Buddha, his delicate fingers were testing the mouths of his cattle. Beside him Harry Belses was buried in the folds of his greatcoat, and in the narrow space at their feet, his head against Sir Turnour's apron, lay the spaniel Benjamin.

They passed through a sleeping hamlet, and debouched from the narrow parish road into the broader Lynn highway. Here Sir Turnour gathered up the ribbons and proceeded to try the quality of his horses. In a trot their paces did not match, and the curricle swayed unpleasantly, but when he sprung them into a short gallop they went better together.

"John was right," said Sir Turnour. "There's blood in both of them, and willing blood. No need for fanning or towelling or chopping 'em. But they're not a sweet pair to drive, and I don't know how the chestnut will last the course. He has come down too often over the sticks, I'll swear, and his off foreleg may give out before we're done with him. The bat-eyed bay is right enough. As they say on the road, he'll go through to hell or Hackney."

The highway climbed from the dim moonlit fields to a ridge of heath, where the going was sandy, and then to a long flat stretch between young woodlands. Harry, with no task to distract his mind, sat twining his fingers with impatience, and grudging every moment when they slowed down at a turn or an ascent. But Sir Turnour, immersed in his proper vocation, seemed to have shed his cares. His manner to Belses had hitherto been civil and stiff, but now it took on the freedom of a comrade. At a rise, when the waning moon gave a prospect, he pointed out the direction where lay his own house of Wood Rising; he expatiated on what he could have provided in the way of horseflesh had his stable been twenty miles nearer; he had tales of the road and of the local hunt, which he recounted as to a brother sportsman; and, as the pearly spring dawn crept up the sky, he burst into a song which he said his own father had composed in honour of a squirrel of a mare called "Iron Devil." "Hirondelle she was christened," he said, "but that Frenchy jargon won't go down in Norfolk."

With that melody disaster came upon them. The off horse, the chestnut, suddenly began to jib and hang back. "Scotching it," Sir Turnour cried. "What on earth is the matter with you? The road's good and the pace is easy." Then in a moment the animal seemed to go dead lame. He pulled up, flung the reins to Belses, and the next second was on the ground, passing his hands over the chestnut's legs.

"God," he cried. "I wouldn't have believed it! He has broken his off thigh—the bone's sticking through the skin. John Cherrybook is an infernal tailor not to have known of this, and I'm another not to have spotted it sooner. The poor devil must have been crocked at the start, and the mild springing I've given 'em has put the cap on the mischief."

Sir Turnour took off his beaver and surveyed the rosy heavens and the wide, empty landscape. "There's an inn a mile on," he said, "a rotten little beer-shop, but we may be able to pick up something. Something we must have, though it be a punch from the plough-tail."

So they limped on for a mile, Sir Turnour being wholly taken up with redressing the extravagance of the bay, who seemed to have developed a vile trick of shouldering. The beer-shop proved to be a very small place, with a half-obliterated sign which seemed to represent a rising or a setting sun. The landlord had to be fetched out of bed, and appeared in a red cotton nightcap, which was hastily doffed at the sight of Sir Turnour. He was very willing to help, for Sir Turnour's was a name to command respect, but he had only the one beast in his stable. "He's not what I'd offer to your honour," he said, scratching his head, "for I dunno as he has ever run in a gentleman's pair. He come to me by way of a bad debt from my cousin Barnaby. But fetch him out, Jim," he told his boy, "and let his honour cast an eye over him."

The horse which was produced was a big, wild-looking brown, all over flea-bites, with a queer uncertain eye. Sir Turnour examined him critically, and nearly had his hand bitten off, while a flying hoof grazed his thigh.

"Pace," he pronounced, "and the strength of an elephant, but as shy as a trout. Don't blame me, Belses, if he pitches us both into a field or kicks this contraption to pieces. But there's no choice before beggars. Put him to, my lad, and quick about it."

The harnessing was a dangerous business, and the innkeeper's final act was to strap over the horse's eyes a piece of black leather like the half of a coal-scuttle. "It's what we call moping," he explained. "It's the only way to drive a hot devil like him. A gentleman like your honour will teach him manners, and I'll be bound he'll carry you to Lynn."

They departed like a whirlwind, the bay disliking his companion and shying violently, and the new horse apparently determined to run a race on his own account. For ten minutes Harry believed that each one would be his last. The curricle swayed and swung like a bough in a gale, and had the road not been straight and smooth there would have been instant disaster, for they needed every inch of its breadth. So erratic was their course that, in spite of their fury, they covered the ground slowly. Sir Turnour's face turned from red to purple, and the muscles stood out in knots on his wrists. He used the whip vigorously, but not all his arts could produce a decent harmony. Finally he slowed down.

"I can hold the brute," he grunted between his clenched teeth, "but, damme, I can't drive him. Soon I'll be reduced to clubbing him, a thing I've never done in my life. He wants weighting—I could manage him in a coach if he were one of four—but in this cursed bandbox he plays cup and ball with me. I apologize, Belses, for giving you such a bucketing."

"Never mind me," said Harry. "All I want is to get on. Can't you spring them again?"

But to get on was just what Sir Turnour could not achieve. The pair would walk uneasily and could even manage a shambling trot, but any increase of pace set the new animal plunging and the bay misbehaving in tune. Fortunately, the road was empty, and they were passing over heathy downs where a prospect could be had for a mile ahead. But soon the country became more enclosed and populous, and farm wagons appeared on it, and now and then a bagman's trap; and at every such encounter there was a performance like a demented circus. . . .

The sun rose higher in the sky, the hours moved towards midday, and Harry's impatience grew beyond bounds.

"We have lost the trail," he cried. "Cranmer will have been out of Lynn by dawn, and we'll never get word of him."

Sir Turnour growled assent.

They passed no villages bigger than a hamlet, and no inn better than an alehouse, but Harry was urgent to stop at one of them and seek better horses.

"No earthly good," said Sir Turnour. "We're out of the horse country now, and could pick up nothing but a farm nag. Besides, I've never yet been beat by anything that walked on four hooves, and I'll be shot if I'll begin now. I swear I'll bring these two devils into Lynn, though I have my arms palsied—they're devilish near it now, I can tell you. Then they can go to the knacker's yard, which is all they're fit for. We'll get something better in Lynn."

"But we'll have lost Cranmer," Harry moaned.

"Very likely. But confound you, Belses, let's take one job at a time."

At last they saw before them a faraway strip of water with the sun on it, which was Lynn Deeps, and nearer the twin towers of a great church, and came into the outskirts of a town.

"We'll leave these brutes at the Three Tuns," Sir Turnour said, "for I'm not going to make a spectacle of myself with them on the Lynn cobbles."

It was very plain that the brutes were of the same mind, for as houses closed in on the road, and a boy appeared trundling a hoop, and a bricklayer with a hod, and a posse of school-children, they became all but unmanageable. The last hundred yards of the journey saw a crab-like motion which took up the whole width of the street. The curricle came to a standstill with the bay on the pavement and his nose inside the inn door.

"Get to their heads," Sir Turnour shouted to a couple of ostlers who, recognizing him, pulled their forelocks. "Get them out of my sight." He and Belses tumbled off different sides of the vehicle, so cramped and bruised that they all but fell on their faces. Sir Turnour felt his forearms as if he were uncertain whether they still belonged to his body. . . . Then the two saw a sight which caused them to forget their aches. For on the side-walk stood the square figure of Eben Garnock, and Bob Muschat in his borrowed blacks, and the wondering Mr. Dott, and Jock Kinloch with a grin of welcome broadening into amusement.

"We have forgathered, sir, as ye observe," said Eben. "Man, I'm blithe to see ye. I was feared ye had fallen by the road."

Sir Turnour strode into the inn, beckoning the rest with a nod over his shoulder. "A room," he cried to the landlord, "and something to eat. Something to drink, too—ale in buckets—for my throat is like the nether millstone." He shepherded the others before him, and, when the ale came, buried his head in a quart pot.

"Now," he said, "what news? Good, I hope, for we've need of it. My lord and I have been enduring the tortures of the damned behind two fiends of the Devil's own siring." He looked round the company, and his eyes fell on Jock, and it was Jock who took up the tale.

"Eben and Mr. Dott arrived two hours ago," he said. "Bob and I have been here since yesterday morning waiting for you, and an anxious wait we've had."

"Where is Mr. Lammas—the Professor?"

"He stayed behind to keep guard. A place called Fenny Horton. We have found the Merry Mouth inn."

"The deuce you have!" Sir Turnour cried, and as Jock expounded the whereabouts of the inn, he got to his feet and strode excitedly about the floor.

"Fenny Horton! I know the place. Not far from Landbeach, where old Madame Horningsea roosts. That is forty miles off—nearer fifty—and the fen roads are not like Norfolk. I know their foul 'droves' as they call 'em, which they plough up when they want to mend 'em. Six inches of black dust and as hummocky as a fallow. But at any rate we know where to point for. We'll have Cranmer out of his earth by tomorrow morning."

"Tomorrow will be too late," said Jock. "This is the day. Tonight is the night." And he told of the great fight at Fenny Horton, at that moment in full blast, of an empty countryside, and of all things secluded and guarded for a secret purpose. He told his tale diffidently, for he knew that Sir Turnour was incredulous about Mrs. Cranmer's revelations.

But Overy had made the sceptic a believer.

"And that poor woman is alone!" he cried. He looked at the spaniel Benjamin, which sat on its haunches gazing at him with languishing eyes, and the sight stirred him to action. "Where do you say Lammas is?" he demanded.

"God knows," said Jock. "I hope he be not in peril of his life. Nanty's a paladin before he's a professor."

Sir Turnour plucked his watch from his fob.

"Half an hour after midday! Your Merry Mouth is five

hours off by the best going—more, for the last part of the way will be a cart track. It means turning from the London road at Ely and bearing west across-country by the Cottam River. There's no great choice of horses in Lynn fit for that pace, and we daren't risk bad cattle. A moment, sirs! At two sharp the Rover Mail starts from the Crown with a team of short-legged cats as prettily matched as Mr. Bicknell's greys on the Holyhead road. I've handled 'em more than once, and I'd wish for none better. It's horsed down the road by old Jabez Bellwether, who has a conscience and an eye for blood. . . . By God, gentlemen, there's but the one way of it. We must play highwaymen and take possession of the Rover. Robin Trimmle will be driving her, and Abel Cross is the guard, both of 'em friends of mine. I have purchase enough in this shire to condone the villainy, and if we save the life of His Majesty's Prime Minister, how the deuce should His Majesty's Post Office complain? Swallow your food, sirs, and let us be off. It's a plaguy long mile through Lynn streets to the spot beyond the South Gate where I hope to have a word with Robin!"

"Sir, I do not like it," said Mr. Dott, alarmed by the fire in the baronet's eye. "Cannot you persuade the proprietor and get lawful possession?"

"Not a chance," said Sir Turnour cheerfully. "Old Utterson is as stiff as a poker, and would keep us arguing till midnight. We're six stout fellows, and might's right in a good cause. Nothing for it but to hold up the Rover. I reckon to persuade Robin and Abel."

"But the seats will be taken. There will be no room for us."

"Then, by Heaven, we'll decant the passengers! Come along. It's the Saturday market, and all the wharf side will be packed like a barrel of herrings. I know the place, and can lead you by quiet streets. Belses, you walk with me, and the rest scatter and follow. Pick up the dog if he looks like straying. Our baggage can abide in the one *Merry Mouth* till we have done with the other. Sharp's the word, for it's neck or nothing."

Half an hour later His Majesty's Mail, in all the glory of crimson paint and gilding, scarlet-coated guard and emblazoned royal arms, drew up sharply at the first turning out of Lynn on the London road. It carried but three passengers—a young gentleman on the box seat, and, inside, a very pretty young lady and an elderly man who held on his knee a portfolio of papers. By the wayside, in the lee of a copse, stood an odd little company of six.

The driver saluted with his whip in response to the imperious summons from the roadside.

"Do I see Sir Turnour Wyse?" he asked. "How can I oblige 'ee, sir?"

"You see Sir Turnour Wyse, and you can oblige him mightily. I and my friends are travelling with you, Robin."

"Have you your tickets took, sir? There's no other names on my waybill."

"No; we're shouldering! We're coming with you, for it's a matter of life and death. When I tell you it concerns His Majesty's service, knowing me you'll take my word for it."

The driver looked embarrassed, and Abel the guard climbed down from his perch.

"I dunno as I can, Sir Turnour. . . . You see, it's amazin' irregular. I've got my orders, and I knows my dooties—"

"Of course, of course. But I promise you it will all be set right. You have my word for it that Abel and you will not be blamed. The responsibility is mine, and you never heard of me backing out of a promise."

"But . . . but . . . I'm bound to say it, Sir Turnour. Supposin' my dooty compels me to refuse?"

"Then my duty will compel me to pitch you off the seat and take the ribbons myself. Call it a highway robbery. I summon you to stand and deliver."

Robin's broad face expanded into a grin at words which at last he understood. "Well, sir, if you puts it that way, I'm bound to give in. Abel, you just present your blunderbuss at his honour for form's sake, so as we can say we made a fight of it. It ain't loaded."

"Good," said Sir Turnour, "and now, for form's sake, we must make room for ourselves. Madame," and he took off his hat with a flourish to the young lady whose face showed signs of alarm. "You are half a mile from the Duke's Head, from which, in one hour's time, the coach called the Norfolk Hero will carry you to whatever destination you desire. I grieve to incommode you, but I and my friends are on a desperate errand which involves the safety of the realm, and we are forced to desperate shifts."

"But I will be too late," she said. "Aunt Tabitha was to send her carriage to meet me five miles beyond Downham, and I was to travel by the Mail."

"Your aunt's horses, my dear, will take no harm from an hour's wait in this brave weather, and I assure you we will take all the harm in the world if we do not instantly start."

She still looked doubtful, but the young man who had descended from the box seat proved an unexpected ally. He was her brother, a member of the University of Cambridge, and of a sporting inclination, as his cravat and waistcoat revealed. Also he recognized Sir Turnour, who had once been gracious to him at a cocking at Holkham.

"Nonsense, Sophy," he said. "Aunt Tabby's fat geldings are not worth a thought, and coachman Rufus will be glad of an extra hour in The Grapes. Sir Turnour, I have the honour of a slight acquaintance with you, and I think you know my father, Squire Petting of Langrish. Sophy, I present to you Sir Turnour Wyse. There's no good Norfolk man who won't bustle to oblige Sir Turnour. If he says his business needs haste, then other business must wait."

The attorney proved more difficult. He flatly refused to budge, maintaining his right as a lawful traveller, quoting the regulations for a Royal Mail, and alleging an urgent duty that night in Cambridge. With the help of young Mr. Petting, Sir Turnour very gently lifted him from the coach and set him by the roadside. His portfolio burst open and his papers flew out, and as he collected them he threatened a variety of actions in tort.

"You'll stand by me and Abel, Sir Turnour," said the alarmed Robin, to whom the legal jargon seemed ominous.

"I'll stand by you against any attorney in England. Hang it, man, don't look so glum. You're more likely to get a letter of thanks from the Government for this than a wigging. Let's see to the harnessing, for we have the devil of a course before us."

Very carefully Sir Turnour went over every detail. He examined the bitting and the coupling, saw that the traces were the proper length, the pole-chain in order, the curb properly adjusted, and the collars, pads, and harness fitting sweetly. He made certain that each buckle and strap was in its right place. Then Eben and Bob and the dog Benjamin ensconced themselves in the inside, where they promptly went to sleep, while the others mounted to the top. Sir Turnour took the reins and gave the team the office. But first he looked at his watch. The time was two o'clock.

Fifty miles away at the same time Nanty had come out of his dazed sleep and was beginning to feel his way round the room of the sheepskins. . . . Miss Kirsty Evandale at Landbeach had spent an unquiet forenoon. Nanty's failure to return the previous night had filled her with anxiety, and, when no news had come of him in the morning, she had been the prey of acute forebodings. As he had predicted, the fight at Fenny Horton had drained the men from the estate. There was not a groom or a gardener left on the place, and in the house only the old butler remained and a consumptive footman. About eleven o'clock she had walked to the Merry Mouth inn, and had found it apparently shuttered and empty. She could not, in spite of much knocking, find the old woman who had received Nanty, though she thought she had a glimpse of a wicked old face at an upper window.

Two hours later she had walked in the same direction, but some instinct had kept her inside the park, and had taken her to a knoll from which she could overlook a patch of road near the inn. There she saw what she feared to see, the bustle of an arrival. Horses were being led round to the stable-yard, and she saw more than one figure by the inn door, though she was too far off to make out the details. She noted that their movements were quiet and furtive, and in a few moments the inn had swallowed them up, and was again a blind face in the sunlight.

The spectacle confirmed her worst fears. That was happening which Nanty had foretold, and not a shadow of doubt remained to her. Nanty, she feared, was dead, the victim of his foolhardy courage. Somewhere in the inn was an unhappy woman, an innocent and unwilling murderess. Some time in the dusk or in the dark would come the victim.

There was nothing she could do, and she wept at her impotence. To her aunt she wearily recounted what were no longer fears, but awful certainties.

"There's just the one thing possible," she said. "I might warn Mr. Perceval. There are horses in the stable, and I could scour the road if I only knew which one he will take. I know what he looks like, and could not miss him. He may come by either of two roads, by Cambridge or by Huntingdon—I can't see any third way if he is coming from London, and poor Mr. Lammas was certain he would. But I can't be on two roads at the same time."

Then Miss Georgie surprised her niece, and maybe surprised herself.

"You're not the only one, my bonny lamb. If there's two roads to ride, there's two folk here to ride them. I'm an auld woman, but you'll admit I'm an active one, and I can back a horse as well as ever. What hinders you to take the one road and me the other? I'll wager if I see anything in the living image of the Prime Minister I'll have it stopped, for I can screech like a wild cat."

So about the time when Sir Turnour took the reins of the Rover outside the town of King's Lynn, two ladies were busy in the stables of the manor of Landbeach. Only one lady's saddle could be found, so Miss Kirsty rode astride. They spun a crown to decide which roads they would take.

*   *   *

Till his dying day Harry Belses remembered the hours which followed, when in the golden afternoon, through a world of essential light and clear spring shadows, he moved swiftly to the place of destiny. The fear which had been consuming him for days, which had made the time on the boat a purgatory, and the hours on the road that morning a hell, seemed to have left him. He had the sense that he was in the grip of fate, and must wait humbly on the pleasure of the gods, since all that man could do had been done. He did not look at his watch, he paid no heed to Sir Turnour's shouted bulletins which chronicled their speed; the smooth, swift movement lulled his aching body into peace and was like an opiate to his nerves. He did not even pray, as he had done fervently for so long. His inward vision was filled with a woman's face, and, whereas the same vision had hitherto shown him tragic eyes and the pallor of death, it now revealed what he had first loved in her, a spring-like innocence and an elfin mirth. He was comforted, but every now and then a pang of terror shot through his heart at his comfort. For the end was not yet. The moment of crisis was still to come.

Sir Turnour had often driven this road, and knew all the times allowed to the stages. He took five minutes to feel the quality of the team and then he handled what he had described as "short-legged cats" in a way which drew from Jock Kinloch a continuous mutter of praise. They were so perfectly balanced that the coach ran on even wheels, the surface was good, the hills easy, and for miles he sprung them in a steady gallop. The horn of Abel the guard advised the toll-keepers well in advance, and there was no slowing down. At the first change, which was done in fifty seconds, a team of blue roans replaced the greys, bigger animals with more promise of pace. "I've knocked three minutes off your time on that stage, Robin," Sir Turnour observed, "and, please God, I'll knock five minutes off the next. We must stretch 'em while the going's good, for the Lord knows what we may find after Ely."

"There's nothing to fear after Ely," said Robin. "We reckons Ely to Cambridge one of the best bits of road, unless the waters be out."

"We're not going to Cambridge," was the answer. "We're for Fenny Horton by the Cottam Dyke."

Robin cried out. "That ain't no road for the Mail. It's one of the wust of the droves."

"All the same it's our road. You cut out Cambridge, but I'll promise you you'll be at the Golden Cross in London up to time. No trouble for you on that score, though the Cambridge folk may complain."

Jock Kinloch sat in an ecstasy of content, watching such coachmanship as he had never dreamed of. Mr. Dott, having overcome his first terrors, fell asleep, for he had much leeway to make up. Harry, wrapped in his own dreams, was only dimly conscious of the celestial landscape through which he swept. Now they were between hedges white with blossom, and in aisles of chestnut just breaking into bloom; now in lush green meadows with sheep and cattle at graze; now skirting a slow stream, where dark currents drowsed among pollarded willows. They passed through hamlets of ancient brick houses festooned with honeysuckle, and through the cobbled streets of little market-towns. And sometimes from a rise they had a glimpse of infinite grassy levels studded with windmills and seamed and laced with shining waters. The afternoon was beginning to mellow towards evening when the white tower of Ely Cathedral rose before them over the plain like a lighthouse at sea.

The change at Ely took time, for Sir Turnour descended and examined afresh every detail of the harnessing. He shook his head over the team, two heavy chestnut wheelers, a black off leader, and for the near leader a big rawboned grey. "The worst match we've had," he said, "for the most critical stage. I don't like the look of that grey. Too young and raw."

Robin also shook his head.

"That's Empson's way. He's the poorest horse-master on the road—always looking to skimp a penn'orth. We don't complain, because it's an easy run to Cambridge."

"It won't be an easy run to Fenny Horton," said Sir Turnour grimly, as he remounted the box.

Their journey now lay through a different land. They left the turnpike for a road which followed a wide dyke, and which was so uneven that it shook Eben and Bob out of their slumbers. To Jock it seemed that the coach, which on the highway had been an elegant, almost a dainty, thing, had now suddenly become top-heavy and out of proportion to the landscape. Down in these flats among the long grasses and the water-weeds it looked a precarious, lumbering contrivance, which any moment might stop from its own unwieldiness. Sir Turnour had difficulties with his cattle, for the road was narrow, and the near leader was only half broken to harness. It had perpetually to be checked as it tried to break its pace into a canter. As for Harry Belses, he noticed none of these things—only that the sun was getting ominously low in the west, and that the twilight was drawing near.

Presently, to Sir Turnour's relief, the road climbed to the edge of a big drain which had been embanked high above the surrounding flats. On one side was a steep descent to marshy fields, and on the other the dyke, carpeted with water buttercups and forget-me-nots and the broad leaves of water-lilies. The surface of the track was inches of powdery dust, and now and then came deep hollows, but it ran as straight as an arrow, and it had no toll-bars or side-ways. Few men would have dared to take a coach along such a road at the speed at which Sir Turnour took it, the more so as the team was not running sweetly. A jib on one side would have sent it into the water, and on the other down forty feet of slope into the marsh.

For the first time that afternoon Sir Turnour showed signs of impatience. He looked at his watch and then at the darkening sky. To Robin the driver he said: "Ten miles to

Fenny Horton—five or six to the Merry Mouth inn, which is short of the town. There we leave you to make up speed on the Huntingdon turnpike. I daren't spring 'em as I would like, partly because of this cursed black soil and partly because of the grey. He's only waiting his chance to get to his tricks."

"Pray God he don't," said Robin, who sat with tight lips. "If I didn't know your honour for the best whip in England, I'd be out of this here concern to save my neck. I've never driven before along the rigging of a roof, and s'help me if I ever does it again."

About this time Nanty was fumbling at the door which led into the cobwebbed room where the Cranmers were at meat. . . . Ten miles away on the road from Cambridge a carriage, with four horses and postilions, was moving northward, a carriage in which sat a slim, elderly gentleman, much wrapped up, for the evenings were chilly and his throat was weak. Beside him sat a younger man, who had the discreet air of a secretary. Suddenly the carriage slowed down, there was a cry from the postilions, and the noise of a ridden horse violently reined up. The elderly gentleman thought for a moment of highwaymen, till he was reassured by the rider's voice, which was clearly that of a woman.

A head most curiously wrapped up in shawls looked in at the window, and out of the shawls an old face showed in the waning light. The voice which spoke had a rasp and a burr which reminded the occupant of the speech of his friend Lord Melville.

"Are you Mr. Perceval? Him that's the Prime Minister? Well, I've a word for you from Landbeach, where I'm biding with the auld Leddy Horningsea. Your cousin, her they call Mrs. Cranmer, is in a sore trauchle. Her scoundrel of a husband is proposing the night to make away with you, and you've been brought here for that purpose, and the poor lassie has no power to prevent it. But word came secretly to us of the ploy, and my niece—that's Miss Christian Evandale, whom you've maybe heard of—her and me came out to warn you. So back you go where you came from. It's not you and your postilion lads that can cope with desperate men."

Mr. Perceval had faced this kind of thing before. One glance at Miss Georgie's face convinced him of her honesty. He hopped from his carriage.

"There is no evil which I would not look for in Justin Cranmer. But my cousin told me she would be alone at the Merry Mouth, and I had many things to discuss with her. I do not know your name, madam, but I know Lady Horningsea well, and I am deeply beholden to you. I shall most certainly continue my journey, for I cannot fail the unhappy child. But I am fortunately in a position to protect myself.

"Unharness the leaders," he told the postilions. "Hibbert," he told his secretary, "take one of them and ride back to the Birdcage Inn. We passed it ten minutes ago. There are ten of our mounted runners there, who have come down on Sir Giles Wintringham's business. Bring them here—the Prime Minister's order. Meantime, madam," and he bowed to Miss Georgie, "I invite you to pass the time of waiting for our escort over a small collation. I have brought the materials for supper with me, for I did not trust a Fenland inn. . . ."

Sir Turnour held his watch close to his eyes, for the dusk had deepened from amethyst to purple. "I must spring 'em again—at all cost—'tis devilish late." And he tickled the leaders under the bar, causing the grey to close up to his neighbour. To Jock, who was watching, it looked as if he was about to stretch them into a gallop, when suddenly there appeared in the road a wooden post, not in the middle, but about three-quarters of the distance between the drain on the right and the steep descent to the left. There was room enough for the coach in careful hands to pass between the post and the water, but, as luck would have it, the near leader, the grey, chose that moment to edge away from his partner. He was going to the left of the post and nothing would prevent him. Jock clutched the rail, confident that the next instant coach and horses would be precipitated down the bank.

But in that instant the impossible happened. Sir Turnour saw that the leader's bar would be caught by the post. He had his wheelers tight in hand and sharply drew back their reins, causing them to throw up their heads, which, acting on the pole chains, jerked the bar over the post's top. At the same moment, hitting the near wheeler, he brought the splinter-bar clear. Neither coach, horse, nor harness touched the post. As Jock drew a long breath of relief, he saw, a mile or two ahead, a gleam of light reflected in water.

"By God, sir," Robin gasped, "that's the nicest bit of coachmanship I ever seen. An everlasting miracle, I calls it."

"Simple enough," said Sir Turnour coolly, "if you keep your head and know the meaning of proper harnessing. I couldn't have done that if the pole chain hadn't been the right length—and the wheelers properly curbed up. That's why I took such pains at Ely, and it's the truth I'm always preaching to you professionals."

Then he too saw the light ahead.

"That's the Merry Mouth," he cried. "That's the glow of the windows in the mere. There you drop us, and get you on to Huntingdon and ask no questions. I owe you ten guineas for this performance, Robin, my lad, and five to Abel. Now for a bit of pace down the straight."

The close shave at the post seemed to have pulled the team together, for the last miles were covered at a gallop which would have been fast on the Bath road. The track left the dyke side and descended into the highway almost opposite the lodge gates of Landbeach. The team turned neatly to the right, and, cheered by the better surface, swung unerringly through the dark of the trees to where the glow from the inn made a ribbon of light.

But the miracle of their escape and the quickened speed produced no exhilaration in the four men on the top of the coach. Suddenly there descended upon them a sense of fate which caught the breath and chilled the heart. The light towards which they were rushing was a bale fire which might beacon desperate things. It was like riding a finish to death rather than to victory. Sir Turnour knew at last the meaning of fear, and, being unfamiliar with the thing, could only set his jaw and curse silently. Jock Kinloch clutched at the rail and kept his eyes fixed on the light ahead, choking down an inclination to scream. Upon the town-clerk of Waucht there fell a sickening apprehension of horror unknown to his sober life. Harry Belses, with pale lips, fell to praying.

Then to Abel the guard came an inspiration. He plucked from its case his yard of tin and blew a rousing blast. That was the sound which Nanty heard as he sat pinioned in the chair.

CHAPTER XIX

OF THE MEETING OF LOVERS AND THE HOME-GOING OF YOUTH

NANTY watched the hand move to the pistol. Cranmer took a long time about it, for he was enjoying himself, and he had still nearly a minute by his watch before the half-hour struck. The echo of the horn was in Nanty's ear, but it might have been a horn of elfland for all that it meant to him. He was shut up in a prison with death. His own fate did not trouble him, for he had that strongest provoker of courage, a burning anxiety about the fate of another.

Cranmer's hand lifted the pistol, and as it did so two other hands closed on it. Gabriel had come out of the shadow—Nanty saw her face white in the green lamplight—and she flung her slight weight upon her husband's arm. Her clutch was so desperate that he could not shake her off. He brought round his left hand and pushed her face away from him, but he did not loosen her grip. Her neck must have been almost dislocated, the slim arms were at a cruel tension, but still the fingers held. Nanty, in a cold sweat of misery, saw the woman he loved in an extreme of bodily pain.

Cranmer saw it too, and there was that in the sight which roused the fiend in him. Perhaps he had never before physically maltreated her; his hate had revealed itself in subtler tortures. But now the sight of her suffering was like the smell of blood to a tiger. To Nanty's eyes his face lost its evil beauty, for it lost humanity. Suddenly the features seemed to dissolve and blur and the eyes to become pits of fire. It was now the face, not of a devil, but of a maniac.

He wrenched his right hand loose and held the pistol at her breast. He had forgotten his deeply meditated plan, by which he had reserved her for a long torment of public shame. He was a wild beast now, hot with the lust to kill. Her arms were bound by his left arm to her side, and the pistol barrel was an inch from her heart. His mad eyes were waiting to exult over her mortal fear.

But fear she showed none. There was no drooping despair now about her, for she was a free woman again. She faced him squarely, her eyes mocking and challenging.

Nanty saw her purpose. She was luring him to shoot, in the hope that her death might be the salvation of the other. The pistol was single-barrelled; if it had to be reloaded there was the chance of interruption, of some miraculous deliverance. He read her soul, and he went crazy. His bonds made movement impossible, but he had his voice. He shouted insults at Cranmer, the hoarded insults which had been shaping themselves for days in his subconscious mind. His voice rang in the silent place with a fury that might well have brought his enemy tooth and claw upon him. But the enemy did not turn his head. He was savouring the obscene delight of the torturer, holding the woman in his madman's grip and gloating over her helplessness. . . .

The shot rang out. . . . Nanty's bursting eyes saw Gabriel stagger backward and collapse on the floor. But he saw another thing. Cranmer had dropped over the arm of a chair and hung limp, while his pistol clattered on the boards. . . .

Then came a riot of confusion. Gabriel, not dead, but living, was kneeling before him. She was tearing at his bonds with weak hands. "Quick, quick," she muttered, as she wrestled with the knots. "Let us get away. God has smitten him. Quick, oh, quick!"

Then a hand not hers slit the cords. Nanty's cramped limbs had no power in them, and he would have fallen out of the chair if strong arms had not sustained him. He dimly recognized that he was being held by Harry Belses.

A face rose like the moon in the green lamplight—a rosy but a solemn moon. He saw that it was Sir Turnour. He was returning a pistol to the case at his belt.

"You have come," Nanty cried. "Oh, thank God! Thank God!"

Sir Turnour was looking at the figure huddled in the chair. "Stone dead," he said. "Pretty shooting in this foul light. It wouldn't have done to miss, or it would have been the lady's turn. Don't let her look this way, for it ain't a pleasant sight. Hold her, Belses. I'll get this thing out of sight. Gad she's going to faint."

But Gabriel did not faint. While Nanty, relieved from his bonds, had leaned forward on the table for support, Belses had taken her in his arms. She seemed to be half in a stupor. She stroked Nanty's face as if to convince herself that he was alive, and then looked blindly round the room. Suddenly she broke from Belses, ran round the table, and stood looking down at her dead husband.

"I killed him," she sighed, and her voice was like a sleep-walker's. "He was mad, but he was my husband, and I killed him. I tried to force the pistol round so that I could shoot him. I did not know I was so strong. . . . Oh, I did not know."

"Nonsense, my dear," said Sir Turnour. "I shot the black-guard just when he was going to pistol you." He picked up Cranmer's weapon from the floor. "See, it is still loaded. Will that convince you?"

But Gabriel was beyond argument. The cumulative anxieties of months and the tension of the last hour had numbed her mind, and left only a fevered imagination. She covered her eyes, and her fortitude broke down in hysterical sobs.

In vain Harry Belses strove to comfort her. She was still living in a nightmare world, and, since action was no more required of her, she was left at the mercy of its terrors. Nanty, watching her with deep concern, feared for her reason. . . . He saw other faces appear in the room—Jock Kinloch, with tousled hair and blood on his cheek—the scared and homely visage of Mr. Dott. He saw Eben's great arms carry away the dead Cranmer. He heard Bob Muschat's voice. "The redbreasts have gotten them a'—a' but Winfortune, wha slippit off on a horse. But first he fired the stables, and soon the hale place will be in a lowe. D'ye no smell the reek?" It was Gabriel only that he thought of, Gabriel hovering on the verge of a mindless horror, and it was plain from the faces of Belses and Sir Turnour that they saw the peril.

Then Sir Turnour had an inspiration.

"Where's that dog? Where's her spaniel? Somebody fetch the dog. It may do the trick."

Into the room rushed Benjamin, squandering himself about the floor, his paws slipping on the boards, his ears flopping dementedly. He found his mistress and leapt on her, pressing a wet nose against her, as she sat crouched in a chair. In a second he was in her lap, wildly endeavouring to lick her face.

She stared at him stupidly, and then something died out of her eye. The panic and horror disappeared, and were replaced by tenderness. Once again she knew the habitable and homely world. "Benjamin," she crooned, as she fondled his head and pressed him to her. "Oh, Benjamin, you clever dog to have found me! I did not think ever to see you again." Tears came, but they were healing tears.

With Benjamin were others, one a slight little man with a kindly pinched face between the high collars of his greatcoat. He sat on the table beside her and stroked her arm. "Courage, my dearest Gaby," he said. "It is all over. You have been a lamb among wolves, but the Lord has shown you His mercy."

He slipped from the table, for two women had entered the room. One was young, and flushed, as if she had just come from the hunt. She flung off her riding gauntlets and took Gabriel in her arms. The other had a head most wonderfully wrapped up in shawls, but her air was that of a grenadier. She issued masterful orders.

"What are you folk staring here for?" she cried. "D'you

not see that the poor lassie is clean forfochen? Bed's the place for you, my bairn. Your cousin's carriage is below, and in an hour we'll have you between the sheets with a hot pig at your feet. Give her your arm, my lord," she told Belses, "and don't stand glowering like a stookie. The house is burning."

As the others turned to follow, Mr. Spencer Perceval addressed Sir Turnour. "You have conferred infinite obligations upon me, sir," he said in his precise tones. "You have preserved my dear ward's life, and you have been the means of bringing to justice a gang of very dangerous miscreants. Also you have saved the State the expense of a hanging. I fear you will have to tarry here for the inquest, when the full story can be told. Be assured that His Majesty's Government owe you a debt of which they will not be unmindful."

"Not me," said Sir Turnour. "My part was only a trifling bit of coachmanship and a lucky shot. There's the fellow that played the master hand," and he pointed to Nanty, who was raising himself on very shaky legs.

The Prime Minister bowed. "Pray, sir, will you tell me the name of my benefactor?"

"My name is Anthony Lammas. I am a minister of the Kirk of Scotland and a professor of logic in a Scottish college."

The little man beamed.

"A divine and a philosopher and a man of deeds. I think your nation has the monopoly of that happy combination."

Two days later Nanty sat in the very summer-house at Landbeach in which he had first talked with the Balbarnit ladies. It was again a morning of sun and light spring airs, and the turf round them was starry with flowers. He himself still bore marks of ill usage in a bandaged head, but his sturdy nerves had suffered little damage, and the healthy colour of youth was back in his cheeks. The woman by his side had undergone an amazing transformation, as if the soul which had been long absent from her body had now returned to it. Her face was pale, but it was no longer a mask of tragedy. The ladies of Landbeach—and Lady Jane in her desire to care for another had forgotten to be an invalid—had provided her with clothes that became her better than the rough garments of the hill and the road in which Nanty had hitherto seen her. He saw that she was lovelier than he had thought, and that she was very young.

Mr. Spencer Perceval, after assuring himself of the safe custody of the prisoners, and sending certain express messages to town, had taken his leave, promising that he would return in a week to claim his ward. To Nanty he had been very gracious in his shy, precise way. He had promised that the St. Andrews business would be expeditiously settled. "You have put us all in bonds of gratitude," he had said. "Lord Snowdoun is your debtor—I knew something about the affair of young Belses—and as for my ward and myself we owe you our lives. Under God, Mr. Lammas," he had added. "Let us never forget the great Disposer."

With him had gone Sir Turnour Wyse, a man once more at peace with the world. Sir Turnour, regretting loudly that more urgent duties had prevented his seeing the championship fight at Fenny Horton, had hastened to that town to get hold of one Tarky Bald, who had won the belt after desperate battles, with a notion of matching him, for the honour of Norfolk, against his own local champion. For Sir Turnour Nanty had now not only that respect due to one who represented in all things his exact opposite, but affection for a human creature so massive and so nobly secure in its own code of life. It was Jock Kinloch who had delivered the final judgment. "Yon's England," he had told Nanty. "We don't breed them like that in the north. We're maybe cleverer and quicker, and we're just as brave when it comes to the pinch, but we're cockleshells compared to yon even keel. If I saw much of him I'd be always differing from him, but, man, I should also be dumb with admiration. I've no fear of Boney when I think of Wyse and his kind. He's like the stone in the

Bible—whoever falls on it will be broken, and on whomsoever it shall fall it will grind him to powder."

Sir Turnour had paid proper homage to Miss Kirsty's charms, but he had departed without regrets, for indeed no woman was ever likely to bulk large in his life. It was as well, for he would have had no chance. Jock was again the chosen cavalier, for the events of the past days seemed to have changed the modish young woman back to the country girl. It was of Fife that they spoke in that foreign lowland place, of Fife and of their childish doings. Jock, too, had altered, and out of the hobbledehoy was emerging the man, a stiff-jawed, masterful, mirthful being, with, as Nanty observed, some of his formidable father's ways. Even Miss Georgie had taken him into her favour. It was comforting to have some one among those kindly alien grandees who spoke her own tongue.

So one love affair seemed to have happy auguries. Nanty approved with a sigh, for he had been forced to admit the downfall of his own. The first sight of Gabriel and Belses together had shown him the truth. Compared with her strength Harry was only a windlestraw, and set against her spiritual fineness no more than a clod. But this was a woman to whom a lover must be a child. Her eyes as she looked on the young man had had the maternal glow of a Madonna's. She would shape him into something worthy, for she had the fire in her to fuse the coarsest ore and draw out the gold. . . . As for Nanty himself he had not the same need of her, and assuredly she had no need of him. The cobbler, having had his vision, must return soberly to his last.

Yet, as she sat by his side, she seemed to have disturbing thoughts.

"I cannot repay you," she said. "You were willing to give your life for me. . . . When I saw you bound in that chair waiting on death, I seemed to be looking at a Crucifixion. I shall never get your face out of my mind. . . . Why did you do it? You did not know me as Harry knew me. We shared nothing together. Your conduct was far beyond the obligation of manhood or chivalry. It exceeded the duty of the most dutiful Christian. I cannot fathom it, and I cannot repay it. . . . What will you do now? You are too great for the common roads of life."

"No," said Nanty. "You flatter me, for I am the commonest clay. But I will say something to you which, as soon as it is uttered, I want you to forget. I have been in love with you since I first saw you that morning on the hill. I have been happy even when I was most afraid, for I would gladly have died for you. I have been living in a dream, and all the time I knew it was a dream. . . . I am wide awake now, and I have put it behind me. Some day you will marry Harry Belses. Be kind to him, for he is my dearest friend—"

Pain was again in her face.

"Oh, I am born to bring unhappiness to those who love me!" she cried. "You have given me everything and I can give you nothing."

"You can sometimes remember me," he said gently.

Round the corner of the summer-house came the apologetic face of Mr. Dott. He had a bundle of parchments in his hand, an ink-horn, and a quill.

"Your pardon, mem," he said. "Your pardon, Professor. If I may make so bold, I would like Mrs. Cranmer's name appended to these documents. Just the scart of a pen and my job is done, and, gudesakes, it has been a weariful job. Little I thought when I started from Waucht that I was to travel through the feck of England, not to speak of fires and slaughterings."

Nanty laughed and was back again in the light of common day.

"Mr. Dott reminds me," he said, "that I, too, must be getting on with my business."

Very early on a morning in mid-May the *Merry Mouth* cutter landed Nanty at the harbour of St. Andrews. He had come north by the Leith packet, and, falling in with Eben Garnock in that port, had been set across the Firth in the summer night, and had reached his destination when the first cocks were crowing in the East Neuk farms. A letter had apprised Mrs. McKelvie of the time of his arrival, but the packet had been slow, and but for Eben he would have been twenty-four hours late. As it was he was only a night behind his time. His landlady, expecting that he would post from Kirkcaldy, would even now be preparing his breakfast. As his feet touched the harbour-side stones the town clock was striking seven.

The familiar smells of salt and tar and herrings greeted him, and on his ear fell the babble of awakening life in the little city. The jackdaws were busy in the tower of St. Regulus, and he could hear the voice of a man crying the morning baps. The housewives in the wynds were fetching water from the pumps—he caught the distant clack of their tongues. The Professor of Humanity, who had a weak digestion, would be returning from his pre-breakfast walk. He felt himself welcomed by the gentle hand of old homely things. Pleasantly he thought of his little study and the drawer with the manuscript of his great treatise on the relation of art and morals, and the poem on Cardinal Beatoun which was to rival Mr. Walter Scott. As he climbed the steep cobbles he reflected that he had successfully accomplished his mission. He saw the pleased surprise in the Principal's face that so much should have been done so expeditiously; he heard his congratulatory words, and observed the sour smile of Dr. Wotherspoon, his Moral Philosophy rival.

The thoughts that had filled his mind on his journey had now dispersed like an early mist. Sad thoughts they had been, some of them—regrets which he tried in vain to stifle. Memories of a face and eyes and voice which were still too vivid for his peace. But he had also had his comforting reflection that he had proved the manhood of which he had not before been wholly certain, and recovered that youth which in a poet must never be suffered to die. There had also been at the back of his head the thought that he was returning to dear and familiar things. Now as he entered

Mid Street this last had dominated and expelled the rest. He was very content to come home.

As he entered his lodgings a faint smell of burning came to his nostrils.

"Babbie," he shouted, "you are letting the porridge burn again. Have I not told you a hundred times that I cannot abide burnt porridge?"